D1616959

A Comparative Study of the Origins of Ethical Thought

A Comparative Study of the Origins of Ethical Thought

Hellenism and Hebraism

SEIZŌ SEKINE
TRANSLATED BY JUDY WAKABAYASHI

A SHEED & WARD BOOK

ROWMAN & LITTLEFIELD PUBLISHERS, INC.
Lanham • Boulder • New York • Toronto • Oxford

A Sheed & Ward Book

ROWMAN & LITTLEFIELD PUBLISHERS, INC.

Published in the United States of America
by Rowman & Littlefield Publishers, Inc.
A wholly owned subsidiary of The Rowman & Littlefield Publishing Group, Inc.
4501 Forbes Boulevard, Suite 200, Lanham, Maryland 20706
www.rowmanlittlefield.com

PO Box 317, Oxford, OX2 9RU, UK

Chapter 11 was previously published by Seizō Sekine as "Research Note: Proverbs as a Catalogue of Virtues: A Comparison with Nicomachean Ethics," *Annual of the Japanese Biblical Institute* XXVIII (2002): 55–86.

British Library Cataloguing in Publication Information Available

Library of Congress Cataloging-in-Publication Data

Sekine, Seizō.
 [Rinri shisō no genryū. English.]
 A comparative study of the origins of ethical thought : Hellenism and Hebraism / Seizō Sekine ; translated by Judy Wakabayashi.
  p. cm.
 Includes bibliographical references and index.
 ISBN 0-7425-3239-9 (alk. paper)—ISBN 0-7425-3240-2 (pbk. : alk. paper)
 1. Ethics—History. 2. Hellenism. 3. Jewish ethics—History. I. Title.
BJ71.S45 2005
170'.9—dc22   2004020422

Printed in the United States of America

♾ ™The paper used in this publication meets the minimum requirements of American National Standard for Information Sciences—Permanence of Paper for Printed Library Materials, ANSI/NISO Z39.48-1992.

Contents

PART III: THE CONSEQUENCES OF HELLENIC AND HEBREW ETHICS

Preface to the English Edition

The main aim of this book is tracing "Western" ethical thought back to its ancient roots and examining its various manifestations and essential content from the viewpoint of comparative thought. The reason I do not specifically use the expression "Origins of *Western* Ethical Thought" in the title is that, although an Eastern version investigating Indian and Chinese ethical thought would also be conceivable when discussing the "origins of ethical thought," the subheading "Hellenism and Hebraism" makes it clear that this book deals with Western ethical thought.

Another factor behind this decision was that today, when internationalization is proceeding apace and the world is being merged into a single entity, the waves of modernization (synonymous with Westernization) are, for better or worse, spreading around the entire world, and Western thought—as typified by the scientific, rational mind; liberal or democratic political and economic forms; and respect for the dignity of the individual and for human rights—is becoming the common foundation of contemporary world civilization. Tracing the origins of Western "ethical thought" might, therefore, lead to an exploration of the "origins" of general "ethical thought" around the world. This is also a reason behind my decision not to restrict the scope of this book to "the origins of *Western* ethical thought."

The above-mentioned features of Western thought also constitute the direct basis of Western *ethical* thought, but just what is "ethics"? It is common knowledge that the European words *ethics* (English), *Ethik* (German), and *éthique* (French) derive from the Latin word *ethica*, which can be traced even further back to the Greek word *ēthika*. In turn, *ēthika* is the adjective neuter plural of *ēthos*, which originally referred to "an accustomed abode," and from this it came to signify "customs and mores" at the level of the group and "personality or personal character" at the level of the individual. If we follow this tradition, then "ethics" is a generic term referring to "matters pertaining to customs and personality." Explanations of "ethics" that trace back to its Greek etymology

were also put forward in early times by Aristotle[1] and others. Noteworthy here is the fact that what was regarded as "ethical" (*ēthikos*) was not
personal attributes or customs that were simply acquired naturally in the
course of things, but those that were intentionally cultivated and developed into habit.

In contrast to the Greek tradition, there is no word in Hebrew that
corresponds directly to "ethics." Nevertheless, all students of the Old
Testament would be unanimous in agreeing that the Hebrews were even
more mindful than the Greeks of the formation of good character and
mores. The modern-day philosopher of Judaism, Abraham Joshua
Heschel, has suggested that *mitswah* (commandments) and *torah* (the
law), both of which appear frequently in the Old Testament, are concepts
that overlap with "ethics." He points out that these entities are linked to
commandments, obligations, good deeds, acts of benevolence, and so
on.[2] The differences from the Greeks are also apparent here, with Hebrew ethics involving "commands" from a personified God and "the
law" as religious law. For the Hebrews, therefore, observing God's commandments is the essence of being "ethical." (For a discussion of the
Japanese equivalent of "ethics," *rinri*, and its meaning in Japan and ancient China, see chapter 8.1 in part II of this book and chapter 1.1 in
Tetsurō Watsuji's *Ningen no gaku toshite no rinrigaku* (Ethics as the
study of man).[3]

Hence the immediate aim of this book is exploring the similarities
and differences in Greek and Hebrew "ethics" in their various contexts
and construing their diverse meanings by means of hermeneutical procedures. This task presents a range of difficulties, particularly in relation to
two issues: (1) the selection of texts representing "ethical thought" and
(2) evaluation of their ideological coloring.[4]

In relation to the first issue, it must be noted that the texts selected
for discussion here are not restricted solely to works that discuss ethics
in an academic way. Even if we are not aware of them in an academic
sense, texts such as laws, literature, and histories also reflect, both explicitly and implicitly, the "ethical thought" of a particular time and people.
This means that exegetical interpretation comes into play right from the
stage of text selection, even prior to any consideration of how the text
itself is to be interpreted. In part I, which deals with ethics in Greece, we
cannot overlook Aristotle's *Nicomachean Ethics*, which represents the
first system of ethics (chs. 5–7; also ch. 15 in part III). The same goes for
the philosophy of Socrates and Plato, whose main concerns lay with
ethics (chs. 3–4). In the remaining pages we are faced with the question
of whether in relation to the pre-Socratic philosophers we should focus

only on a brief discussion of those thinkers such as Democritus who discussed ethics proper, pick out ethics-related passages from Homer's epic poems and the Greek tragedies or Thucydides' historical accounts, or alternatively, trace the scholastic lineage consisting of the close ties among the pre-Socratic philosophers and seek in this the early signs of ethical thought and traces of its subsequent development. It is this third approach that I have chosen. Although there are various technical grounds for doing so, the most fundamental reason is that, having identified "wonder" as a keyword in the ethical thought that underpins both Hellenism and Hebraism, as I will discuss later, I believe that its original form appears most strikingly in the pre-Socratic philosophers' thinking on ontology. Note that this decision already involves interpretation on my part, and note also the limitations imposed by this choice, so that a discussion of such fields as epic poetry, tragedies, and history has not been possible here. Ever since *Geschichte des Hellenismus* (A history of Hellenism) (1836–43), by the German historian Johann Gustav Droysen, there have also been strong views that instead stress Hellenism (hellenized culture) as the period of decline in Greek history over the three centuries after Alexander's accession to the throne (336 BCE). With that approach, the focus in terms of ethical thought would turn, for example, to the Epicureans, the Stoics, and the Skeptics, but space limitations do not allow me to discuss this here. Hence the texts examined in part I are restricted to the "practical philosophy of classical Greece."

In *Culture and Anarchy* (1869), Matthew Arnold, an English poet and cultural critic who was Droysen's contemporary, interpreted Hellenism in a somewhat broader sense as the spiritual basis relating to the essence of Greek culture in general, and he contrasted it with Hebraism, the source of Judaic and Christian thought. In part II, I have chosen the most important texts concerning the "religious ethics of the ancient Hebrews" from three sources in Judaism's Bible, or Christianity's Old Testament: the Law, the Prophets, and the Writings. There are no narratives related to the *discipline* of ethics in the Old Testament, which lacks even the word "ethics," but I have attempted to interpret the meaning of the ethical fragments scattered throughout the Old Testament, at the same time contextualizing them within the surrounding text. From the Law, I have singled out the Ten Commandments (chs. 8–9), as well as the Book of the Covenant, the Deuteronomic Code, and the Holiness Code (ch. 10); from the Writings, I have selected Proverbs (ch. 11), the book of Job (ch. 12), and the Qohelet (Ecclesiastes) (ch. 13 in part III); and from the Prophets, I have chosen the books of Isaiah and Deutero-Isaiah (ch. 14). In the first two chapters of part III, "The Consequences of Hellenic and Hebrew Ethics," I have made a particular effort to open up a coherent perspective on the lineage and essence of Hebrew ethical thought, incorporating other texts as well. Again, space restrictions mean that texts such as the story of Adam and the tree of the knowledge of good and evil (Gen 2–3) or the story of Abraham's offering of Isaac (Gen 22) had to be omitted. I had no choice but to overlook several such texts that richly convey the sense of ethical thought. Nevertheless, rather than treating a wide range of texts in a cursory manner, I decided to narrow the focus to a few key classic texts and to carry out a more in-depth reading of these in the belief that this would reveal the "origins of ethical thought" more clearly. As with part I, therefore, those texts not regarded as indispensable were decisively set aside. On another occasion I would like to discuss those texts that could not be covered here, and I would ask readers to refer directly to texts that I have already discussed elsewhere.[5]

Here we have noted the problematic aspects relating to the first point, text selection, but the ideological nature of ethical thought must also be mentioned. By "ideology" I mean the ideological tendencies specific to a certain society (class) in a particular period and the misrepresentation of this ideology as universal, whether or not people are aware of its particularity, so as to legitimize the existence or interests of the society that forms its own basis. When interpreting texts relating to ethical thought, it is important to be aware that to a greater or lesser extent these texts carry ideological overtones; but this awareness is a double-edged sword, and we need to realize that those who criticize a particular way of thinking as ideological are themselves also embedded in a certain society and are perhaps basing their critique on a particular ideology.[6] For instance, when Aristotle states that the possibility of happiness does not extend to slaves, it seems self-evident that he is maintaining his own privileges as a free citizen, and when Deutero-Isaiah talks of the redemptive significance of the people of Israel, it is highly likely that at work here is an awareness that "glorifies" and legitimizes what Max Weber has referred to as Israel's "state as a pariah nation," a state in which Deutero-Isaiah himself was mired. It is possible that evident at such times is not just the social ethos forming the basis of the ethical thought glimpsed here, but also the contemporary ethos surrounding those who critique this. In other words, critics of Aristotle's discrimination against slaves are unaware that they are also acting self-righteously on the self-evident premise of a modern democratic ideology consisting of respect for human rights, while those who judge Deutero-Isaiah's redemptive faith as a delusion legitimizing the *ressentiment* that turned the tables on religious awareness might need to reexamine their own scientific, rationalistic assumptions and the validity and scope of the very ethics of the strong. People who criticize a particular way of thinking must obviously be open to such counterquestions in relation to the basis of their own thinking. The ethical thought of the past can also act as a mirror reflecting our contemporary ethos, and interpretations of past ethical views should contain the potential to encompass the (empathetic or antagonistic) resonance between past and present. As Hans-Georg Gadamer[7] has pointed out, this is generally a task that hermeneutics should take on voluntarily, and while on one hand the exegete needs to read a text's meaning as objectively as possible, on the other hand it is also acceptable—even desirable—to attempt a bold reading based on the exegete's own horizon and arrive at a hermeneutical experience that consists of a clash or a fusion of the exegete's horizon with that of the text. As a deliberate attempt to come to grips with this, the discussions in part III and in the introduction and conclusion that frame the main text will, I hope, act as a stimulus for readers in their own considerations of our contemporary ethos.

The ethical situation in Japan at the turn of the twenty-first century, when I was working on the Japanese edition of this book, gave little cause for optimism. Young boys were committing murder and young girls were prostituting themselves. They blatantly questioned why such behavior was wrong, and adults could offer no answer. If it is adults who use the services of prostitutes, it was also adults who raised them. The irresponsible attitude on the part of the police, who should be controlling such crimes, is simply deplorable, and it has long been an open secret that quite a few politicians and bureaucrats are involved in fraudulent money-making and looking after their own interests. The behavior of academics and doctors is also problematic, as they have failed to admit their error in colluding with pharmaceutical companies, whose main priority is profits, in spreading killer viruses. Manipulated by attorneys who protect only the rights of the offenders, the judiciary long ago lost any sensitivity to the suffering of victims, and it has failed to make offenders take responsibility befitting their crimes. Even in cases where an offender rejoins society several years later and reoffends, I have not heard of any judge or attorney accepting responsibility for this. Although most people regard this system as anachronistic, the framework that does not allow reform of this structure is blocking reform in all areas of society. The sense of helplessness today has virtually reached a critical point.

How are the "origins of ancient ethical thought" relevant to our times and societies? If we regard these "origins" as referring not just to the historical roots but also to the very source of thought—while acknowledging that this might result in ideological dogmatism—then it is tempting to regard this subject as having the potential to transcend time and place so as to resonate with contemporary society. It seems to me that the problematic situations facing the ancients are not essentially all that different from our circumstances today. Socrates said to the Athenians, "are you not ashamed that you care for having as much money as possible, and reputation, and honor, but that you neither care nor think about prudence, and truth, and how your soul will be the best possible?"[8] Aristotle complained about "ordinary men," commenting that "by leading a life of passion such men pursue the corresponding pleasures and the means to them but avoid the opposite pains,"[9] while Amos censured the nobility who "afflict the righteous, who take a bribe, and push aside the needy in the gate" (Amos 5:12) and Isaiah shuddered at the sins of those who had lost their sense of holiness, lamenting, "Woe is me! I am lost" (Isa 6:5). In this situation, the origins of ancient ethical thought call for us, above all, to return to the reality that we have been given life by a Being who transcends us and to regain our sense of wonder at this. Becoming aware of this transcendental agency operating behind various phenomena in nature and history, let us cultivate joy at being influenced by this Being and also a clear desire to coexist with others who are likewise influenced in this way. Entertaining a sense of wonder full of empathy toward others who transcend our expectations, an appreciation for the fact that our innate egoism is rejected and our vivid interest in others revived, and astonishment at the mystery of the death of the one who, after unreasonable suffering, died with love for others, let us too begin to love. Even if humans are by nature closed to such love and carry a fundamental sinfulness whereby we must deprive others of their lives for the sake of our own existence and must attempt to win out in the struggle for survival of the fittest, the very fact of such sin is all the more reason at least to continue exploring the inescapable question of ethics as a means of transcending this. It seems to me that the origins of ethical thought strongly urge this on contemporary times.

Finally, let me close by commenting on how this book was written. This is my fourth independently authored book, but its form differs in one striking respect from my previous three books. In the past, I labored under at least two constraints arising from the nature of those books as individual studies in my own specialization of Old Testament studies.

One of these constraints relates to the fact that, to believers, the Bible is a canonical work and hence authoritative. Scholarship, however, must set out by casting doubt on this authority. Scholarly research into the

Bible must at least pass through a historical-critical analysis. It is in my nature, after having set forth various criticisms, to try to arrive at a position where I can recapture the revelational force that remains after such criticisms; but in any case, without some kind of critical viewpoint, the discussion will end up as a sermon or work of apologetics. In other words, my writing is usually constrained in that I cannot simply be carried away naïvely by how wonderful a text is the Bible.

Another constraint is that, although I may arrive at a conclusion by myself, it is necessary to examine existing studies to determine whether my findings have already been expounded elsewhere. If that is the case, I must abandon my plans to present that conclusion. And, no matter how interesting the text might be, unless it offers the potential to move beyond existing studies, I must abandon plans to study it. In other words, I cannot ignore the further constraint that research must be original.

In this book, however, which is somewhat outside my own specialty and which also has the nature of an introductory work, I deliberately freed myself from both of these constraints. Of course, even when following existing research I have done so only after examining the text in detail myself, and I have tried to mention in a note whenever I am aware of a discrepancy between what I have learned from previous scholars and my own ideas, but I have not dwelt excessively on my own original thinking. Doing that would have resulted in a patchy outline full of holes. Here I thought it more important to convey in a straightforward manner, with no preconceived notions, what I have identified with, sharing with readers in easily understood language what I have learned and been awed by, namely, that there are thinkers who have held these ideas and that they have said such wonderful things. Naturally, I have no intention of using this as a pretext for lowering the academic standard, but I would simply like to note that this was my focus and motivation in writing this book.

It was my mentor, University of Tokyo Emeritus Professor Jirō Watanabe, who invited me to take up this task and who—when I hesitated, suggesting that at least the section on the Greeks be written by a different specialist—proposed the need for a unified perspective encompassing the Hebrews, thereby prompting me to take on this new challenge. I would like to express my respect and heartfelt gratitude for his great kindness. This book is an English translation of *Rinri shisō no genryū—Girishia to Heburai no baai*, which was originally published by Hōsō Daigaku Kyōiku Shinkōkai (Tokyo) in 2001, on Professor Watanabe's recommendation. It is my great pleasure to have Dr. Judy Wakabayashi, an associate professor at Kent State University, complete another meticulous and smooth translation after her earlier rendition of my book *Kyūyaku ni okeru chōetsu to shōchō*, translated as *Transcendency and Symbols in the Old Testament*. In addition, J. Randall Short, a young friend who is currently writing his doctoral dissertation in Old Testament studies at Harvard Divinity School, has kindly taken the trouble to read carefully through the translation. I would like to express my deep gratitude to both of them for their efforts. My desire for a dialogue with scholars around the world has been achieved through this English translation, which has been sponsored by a Grant-in-Aid for Scientific Research (Grant-in-Aid for Publication of Scientific Research Results) from the Japan Society for the Promotion of Science in 2003 and 2004. I greatly appreciate this opportunity to reach a new international readership.

Finally, I would like to conclude this preface with the wish that this book might motivate each individual reader, on learning of the rich contents of the various ethical ideas of the ancient Greeks and Hebrews, to develop his or her own thinking about modern-day ethics. As the author, I would be deeply gratified if this book were to stimulate readers to let me know their honest opinions and criticisms.

Seizō Sekine
Advent 2003

Notes

1. Aristotle, *Nicomachean Ethics*, book 2, ch. 1, 1103a18–19.
2. A. J. Heschel, *God in Search of Man: A Philosophy of Judaism* (New York: Farrar, Straus & Cudahy, 1955), ch. 35.
3. Tetsurō Watsuji, *Ningen no gaku toshite no rinrigaku* (Ethics as the study of man), vol. 9 of *Watsuji Tetsurō zenshū* (Watsuji's collected works) (Tokyo: Iwanami Shoten, 1934).
4. See Yōnosuke Katayama, "Rinri to rinri shisō-shi" (Ethics and the history of ethical thought), in *Rinri shisō jiten* (Dictionary of ethical thought), ed. Tsutomu Hoshino, Teruo Mishima, and Seizō Sekine (Tokyo: Yamakawa Shuppansha, 1997).
5. For instance, see chs. 5 and 6 in my *Kyūyaku seisho no shisō* (The thought of the Old Testament) (Tokyo: Iwanami Shoten, 1998), in relation to the story of the offering of Isaac; ch. 4 in my *Transcendency and Symbols in the Old Testament* (Berlin: Walter de Gruyter, 1999), in relation to the story of Adam; and the introduction to ch. 3 in that same book in relation to Thucydides.
6. K. Mannheim, *Ideologie und Utopie* (Bonn: Cohen, 1929).

7. Hans-Georg Gadamer, *Wahrheit und Methode* (Tübingen, Germany: Mohr, 1960).

8. Plato, *Apology of Socrates* 29D–E, trans. T. G. West (Ithaca, NY: Cornell University Press, 1979), 36.

9. *Nicomachean Ethics* X, 9, 1179b13–16, trans. H. G. Apostle (Boston: Reidel, 1975).

Explanatory Notes

The main source used for the pre-Socratic philosophers discussed in chapters 1 and 2 was H. Diels and W. Kranz's *Die Fragmente der Vorsokratiker*, 3 vols. (Berlin: Weidmann, 1951–52). The English translations of this work are taken from Kathleen Freeman's *Ancilla to the Pre-Socratic Philosophers* (Oxford: Blackwell, 1952). The Japanese translations were mostly based on Katsutoshi Uchiyama's edited collection, *Sokuratesu izen tetsugakusha dampen-shū* (Collection of fragments from pre-Socratic philosophers; abbreviated here as *Collection of Fragments*), vols. 1–5 (Tokyo: Iwanami Shoten, 1996–98), which is also based on Diels and Kranz. The notation " = A" after citations indicates the number in the "A" texts about the "life and doctrines" of each philosopher in Diels–Kranz or *Collection of Fragments*. The notation " = B" indicates the number in the "B" texts, which are a collection of the philosophers' "written fragments."

The main source for Plato, who is discussed in chapters 3 and 4, was J. Burnet's *Platonis Opera*, Oxford Classical Texts, 5 vols. (Oxonii: E Typographeo Clarendoniano, 1905–13). The Japanese translations are based on *Puraton zenshū* (The complete works of Plato), edited by Michitarō Tanaka and Norio Fujisawa (Tokyo: Iwanami Shoten, 1974–78). In particular, in most cases I follow Fujisawa's translation of *The Republic* in vol. 11. For *Apology of Socrates*, I referred not only to Michitarō Tanaka's translation in the complete works but also to a translation by Teruo Mishima (Tokyo: Kōdansha gakujutsu bunko, 1998), while for *Phaedo*, I referred not only to Yūji Matsunaga's translation in the complete works, but also to that by Mie Ikeda in *Sekai no meisho 6 Puraton I* (Great books of the world 6, Plato I) (Tokyo: Chūō Kōron, 1978).

The main source for Aristotle's *Nicomachean Ethics*, which is discussed in chapters 5–7 and chapter 15, was I. Bywater's edition, *Aristotelis Ethica Nicomachea: Recognovit brevique adnotatione critica instruxit I*, Oxford Classical Texts (Oxonii: E Typographeo Clarendoniano, 1894). The Japanese translations that I used draw heavily on *Niko-makosu rinrigaku* (Nicomachean Ethics), trans. Saburō Takada (Tokyo: Iwanami Bunko, 1971–73), and *Nikomakosu rinrigaku* (Nicomachean Ethics), *Arisutoteresu zenshū* (Complete works of Aristotle), trans. Shinrō Katō, vol. 13 (Tokyo: Iwanami Shoten, 1973). In some places I have adopted the equivalents and translations of Yasuo Iwata, *Arisutoteresu no rinri shisō* (The ethical thought of Aristotle) (Tokyo: Iwanami Shoten, 1985). English translations are from *The Nicomachean Ethics*, trans. H. G. Apostle (Dordrecht, Netherlands: Reidel, 1975). For other works by Aristotle, I have used the texts in the Loeb Classical Library, and I referred to the various translations in Takashi Ide and Mitsuo Yamamoto's edited collection, *Arisutoteresu zenshū* (Complete works of Aristotle) (Tokyo: Iwanami Shoten, 1968–73). Where possible and unless otherwise indicated, the translations in the Loeb Classical Library are also used for other writers.

For the biblical sources discussed in chapters 8–14, I have mainly used *Biblia Hebraica Stuttgartensia*, edited by K. Elliger and W. Rudolph (Stuttgart: Deutsche Bibelstiftung, 1976), for the Old Testament and *Novum Testamentum Graece*, 27th ed. (Stuttgart: Deutsche Bibelstiftung, 1993), edited by Eb. Nestle, Er. Nestle, K. Aland, and B. Aland, for the New Testament. For Japanese translations, I mostly used the Japanese *Shin-kyōdōyaku* (New common Bible translation) (Tokyo: Japan Bible Association, 1987), and where appropriate, I referred to the following various translations: *Shin-kaiyaku seisho* (New revised Bible) (Tokyo: Nihon Seisho Kankōkai, 1970); *Kyūyaku Seisho* (The Old Testament), trans. Masao Sekine (Tokyo: Kyōbunkan, 1997); Iwanami's already-completed *Shin'yaku seisho* (The New Testament) (Tokyo: Iwanami Shoten, 1995–96); and its *Kyūyaku seisho* (The Old Testament) (Tokyo: Iwanami Shoten, 1997–). Unless otherwise stated, all English translations are from the New Revised Standard Version of the Bible, copyright 1989 by the Division of Christian Education of the National Council of the Churches of Christ in the U.S.A.

When readily available, English translations of the German and French works quoted here have been used. All translations from Japanese works are by Judy Wakabayashi.

Japanese names are written in Western order, with the surname last.

In closing, I would like to express here my deep appreciation for the text criticism and translations of these earlier scholars, for whose work I feel a renewed respect and sense of gratitude.

"Wonder"

Wonder

Let us begin by noting that the concept of "wonder" constitutes the fountainhead of Greek and Hebrew ethical thought. Little has been made of "wonder" as a fundamental concept in ethics. Yet insofar as ethics is a practical philosophy, it is by no means particularly far-fetched to regard it as having originated in "wonder," just as was the case with philosophy. In fact, an exploration of the origins of ancient ethical thought leaves one greatly impressed by its rich sensitivity to "wonder."

Greek "Wonder"

It is well known that the first person to discuss philosophy as originating in wonder was Plato.[1] In *Theaetetus*, one of his later dialogues, Plato has Socrates say: "this is an experience which is characteristic of a philosopher, this *wondering* [*thaumazein*]: this is where philosophy [*philosophiā*] begins and nowhere else."[2] This was in reply to a comment by the young Theaetetus that "I often wonder [*thaumazō*] like mad" and "I begin to feel quite giddy" at the various views put forward on the main theme of this particular dialogue, that is, "What is knowledge?"

In one of the middle dialogues, *Phaedrus*, which discusses the remembering of ideas seen in a previous existence, Socrates says: "yet when they see here some resemblance to those former sights, they are stricken with *amazement* [*ekplēttō*]."[3] As if in response to these comments, Aristotle similarly observes in *Metaphysics* that

> It is through *wonder* [*thaumazein*] that men now begin and originally began to philosophize [*philosophein*]; *wondering* in the first place at obvious perplexities, and then by gradual progression raising questions about the greater matters too, e.g., about the changes of the moon and of the sun, about the stars

1

and about the origin of the universe. Now he who *wonders* and is perplexed feels that he is ignorant (thus the myth-lover is in a sense a philosopher, since myths are composed of *wonders*); therefore if it was to escape ignorance that men studied philosophy, it is obvious that they pursued science for the sake of knowledge, and not for any practical utility.[4]

Here "the first place" that men "began to philosophize [*philosophein*]" refers to the natural philosophy of Ionia that began with Thales, whom Aristotle was shortly afterward to dub the "founder of this school of philosophy."[5] Yet this natural philosophy was not merely a pursuit of the fundamental principles of Nature, but also a supreme ethics that explored how people should live on the basis of a fundamental wonder as to what constitutes Nature. Anaximander hit on the concept of "the Boundless" and considered it in relation to such ethical concepts as "injustice," "punishment," and "atonement." Xenophanes attacked the unethical ignorance represented by anthropomorphism and regarded ethical dread and wonder toward God as "good." He also had a clear view of human beings' station in life, rather along the lines of what Socrates later called "knowledge of ignorance," and from that perspective Xenophanes spoke of an unrelenting intellectual "seeking" for ethically "better things." There are countless such examples in Greece, but let us turn now to the situation in the land of the Hebrews.

Hebrew "Wonder"

Although Hebrew ethical thought should probably be characterized not as a practical philosophy but as a religious ethic, Abraham Heschel, a modern philosopher of Judaism, demonstrated that a "wonder" comparable to Greek *thaumazein* lies at the root of Hebrew ethical thought.[6] He called attention to the fact that when religion loses the sense of wonder as a primal emotion before an established position of faith has been adopted, it has no option but to become an empty ritual.[7] This same feeling of wonder should also constitute the source of religious ethics.

For instance, the prophet Jeremiah extols the work of God, who gives "according to" ethical "doings" as something "wonderful":

Ah Lord God! It is you who made the heavens and the earth by your great power and by your outstretched arm! Nothing is too *wonderful* [*pala'*] for you![8] You show steadfast love to the thousandth generation, but repay the guilt of parents into the laps of their children after them, O great and mighty God whose name is the LORD of hosts, great in counsel and mighty in deed; whose eyes are open to all the ways of mortals, rewarding all *according to their ways* and according to the fruit of their *doings*.[9]

If we assume that Jeremiah[10] is also basing this on the creation myth,[11] then we could say he spoke of "wonder" as a "myth-lover," to borrow Aristotle's expression. It seems, however, that Hebrew narrators' sense of "wonder" was triggered more by historical events than by the genesis, principles, and creation of Nature. An examination of all twelve Old Testament occurrences of *pele'*, the Hebrew word that expresses "wonder," or of all seventy-one instances of its verb form, *pala'*, shows that very few occurrences relate to Nature,[12] with nearly all of the remaining cases referring to God's acts in history, particularly to the event of salvation embodied in the exodus from Egypt. For instance,

Both we and our ancestors have sinned;
  we have committed iniquity, have done wickedly.
Our ancestors, when they were in Egypt,
  did not consider your *wonderful [pala']* works;
they did not remember the abundance of your steadfast love,
  but rebelled against the Most High at the Red Sea.
Yet he saved them for his name's sake,
  so that he might make known his mighty power. . . .
But they soon forgot his works;
  they did not wait for his counsel.
But they had a wanton craving in the wilderness,
  and put God to the test in the desert;
He gave them what they asked,
  but sent a wasting disease among them.[13]

The psalmist seems to be arguing that when people forget that their escape from slavery in Egypt was in fact a "wonderful work" on the part of God, they fall into religious disobedience and ethical decline. Similar claims were made repeatedly by the prophets.[14]

Yet do the wonderful works of God really govern history? Rather, is it not the way of the world that the just perish and sinners prosper, with ethical retribution not carried out and the workings of God remaining hidden, with no wonderful occurrences at all? It is inconceivable that the Hebrews, particularly the later writers of wisdom literature, would have been unaware of such nihilistic questions. For instance, Qohelet says:

there are righteous people who are treated according to the conduct of the wicked, and there are wicked people who are treated according to the conduct of the righteous. I said that this also is vanity.[15]

All things are wearisome; . . . there is nothing new under the sun.[16]

How can Hebrew ethics generally respond to such refutations? Qohelet's wisdom is already heavily influenced by Greek thought,[17] but just how does Hebrew thought interact with Greek thought in such radical questions? If, nonetheless, "wonder" can still be regarded as forming the undercurrent of ancient ethical thought, then in what sense is this so? What is the object of "wonder" in the first place, and, more specifically, how does this relate to ethical issues?

Aim of This Book

With such questions in mind, in this book I would like to unravel the strands of ancient ethical thought. Naturally, it is not my intention to attribute all the different forms of ethical thought to the sole concept of "wonder." As stated in the preface, the main purpose of this book lies in closely analyzing the initial forms of ethics in the "origins of ethical thought" of the Greeks and Hebrews—roots that extend into the present—and in ascertaining the diverse ideas surrounding these forms. In this process, rather than contrasting the differences and highlighting the diversity to no useful end,[18] I would prefer to focus on ascertaining what their underlying similarities can collectively tell us today. When from the outset we pay attention to "wonder" as a trait loosely common to both the Greeks and the Hebrews, and when we repeatedly return to this both implicitly and explicitly and finally again question its meaning, perhaps the essential qualities of the "origins" that contemporary ethics tends to overlook might also become more apparent. That is my outlook here.

Let us move on now to our main discussion.

Notes

1. Line 780 of Hesiodos' *Theogonia* also records that Iris (the rainbow) was the child of Thaumas (whose name means "wonder"), but the connection between the rainbow and philosophy is unclear.

2. Plato, *Theaetetus*, trans. Myles Burnyeat (Indianapolis: Hackett, 1990), 55D; emphasis added.
3. Plato, *Phaedrus*, trans. W. C. Helmbold and W. G. Rabinowitz (Indianapolis: Bobbs-Merrill, 1956), 250A; emphasis added.
4. Aristotle, *Metaphysics*, Loeb Classical Library (1933), I, 2, 982b12–21; emphasis added.
5. *Metaphysics* I, 2, 983b20–21.
6. A. J. Heschel, *God in Search of Man: A Philosophy of Judaism* (New York: Farrar, Straus & Cudahy, 1955), 45.
7. Heschel, *God in Search of Man*, 3ff.
8. A literal translation would be "Nothing would surprise you." Usually this is rendered freely along the lines of "Nothing is too hard for you," but here I have taken into account the connection with the usage of *pala'*, which is discussed immediately after this, and the meaning of the nominal form *pele'*. I have adapted the New Revised Standard Version (NRSV) of the Bible accordingly.
9. Jer 32:17–19; emphasis added.
10. Jer 33:20–25.
11. Gen 1:1–5; 9:9.
12. In addition to the instance in Jeremiah above, there are Isa 28:29, Job 37:11–14, and perhaps Job 42:1–6.
13. Ps 106:6–8, 13–15; emphasis added.
14. For instance, see Mic 7:11–20 and Jer 32:20–24.
15. Qoh 8:14.
16. Qoh 1:8–9.
17. Cf. C. F. Whitley, *Koheleth: His Language and Thought* (BZAW 148; Berlin: Walter de Gruyter, 1979). Also see N. Lohfink, *Kohelet* (NEB; Würzburg: Echter Verlag, 1980). There are, however, many problems. For instance, see my *Transcendency and Symbols in the Old Testament: A Genealogy of the Hermeneutical Experiences*, trans. Judy Wakabayashi (BZAW 275; Berlin: Walter de Gruyter, 1999), 94, originally published as *Kyūyaku ni okeru chōetsu to shōchō: kaishakugaku-teki keiken no keifu* (Tokyo: University of Tokyo Press, 1996).
18. One classic that adopts such an approach and that will be repeatedly mentioned in the notes below is Thorleif Boman, *Das hebräische Denken im Vergleich mit dem Griechischen*, 2nd ed. (Göttingen: Vandenhoeck & Ruprecht, 1954).

Part I

THE PRACTICAL PHILOSOPHY OF THE ANCIENT GREEKS

Timeline of Ancient Greece

Eighth Century BCE
First half: Establishment of *poleis* (city-states) in Greece
Midcentury: Homer (dates unknown)
Latter half: Hesiod (dates unknown)

Seventh Century BCE
First half: Establishment of an aristocracy in Athens
Midcentury: Conflicts between the nobility and the people

Sixth Century BCE
594 BCE: Solon's reforms (his mediation in the conflicts between the nobility and the people)
First half to first half of fifth century BCE—Ionians:
                   Thales (ca. 624–546 BCE), Anaximander (ca. 610–557 BCE), Anaximenes (ca. 587–547 BCE), Xenophanes (ca. 560–470 BCE), Heraclitus (535–475 BCE)

Fifth Century BCE
First half to first half of fourth century BCE—Italian Thracians:
                   Parmenides (ca. 515–450 BCE), Empedocles (ca. 490–430 BCE), Democritus (ca. 460–370 BCE) [Pythagoras (ca. 570 BCE–?)]
490 BCE: First Persian War (Battle of Marathon)
480 BCE: Second Persian War (Battle of Salamis)
Latter half: Herodotus (dates unknown), Thucydides (471–400 BCE), Socrates (470–399 BCE)
Latter half to first half of fourth century BCE—Sophists:
                   Protagoras (ca. 500–ca. 400 BCE), Gorgias (ca. 484–ca. 375 BCE), Hippias (483 BCE–?), Thrasymachus (fifth century–fourth century BCE), Hippocrates (470–ca. 375 BCE)
443–429 BCE: The Age of Pericles (establishment of Athenian democracy)
431–404 BCE: Peloponnesian War

Fourth Century BCE
First half: Xenophon (428–354 BCE), Plato (427–347 BCE)
385 BCE: Founding of Plato's Academy
Midcentury: Diogenes of Sinope (400–325 BCE), Aristotle (384–322 BCE)
335 BCE: Founding of Aristotle's Lyceum
323 BCE: Death of Alexander the Great

Third Century BCE
First half: Pyrrhon (360–270 B.C.E.), Epicurus (341–270 BCE), Zenon of the Stoic school (335–263 BCE)

CHAPTER 1

The Pre-Socratics (1): The Ionians

Ethics as a practical philosophy arose at the same time as philosophy. There is a tendency to think that Ionian natural philosophy had nothing to do with ethics and that Democritus was the first pre-Socratic philosopher to speak of a clear ethics; but in my opinion, ideas constituting an important core of ethics can already be found in Ionian philosophy. We will be able to verify this at the end of the chapter.

It is customary in academic circles to lump the various scholars from Thales (the originator of philosophy) to Democritus (a contemporary of Socrates) together under the rubric of "the pre-Socratics." Opinion differs, however, on how to subdivide these philosophers further. Since categorization by birthplace more or less accords with the chronological division, here I will divide pre-Socratic philosophers into the Ionians and the Italian Thracians.

In other words, I will group together as the Ionians the three philosophers who appeared in the Ionian city of Miletus—Thales (ca. 624–546 BCE), Anaximander (ca. 610–557 BCE), and Anaximenes (ca. 587–547 BCE)—along with Xenophanes (ca. 560–470 BCE), who although he spent the latter part of his life wandering mostly in southern Italy was a native of Colophon in Ionia, and also Heraclitus (535–475 BCE), who was born in Ephesus in Ionia.

Under the designation of Italian Thracians I will start with Parmenides (ca. 515–450 BCE), from the colonized city of Elea in southern Italy, followed by two philosophers under his influence. In Italy there was Empedocles (ca. 490–430 BCE), from Akragas in Sicily, and Democritus (ca. 460–370 BCE), who was born in the colonized city of Abdera in Thrace on the northern Aegean coast and later traveled widely. Pythagoras (ca. 570 BCE–?), who was a native of Samos near Miletus and later moved to Croton in eastern Italy, falls in both periods and both regions, but in line with the convention of referring to Pythagoras as a member of the Italian School, I will include him in this latter group.

Either way, this division means that the Ionians were active mainly in the sixth century BCE and the Italian Thracians in the fifth century BCE. In this chapter I will study the Ionians, leaving the examination of the Italian Thracians for the following chapter.

1. The Milesian Natural Philosophers—Thales, Anaximander, and Anaximenes

It is commonly accepted that a wave of philosophers who gave rational consideration to the origins of the world appeared in the sixth century BCE in the Greek colony of Ionia on the coast of Asia Minor, and that Ionia was the cradle of philosophy. Of these Ionian philosophers, three who appeared in Miletus—Thales, Anaximander, and Anaximenes—formed the Milesian School, or the Ionian School, in its narrow sense, and were its pioneers.

THALES' "WATER"

Thales was the founding father of the Milesian school, and Aristotle was to dub him the "founder of this school of philosophy."[1] The Greeks have an abundance of anecdotes about Thales, the first on the list of the seven sages.[2] For instance, he immersed himself in the study of astronomy, and one night when he was out strolling and gazing up at the sky he fell into a well, leading a servant girl to mock him because he was so eager to know about what was in the sky that he paid no attention to his own surroundings.[3] Then there is the story about how Thales used his knowledge of astronomy to predict a bumper crop of olives. He bought up all the olive presses in the winter and then made a fortune by renting them out at high rates during the harvest. This prompted him to boast that philosophers can make a go of things if they try, but that it was not worth the effort.[4] Apparently, however, Thales produced no writings, leaving behind not even fragments. All that has been handed down is a riddle-like pronouncement by Aristotle—who first mentioned Thales' philosophical achievements and recorded the source of what subse-

quently became lore[5]—to the effect that Thales, the founder of philosophy, said the principle underlying things is water.[6]

If, however, we concur with Nietzsche that Thales' achievement lay
not in his answer that "water" is the origin of all things but in his very
asking of this unprecedented question as to just what comprises the fundamental principle underlying the world,[7] and if we can say that "the
word emitted in the midst of the strange silence of amazement and tension when people suddenly encountered" the "*something* that revealed
itself to Thales" was "water!"[8] then this constitutes evidence that the
light of philosophy subsequently handed down to Anaximander had
been well and truly lit.

ANAXIMANDER'S "INFINITE"

In other words, "Anaximander, . . . a fellow-citizen and associate of
Thales, said that the material cause [*archē*] and first element of things
[*stoicheion*] was the Infinite [*to apeiron*], he being the first to introduce
this name for the material cause."[9] We can interpret this as meaning that
Thales sought "something" underpinning human existence and gave a
tentative answer in the form of the finite object, "water," while Anaximander took a step further by speculating that what grants us finite beings our existence in this relative world must be an absolute infinite being
that transcends us. If questioning this infinite being is the task of philosophy as metaphysics,[10] then Thales was the pioneer in this respect, and
Anaximander rightly inherited and further developed this view. (By contrast, Anaximander's pupil, Anaximenes, is regarded as having reverted
to Thales' stage, because he posited the finite entity of air (*aēr*) as the
fundamental material substance,[11] postulating that the process of conden-
sation and rarefaction of air results in becoming and change in the universe.)[12]

Anaximander's fragment continues as follows, so it is also noteworthy from the viewpoint of ethical thought.

> [T]he source from which existing things derive their existence
> is also that to which they return at their destruction, according
> to necessity; for they give justice and make reparation to one
> another for their injustice, according to the arrangement of
> Time.[13]

According to the commentary Simplicius attached to this fragment, generation takes place by the four elements changing into one another and

by opposites separating,[14] which means that Anaximander was still discussing physics. Yet it was not until a century later, with Empedocles, that the four basic elements (*stoicheia*) of earth, water, fire, and wind were first mentioned,[15] as will be discussed later. Given the fact, then, that Simplicius's actual commentary is problematic and that the expressions "injustice" and "make reparation" are more suited to human relations than physical matter and that the expression "things" includes humans,[16] it seems plausible that an ethical analogy is at least being implied here. If so, this means that Anaximander believed a balance is maintained between the forces of the natural world and the human world, as a "repayment of excess earnings,"[17] just as, for instance, dryness itself becomes moist and disappears when it invades moist areas[18] or as dying people leave their life savings to those who survive them.

Another important point in Anaximander's thinking is that he also considers the infinite "to be divine."[19] Here we can see the germ of a philosophical view of God—a view that took its next landmark stride with Xenophanes and was passed on down to Heraclitus.

Augustine was of the view that Anaximander did not "attribute anything to a divine mind in the production of all this activity of things,"[20] but this merely seems to illustrate how Augustine's view of God, which had its roots in Hebraism, was concerned less with God's philosophical infiniteness than with his anthropomorphic nature.

2. Xenophanes

CRITICISM OF ANTHROPOMORPHIC VIEWS OF GOD

Xenophanes spent the latter half of his life wandering, mostly in southern Italy, but he originally hailed from Ionia and can be considered as an Ionian in the broad sense of the term. In fact, Xenophanes was strongly influenced by his Ionian School predecessors from Miletus, and he can be regarded as having developed their natural philosophy from a theological perspective.

> But mortals believe the gods to be created by birth, and to have their own (*mortals'*) raiment, voice and body.[21]

> Aethiopians have gods with snub noses and black hair, Thracians have gods with grey eyes and red hair.[22]

> Both Homer and Hesiod have attributed to the gods all things
> that are shameful and a reproach among mankind: theft, adul-
> tery, and mutual deception.[23]

These fragments by Xenophanes were sharply critical of the existing anthropomorphic view of God. As Anaximander had pointed out, if the
gods are infinite beings transcending finite humans, then it could not be
right to portray God in terms of an analogy with humankind. If we can
trace further back and say that Thales too was of the "view that everything is full of gods"[24] and that "Anaximenes proposed that god was air,
that it is . . . unbounded, infinite,"[25] and if, as will be discussed later,
Heraclitus was also a seeker of divine wisdom, then on the whole the
Ionian natural philosophers spoke of God as the "basic principle of nature."[26] Within this tradition, Xenophanes consciously refined and developed this view of God and presented a revolutionary rejection of the
tradition of perceiving God in humankind's own image.

So what view of God did Xenophanes propose in place of such anthropomorphic views?

> Xenophanes taught that God is one and incorporeal, saying
> "There is one god, among gods and men the greatest, not at all
> like mortals in body or in mind."[27]

> But without toil he sets everything in motion, by the thought
> of his mind.[28]

> And he always remains in the same place, not moving at all,
> nor is it fitting for him to change his position at different
> times.[29]

Hence this God forms a relative relationship with relative beings in the
sense that he still has a "body" and "remains" somewhere and "sets
everything in motion" in this world. In that sense Xenophanes has not
attained an understanding of an absolute being who is truly beyond the
relative. There is, however, a suggestion[30] here of a view of God that
foreshadows Aristotle's "immovable Mover,"[31] and this also clearly represents a distinct advance on the view of unethical gods held by Homer
and Hesiod. What effect, then, did this development have on ethical
thought?

REVERENCE FOR GOD, AND INTELLECTUAL
SEEKING

The first important point is that finding a god who has nothing to do
with "theft, adultery, and mutual deception" engendered a feeling of
reverence for God.

> It is proper for men who are enjoying themselves first of all to praise God with decent stories and pure words. . . . [B]ut always to have respect for the gods, *that* is good.[32]

And as long as that god is a superior being in terms of "thinking" and "thought," then people should emulate him even a little and should emphasize the spirit over the flesh and knowledge over physical strength.

> [I]t is not right to prefer physical strength to noble Wisdom.[33]

Mere mortals have no recourse but to grow in wisdom through seeking.

> Truly the gods have not revealed to mortals all things from the beginning; but mortals by long seeking discover what is better.[34]

> And as for certain truth, no man has seen it, nor will there ever be a man who knows about the gods and about all the things I mention. For if he succeeds to the full in saying what is completely true, he himself is nevertheless unaware of it; and Opinion (seeming) is fixed by fate upon all things.[35]

Here is an understanding of human beings' station in life that is comparable to Socrates' "knowledge of ignorance."[36] Discovering a god who truly transcends human beings leads to insights into the finiteness of human knowledge, and these insights do not stop at renouncing relativism but urge people on to a constant "seeking" for "better things." It is here that Xenophanes' seminal significance in the history of ethical thought is apparent.

3. Heraclitus

"PURPOSE WHICH STEERS ALL THINGS"

Heraclitus was the last of the Ionian School, but he criticized his Ionian predecessor, Xenophanes, and his contemporary, Pythagoras, as well as others from the Italian School, who will be discussed in chapter 2, because of their erudition.

> Much learning does not teach one to have intelligence; for it would have taught Hesiod and Pythagoras, and again, Xenophanes and Hecataeus.[37]

Insightfulness is acquired not through sundry knowledge of different phenomena but also through wisdom about what underlies these phenomena.

> That which is wise is one: to understand the purpose which steers all things through all things.[38]

What is this "purpose which steers all things" to which Heraclitus is referring? It is by no means easy to interpret this. No doubt Heraclitus was dubbed "the obscure one" (*skoteinos*)[39] not only because of his dour and critical personality, but also because of the difficulty of his expression, which caused even Aristotle to lament its impenetrability.[40]

EVERYTHING FLOWS

Ever since Plato linked the idea of "everything flows" (*panta rhei*) to Heraclitus,[41] there has been a tendency to sum up Heraclitus's central idea in this catchphrase and to regard it as the embodiment of "the purpose which steers all things." Yet this phrase is nowhere to be found in any of Heraclitus's surviving fragments. The fragment "In the same river, we both step and do not step, we are and we are not"[42] brings to mind the opening sentence of Chōmei Kamo's *Hōjōki*: "Ceaselessly the river flows, and yet the water is never the same, while in the still pools the shifting foam gathers and is gone, never staying for a moment."[43] For Japanese in particular, it is tempting to read the ideas of impermanence and transience into this. There is debate, however, over the interpretation of this fragment, with some taking the view that the emphasis is on how the river remains the "same" even though its flow changes, while others see in how the "flow of the same river" is always turning into something else the idea of "the unity of opposites," which is described in the following section.[44] Even if this fragment is in fact expounding on the idea of *panta rhei*, there are insufficient examples to regard this as Heraclitus's central idea. Out of the 126 fragments of varying lengths that are attributed to Heraclitus, apart from this particular fragment the only ones that hint at this idea are two short passages that are thought to be variations of this fragment.[45]

THE UNITY OF OPPOSITES

So let us return to the question of what is the "purpose which steers all things," which was mentioned by Heraclitus.

From among the erudite he had earlier criticized, Heraclitus singled out Hesiod for further censure: "Hesiod is the teacher of very many, he who did not understand day and night: for they are one."[46] Other fragments by Heraclitus—such as "The way up and down is one and the same"[47] or "And what is in us is the same thing: living and dead, awake and sleeping, as well as young and old; for the latter (*of each pair of opposites*) having changed becomes the former, and this again having changed becomes the latter"[48]—reveal that Heraclitus is speaking of "the insight that . . . things that should by rights be one and the same become manifest in our world as diametrically opposite aspects."[49] This is what is known as the idea of the "unity of opposites."[50] Although miscellaneous erudition about the seemingly antithetical phenomena of all things overlooks this fact, in reality there is a "comprehensive" entity that transcends and unifies such "opposites." Then perhaps we could set out from the perspective that the "purpose which steers all things" lies in the very awareness of this fact.

The following fragment about this "universal Law" is noteworthy:

> Therefore one must follow (the universal Law, namely) that which is common (*to all*). But although the Law [*logos*][51] is universal, the majority live as if they had understanding peculiar to themselves.[52]

Now if we assume that we should regard God as the agent who does the "steering" in the "purpose which steers all things,"[53] then we need to question further the relationship between this "universal Law" and God. According to the commentary by Clement,

> Heraclitus . . . considered that . . . fire is by the Word [Law] of God, which governs all things, changed by the air into moisture, which is, as it were, the germ of cosmical change.[54]

Hippolytus generalizes this situation further:

> Heraclitus then says that the universe is [one], divisible and indivisible; generated [and] ungenerated; mortal [and] immortal; reason, eternity; Father, Son, and justice, God. "For those who hearken not to me, but the doctrine, it is wise that they acknowledge all things to be one," says Heraclitus.[55]

DIVINE WISDOM

Looked at in this way, the "purpose which steers all things" is the wisdom of God as *logos*, an awareness of the sole thing underpinning all variously manifested things. Heraclitus adds that this sole thing is "fire,"[56] but in ethical terms what is more important than such physical explanations of phenomena is the fact that Heraclitus regarded this very questioning about the source that constitutes phenomena as a vital act that transcends erudition. And this source actually consisted of God's knowledge—an idea that Heraclitus shared with Xenophanes, whom he had criticized, and that constitutes the object of ceaseless pursuit.

> You could not in your going find the ends of the soul, though you traveled the whole way: so deep is its Law (*Logos*).[57]

> I searched into myself.[58]

The latter fragment also has something in common with "All men have the capacity of knowing themselves and acting with moderation,"[59] and as various commentators have pointed out,[60] it resonates with the inscription "Know thyself" (*gnōthi seauton*) on the temple of Apollo at Delphi. Heraclitus, who anticipated the ideas of Socrates,[61] who made self-knowledge his lifelong topic, is known to have been critical of others and arrogant and aloof, yet he also had humbleness in the form of a "knowledge of the unknown" that was aware of the "ends" of the soul that "you could not . . . find." Heraclitus the man and philosophy itself constituted a "unity of opposites."

This would indicate that the Ionians, the originators of philosophy, were inspired throughout by the thought of transcendency and by a reverence for this, starting with Thales' awe, passing through Anaximander's discovery of "the Infinite" and Xenophanes' criticism of anthropomorphic views of God, and going right up to Heraclitus's contrast here between God's knowledge and human ignorance. It also indicates that the Ionians continued to question how people should live, that is, they were concerned with ethics. Here we can tentatively recognize the fountainhead of Greek ethical thought.

Notes

1. Aristotle, *Metaphysics* I, 3, 983b20–21 = A12. For an explanation of the notations " = A" and " = B" used from here on, refer to the "Explanatory Notes" at the beginning of this book.

2. See, for example, Plato, *Protagoras* 343A; Diogenes Laertios, *Lives of the Philosophers* I, 22ff. = A1.

3. Plato, *Theaetetus* 174A = A9.

4. Aristotle, *Politics* A11; 1259a9–18 = A10.
5. See, for example, Seneca, *Quaestiones naturales* III, 14p 106, 9 = A15.
6. *Metaphysics* I, 3, 983b20–21 = A12.
7. F. W. Nietzsche, *Die Philosophie im tragischen Zeitalter der Griechen* (Leipzig: Kroner, 1925), 1.
8. Tadashi Inoue, *Konkyo yori no chōsen* (A factual challenge) (Tokyo: University of Tokyo Press, 1974), 15–16.
9. Simplicius, *On Aristotle's "Physics"* 24, 13 = A9, B1; see translation in John Burnet, *Early Greek Philosophy*, 4th ed. (London: Black, 1963), 52.
10. *Metaphysics* IV, 1.
11. *Metaphysics* IV, I, 3, 984a5–7 = A4.
12. *On Aristotle's "Physics"* 24, 26 = A5.
13. *On Aristotle's "Physics"* B1. Unless otherwise noted, the English translations for the pre-Socratic philosophers are from Kathleen Freeman, *Ancilla to the Pre-Socratic Philosophers* (Oxford: Blackwell, 1952).
14. *On Aristotle's "Physics"* A9.
15. Katsutoshi Uchiyama, ed., *Sokuratesu izen tetsugakusha dampen-shū* (Collection of fragments from pre-Socratic philosophers; hereinafter referred to as *Collection of Fragments*), vol. 1 (Tokyo: Iwanami Shoten, 1996), 165, n. 2.
16. This brings to mind M. Heidegger's interpretation in "Der Spruch der Anaximander" (The Anaximander fragment), in his *Holzwege* (Frankfurt: Klostermann, 1950), that Anaximander's "injustice" referred to how once "things" come into existence, immediately they can no longer be satisfied and hence strive for everlasting continuance. See also Yasuo Iwata, *Seiyō shisō no genryū* (The origins of Western thought) (Tokyo: Hōsō Daigaku Kyōiku Shinkōkai, 1997), 84–86.
17. Iwata, *Seiyō shisō* (Western thought), 83.
18. See Aristotle, *Meteorology* B1, 353b6–11; Aetius, *Placita* III, 16, 1 etc. = A27.
19. Aristotle, *Physics* III, 4, 203b13 = A15.
20. Augustine, *City of God* VIII, 2 = A17; see St. Augustine, *The City of God*, trans. Marcus Dods (New York: Modern Library, 1950), 245.
21. Clement, *Stromata* V, 109, 2 = B14.
22. *Stromata* VII, 22, 1 = B16.
23. Sextus Empirucus, *Against the Physicists* B11.
24. Aristotle, *De Anima* I, 5, 411a7 = A22.
25. Cicero, *De Deorum Natura* I, 10, 26 = A10; see Cicero, *The Nature of the Gods*, trans. P. G. Walsh (Oxford: Clarendon, 1997), 12.
26. Iwata, *Seiyō shisō* (Western thought), 87.
27. *Stromata* V, 109 = B23.
28. *On Aristotle's "Physics"* 23, 19 = B25.
29. *On Aristotle's "Physics"* 23, 10 = B26.
30. Iwata, *Seiyō shisō* (Western thought), 89.
31. *Metaphysics* XII, 6, 7, 8, 1071b4–5, 1072a25, 1073a32–34.
32. Athenaeus, *The Deipnosophists* XI, 462C = B1.
33. *The Deipnosophists* X, 413F = B2. See also Plato, *Meno* 80D; *Apologia Socratis* 36D–E.

34. Stobaeus, *Eclogae* I, 8, 2 = B18.

35. *Against the Physicists* VII, 49 = B34.

36. See also *Meno* 80D.

37. Diogenes Laertius, *Lives of Eminent Philosophers* IX, 1 = B40; see also B35. For reference sake, compare also Protagoras' fragments 80–84 in *Collection of Fragments*.

38. *Lives of Eminent Philosophers* B41.

39. *Collection of Fragments* A 1a, 3a.

40. *Collection of Fragments* A 4; Hiroyuki Ogino, *Tetsugaku no gen-fūkei: kodai Girishia no chie to kotoba* (The current scene in philosophy: wisdom and words in ancient Greece) (Tokyo: Nihon Hōsō Shuppan Kyōkai, 1999), 84.

41. B88. *Theaetetus* 152D–E, 160D, 179D; Plato, *Cratylus* 402A = A6.

42. Heraclides Ponticus, *The Allegories of Homer* 24 = B49a.

43. Chōmei Kamo, *The Ten Foot Square Hut and Tales of the Heike*, trans. A. L. Sadler (Rutland, Vermont & Tokyo, Japan: Charles E. Tuttle Company, 1972), 1.

44. See *Collection of Fragments*, vol. 1, 322–23, n. 1.

45. *Collection of Fragments* B12, 91.

46. Hippolytus, *Refutation of All Heresies* IX, 10 = B57.

47. *Collection of Fragments* B60.

48. *Collection of Fragments* B88.

49. Ogino, *Tetsugaku no gen-fūkei* (Current scene in philosophy), 94.

50. See also, for example, *Collection of Fragments* B23, 50, 51, 62, 67, 103, 106.

51. Depending on the context, *logos* has a wide range of meanings, such as "norm or ratio," "rule or order," "speech or discourse." See *Collection of Fragments*, vol. 1, 321, n. 1, concerning B45; 323, n. 2, concerning B50; Ogino, *Tetsugaku no gen-fūkei* (Current scene in philosophy), 95–96, etc.

52. *Against the Physicists* VII, 113 = B2.

53. See *Collection of Fragments*, vol. 1, 320, n. 1, concerning B41.

54. *Stromata* V, 105 = B31.

55. Hippolytus, *The Refutation of All Heresies* IX, 9 = B50; trans. J. H. MacMahon (Edinburgh: Clark, 1898), 331.

56. *Collection of Fragments* B30, 31, 63–67, A1, 5, etc.

57. *Lives of Eminent Philosophers* IX, 7 = B45.

58. Plutarch, *Adversus Colotem* (*Against Colotes*) 20, 1118C = B101.

59. Stobaeus, *Florilegium* III, 5, 6 = B116.

60. See, for example, *Collection of Fragments*, vol. 1, 338, n. 1, on B101; Ogino, *Tetsugaku no gen-fūkei* (Current scene in philosophy), 98–99.

61. Plato, *Phaedrus* 229E.

CHAPTER 2

The Pre-Socratics (2): The Italian Thracians

1. Parmenides

ANALYSIS OF BEING

Through his innovative analysis of Being (i.e., existence), Parmenides marked a new era in the history of Greek philosophy and has had a far-reaching influence right down to Heidegger's ontology in modern times.[1] From the viewpoint of ethical thought, however, Parmenides' ideas were not as diverse as those of his successor, Democritus, so here I will restrict myself to summarizing his analysis of existence and the significance of this analysis in the history of ethical thought.

> One should both say and think that Being Is; for To Be is possible, and Nothingness is not possible.[2]

> For this (*view*) can never predominate, that That Which Is Not exists.[3]

Of course, nor can it be proved that "That Which Is" exists. Existence must simply be understood and spoken of as an absolute given.[4] Yet Parmenides' starting point was his claim that since non-Being is impossible and meaningless, we should be "debarred" from this "way of search."[5] What, then, becomes evident upon an inquiry into Being?

> Being has no coming-into-being and no destruction. . . . And it never Was, nor Will Be, because it Is now.[6]

Being was not created from non-Being, because non-Being was impossible. Yet even if Being were created instead from Being, there would be a self-contradiction whereby Being was not Being. Hence we know that Being is not something created. And if Being cannot become non-Being and the self-contradiction whereby Being ceases to be Being is also impossible, then nor can Being be destroyed. In this way we know that Being is uncreated and indestructible. The fact that it is uncreated and indestructible means that time in terms of the past and future has no meaning for Being. This is why Parmenides says that Being is the origin of "it Is now."[7]

> Nor is Being divisible, since it is all alike. . . . [I]t is motionless
> . . . remaining the same in the same place.[8]

This is so because if Being were not uniform and if it moved, then a particular being would differ in the extent of its beingness from other beings and would become non-Being to some degree, resulting in another self-contradiction. This leads to the conclusion that Being is uncreated and indestructible, homogeneous and motionless, something "like the mass of a well-rounded sphere."[9]

HEIDEGGER'S INTERPRETATION OF BEING AND THINKING

Parmenides conveys these insights into Being in the form of revelations from a goddess. At the start of the revelations she utters the famous pronouncement that "it is the same thing to think [noein] and to be [einai]."[10] This is usually construed as anticipating a Kantian subjective realism whereby existence is prescribed by thought, but Heidegger declared that this was not the case.[11] According to Heidegger, such subjective realism eventually leads to a humanistic worldview where technology (reason) governs Nature (beings), and this is what is laying waste to the modern world. In this world, beings are no more than a resource (Bestand) for use by humans, in what is tantamount to a forgetfulness of Being (Seinsvergessenheit).[12] Heidegger argues that the true meaning of this fragment from Parmenides cannot possibly be a declaration of such a position on the forgetfulness of Being.[13] Here I will not question the merits of translating this fragment along the lines of "There is a reciprocal bond between apprehension [taking a receptive attitude] and being,"[14] as did Heidegger.[15] Even if we construe this in its unvarnished sense of "it is the same thing to think and to be," it does not necessarily have to be interpreted as a profession of subjective realism. It could be understood as follows: "Even in everyday Greek usage 'noein [thinking]'—that is, the functioning of '*nous* [*nūs*]', which is always translated as 'reason'—has overtones of 'intuitive knowledge' in the sense of 'inspiration whereby one penetrates the outward appearance to discern the true identity.' In Parmenides this function is particularly emphasized as 'a force that goes beyond sensory phenomena to apprehend the true essence of things directly.' . . . Fragment 3 discusses how only things that have been apprehended through reason [rational thinking] truly exist."[16] Indeed, as long as Parmenides' philosophical poem (which later generations came to refer to as "On Nature") where this fragment occurs contrasts sensory "opinions" (*doxa*), which regard the world as consisting of moving and changing phenomena, with the "Truth" (*alētheiē*) of reason, which transcends this illusion and perceives true Being as an uncreated and indestructible sphere (e.g., B1, lines 29–30), then it seems to me that this interpretation is valid.

2. Empedocles

"ON NATURE"

Empedocles penned two lengthy philosophical poems, "Poem on Nature" and "Purifications," but today they are mostly scattered and lost, with only fragments surviving. Although based on Parmenides' understanding of existence, Empedocles' "Poem on Nature" emphasizes the senses and seeks out physical principles. "Purifications" portrays the pilgrimage of the divine soul, while suggesting an affinity with the Orphic-Pythagorean cult.

Fragment 12 from "Poem on Nature" clearly inherits Parmenides' ontological truth:

> From what in no wise *exists*, it is impossible for anything to come into being; and for *Being* to perish completely is incapable of fulfillment and unthinkable.[17]

Empedocles is of the view that ultimate existence is uncreated and indestructible in this way, but that the real world is sensed as something created and destructible. In order to explain this world of the senses, Empedocles—who was critical of Parmenides' contempt for this sensory experience[18]—attempts to rethink ultimate existence in a multidimensional manner. This was his theory of the four elements of earth, water, fire, and air.[19] All things are created and destroyed through the coming together and separation of these four uncreated and indestructible "roots [*rhizōmata*]":

> these [four elements of earth, water, fire, and air] never cease their continuous exchange, sometimes uniting under the influence of Love [*philie*],[20] so that all become One, at other times again each moving apart through the hostile force of Hate [*neikos*].[21]

Empedocles seems to have envisaged four phases eternally taking turns—a time of harmony when Love rules, followed by a gradual shift to a time of Hate, then a time when Hate holds sway, and a subsequent shift to Love.[22]

"PURIFICATIONS"

In "Purifications," his other poem, Empedocles speaks of how he committed a crime as a result of hate and how he was condemned to metempsychosis:

> [W]hen one of the divine spirits [*daimōn*] whose portion is long life sinfully stains his own limbs with bloodshed, and following Hate has sworn a false oath, these must wander for thrice ten thousand seasons far from the company of the blessed, being born throughout the period into all kinds of mortal shapes, which exchange one hard way of life for another. . . .
> . . . Of this number am I too now, a fugitive from heaven and a wanderer, because I trusted in raging Hate.[23]

Here one would expect that the self that experiences metempsychosis would be thought of as a continuation of the same agent who bears ethical responsibility, but in his discussion of the four elements in "On Nature," Empedocles stated that all living creatures are born from these elements and "these (*Elements*) alone exist, but by running through one another they become different."[24] In other words, it is as if the agent breaks down and returns to the four elements. Perhaps in the latter poem Empedocles is thinking of the corporeal dimension, while in the former he is thinking of the dimension of the soul; or perhaps this represents a development in his thought between the writing of these two poems. With the extant fragments, which are all we have, it is impossible to do more than speculate. Nevertheless, what is important from the perspective of ethical thought is the fact that the forces of Love and Hate, in the physical sense that Empedocles used them in "On Nature," crystallized in "Purifications" in a shift to an awareness of crimes caused by hate, and in turn this was transformed into a consciousness of an ethical responsibility to atone for these crimes—by whatever process that might be—and this then changed again to the viewpoint of a return to the harmony of the love visible from there. It is noteworthy that Empedocles regards this return to the blessedness of love as becoming possible by avoiding bloodshed and meat eating[25] and by contemplating the truth of the universe that is in the "gods,"[26] and that he discusses this in the context of an affinity with the religion of Orpheus and Pythagoras.[27]

3. Pythagoras and the Pythagoreans

Born in the sixth century BCE, Pythagoras hailed from the isle of Samos in Ionia, but since he was later active in southern Italy we will follow convention and include him among the Italians. In any case, we lack detailed information about Pythagoras. A believer in metempsychosis, he founded in Croton in eastern Italy a religious society that observed laws for purifying the soul. This society was secret, and neither its founder nor the Pythagoreans in the following century made his writings public, so the details and matters such as the society's ties with the Orphean community remain shrouded in mystery. We can surmise that in order to purify the soul the Pythagoreans engaged not only in the practice of the laws and mysteries but also in the study of mathematics, music, astronomy, and so on; that as a result their founder in particular is known to have been a man of astonishing erudition; and that Pythagoras's idea of transmigration and his discussion of space, for instance, apparently had an enormous impact on Plato and his successors. Nevertheless, it seems that no particularly noteworthy ethical ideas have been handed down from Pythagoras.

4. Democritus: "The Jovial One"

Democritus was a contemporary of Socrates. Although he was known for his extensive knowledge and writings in various fields such as natural philosophy, medicine, mathematics, botany, musical theory, and ethics, today only fragments of his writings survive. In order to study these various disciplines Democritus traveled from India through Greece as far as Ethiopia, but there are no definite records of him having talked with Socrates in Athens.[28] Democritus's erudition led to him being "given the nickname of 'wisdom [sophiā],' and he was also referred to as 'the jovial one [gelasinos],' because he was amused at how people become caught up in petty things."[29] Unlike Heraclitus, "the obscure one" (skoteinos), Democritus did not criticize people outright, instead laughing cheerfully at them, which shows that he was a "cheerful" (euthumiē) person.[30] Western paintings of Democritus are likewise fond of portraying him as "jovial," and in most pictures, as in the painting by Velasquez, he has a humorous smile, not a derisive one.

Of Democritus's wide-ranging scholastic legacy, here I would like to focus on how the Ionian natural philosophy that started with Thales was rounded off by Democritus two centuries later, and also on how Democritus paved the way for the moral philosophy that was developed by his contemporary Socrates and others down through to Aristotle half a century later.

ATOMIC THEORY

With Parmenides, Ionian natural philosophy discovered the existence of the uncreated and indestructible and the homogeneous and motionless, but with Empedocles' hypothesis of the coming together and separation and the collection and distribution of the four elements (or of innumerable seeds [spermata], according to his contemporary Anaxagoras, ca. 500–428 BCE, omitted here for reasons of space), Empedocles attempted to capture the world of the senses, which is created and destructible. Is it impossible, though, to envisage the world of the senses from a fresh perspective while still adhering to a Parmenidian line of thinking? Democritus (or Leukippos, ca. 435 BCE, who is said to have been Democritus's teacher, although there are few documents available on the details of Leukippos's ideas) responded to this question with his atomic theory. He argued that the ultimate reality, which ought to be not only uncreated and indestructible but also homogeneous and motionless, is restored to life in the phenomenal world not through heterogeneous elements or seeds, but through homogeneous "atoms" (atomon, atoma).[31] In other words, although atoms are homogeneous, through their configuration, orientation, and arrangement[32] they are perceived as the appearance and disappearance of innumerable different phenomena. In this respect Democritus broke Parmenides' "mass of a well-rounded sphere"[33] down into atoms and parted ways with Parmenides, who believed that "Nothingness is not possible."[34] Democritus argued that "Naught [nothing; nothingness] exists just as much as Aught [existence]" as a venue for the movement of atoms.[35]

Then how and why did space, where atoms fly around in a void, come into existence? Democritus did not, however, "discuss such teleological concerns, attributing all matters in which Nature is involved to necessity [*anankē*]."[36] Or he "regards this [space] as having been created by chance and accident [*tychē*]."[37] In either case, Democritus made no attempt to discuss causes and purposes, instead attributing all things to the movement of matter.

EUTHUMIĒ

There might seem to be no room for ethics in such a theory of purposeless necessity, but in fact Democritus laid great stress on ethics. It is true that there is little systematic connection between his study of Nature and his ethics.[38] It is not clear today whether Democritus viewed the former as being about matter and the latter as about the soul, regarding them as having separate frameworks, or whether he believed that it is a purposeless life that particularly requires guidelines for escaping disorder and chaos. In any case, many of his surviving fragments are devoted to this topic, so let us move on now to a consideration of Democritus's ethical views.

> Happiness, like unhappiness, is a property of the soul. Happiness does not dwell in flocks of cattle or in gold. The soul is the dwelling-place of the (*good and evil*) genius [*daimōn*].[39]

> It is right that men should value the soul rather than the body; for perfection of soul corrects the inferiority of the body, but physical strength without intelligence does nothing to improve the mind.[40]

Such fragments postulate a dimension of the soul separate from that of the appearance and disappearance of matter as a result of the inevitable coming together and separation of atoms. This is discussed in relation to *daimōn*, and together with the "intelligent" "valu[ing]" of this, one is led to expect an ethical perspective similar to that of Socrates. This expectation is not met, however, possibly because the extant fragments are biased in content, or perhaps because Democritus's intrinsic interest in this question was limited—again the reasons are unclear. What the remaining ethical fragments offer is not an indefatigable dialogue and quest for virtue à la Socrates or Plato, but merely a compendium of human wisdom similar to aphorisms. Specifically, Democritus's Doctrine of the Mean, which acted as a precursor to that of Aristotle, and his atomism both present ideals along the lines of the "tranquility" (*ataraxia*) inherited by the Epicureans. Democritus, the "jovial one," refers to this in more positive terms as "cheerfulness" (*euthumiē*).

> The best way for a man to lead his life is to have been as cheerful as possible and to have suffered as little as possible. This could happen if one did not seek one's pleasures in mortal things.[41]

> Cheerfulness is created for men through moderation of enjoyment and harmoniousness of life. Things that are in excess or lacking are apt to change and cause great disturbance in the soul. Souls which are stirred by great divergences are neither stable nor cheerful. Therefore one must . . . be content with what one has, paying little heed to things envied and admired, and not dwelling on them in one's mind.[42]

> The brave man is not only he who overcomes the enemy, but he who is stronger than pleasures. Some men are masters of cities, but are enslaved to women.[43]

> All who derive their pleasures from the stomach, overstepping due reason in eating or drinking or sexual pleasure, have pleasures that are but brief and short-lived, only while they are eating and drinking, but pains that are many.[44]

Thus "cheerfulness" is lost when one indulges to excess in the pleasures of eating, drinking, or sexual desire. Democritus's exhortation to "cheerfulness" is linked to his exhortation to "the mean."

> He is fortunate who is happy [*euthumeō*] with moderate means, unfortunate who is unhappy with great possessions.[45]

> The cheerful [*euthumos*] man, who is impelled towards works that are just and lawful, rejoices by day and by night, and is strong and free from care. But the man who neglects justice, and does not do what he ought, finds all such things disagreeable when he remembers any of them, and he is afraid and torments himself.[46]

Democritus further links these ethical exhortations to his noting of the importance of education. With these fragments, which are equally applicable today, I would like to close here by verifying the other threads of Democritus's ideas.

> The man who employs exhortation and persuasion will turn out to be a more effective guide to virtue than he who employs law and compulsion. For the man who is prevented by law from wrongdoing will probably do wrong in secret, whereas the man who is led towards duty by persuasion will probably not do anything untoward either secretly or openly. Therefore the man who acts rightly through understanding and knowledge becomes at the same time brave and upright.[47]

> Worst of all things is frivolity as the educator of youth, for it breeds those pleasures from which wickedness comes.[48]

> If children are allowed not to work, they cannot learn letters or music or gymnastic, nor that which above all things embraces virtue, [namely] reverence [aideisthai]. For it is precisely from these studies that reverence [aidōs] usually grows.[49]

Note that here it is "reverence" (aideisthai)—which leads to "wonder" (thaumazein)—that "embraces virtue [aretē]." This could be construed as a feeling of shame toward oneself,[50] but it would be more natural to interpret it as reverence based on a sense of wonder toward things transcending oneself. This is why Diels and Kranz render this as Ehrfurcht.[51] There are no other surviving examples of aideisthai or aidōs being used in this sense, but as is evident in the quote above, what Democritus meant by "virtue" is the act of being "brave and upright"[52] and also the desire to "benefit men's life."[53] We can take this to mean that Democritus, who knew to "pray" to meet with "fortunate images" (eidōlon),[54] is suggesting here that virtues such as bravery, uprightness, and good faith derive fundamentally from a "reverence" for such divine beings.

Notes

1. Yasuo Iwata, Seiyō shisō no genryū (The origins of Western thought) (Tokyo: Hōsō Daigaku Kyōiku Shinkōkai, 1997), 103–4.
2. Fragment 6 = B6; Iwata, Seiyō shisō (Western thought), 101. See n. 1 of the "Explanatory Notes" regarding English translations of the pre-Socratic writings.
3. Fragment 7 = B7.

4. Iwata, *Seiyō shisō* (Western thought), 101.

5. Fragment 6 = B6.

6. Fragment 8 = B8, lines 3 and 5.

7. Tadashi Inoue renders lines 5b–6a along the lines of "Being is, because here and now the whole exists all at once as a single amalgam." He takes the view that "the opening of Being . . . is simply as something right now." *Parumenidesu* (Parmenides) (Tokyo: Seido-sha, 1996), 175–77.

8. Fragment 8 = B8, lines 22, 26, and 30.

9. Fragment 8 = B8, line 43. According to Inoue (*Parumenidesu* [Parmenides], 240): "In other words, Being, as [my] Idea, rejects the horizon of the reality of birth and death, which has a time line, and draws close to the constraints of Fate and [appears] 'here now,' and unlike the variedness of the horizon of birth and death, it manifests the universe of an amalgam that is homogeneous and uniform, indivisible and motionless. This is not a sphere that becomes fossilized; it is nothing less than [my] linguistic space that establishes self-identity with its basis while being made into a self-model as a sphere that is perfect from any angle and that continues to overflow with strength from its innerness, its very center, to the nooks and crannies of the Bounded, through the self-identity mechanism of its basis."

10. Fragment 3 = B3.

11. M. Heidegger, *Einführung in die Metaphysik* (Tübingen, Germany: Niemeyer, 1953), 104f.

12. M. Heidegger, *Vorträge und Aufsätze* (Pfullingen, Germany: Neske, 1954), 25. See also Jirō Watanabe, *Haideggā no sonzai shisō* (Heidegger's ontology), 2nd ed. (Tokyo: Keisō Shobō, 1985), 477–80.

13. Iwata, *Seiyō shisō* (Western thought), 103.

14. M. Heidegger, "Zusammengehörig sind Vernehmung wechselweise und Sein," in *Einführung in die Metaphysik*, 111; for an English translation, see M. Heidegger, *An Introduction to Metaphysics*, trans. R. Manheim (New Haven, CT: Yale University Press, 1959), 145.

15. For details, see Watanabe, *Haideggā no sonzai shisō* (Heidegger's ontology), 405–15.

16. Iwata, *Seiyō shisō* (Western thought), 100–101.

17. Fragment 12 = B12; emphasis added.

18. Concerning B3, *Collection of Fragments*, Vol. II, 233, nn. 2 and 7 (see "Explanatory Notes").

19. Fragment 17 = B17.

20. *Philie* is synonymous with *philiā*. Fragments 17, 18, and 20 use *philie*, while fragment 19 and other fragments use *philotēs*.

21. Fragment 17 = B17.

22. See the commentary by Simplicius from *Collection of Fragments* B27 onward.

23. Fragment 115, lines 3–8, 14–14 = B115.

24. Fragment 21 = B21.

25. *Collection of Fragments* B128, 136, 137.

26. *Collection of Fragments* B129, 131, 146.

27. See *Collection of Fragments*, Vol. II, 130, n. 1.
28. *Collection of Fragments*, Vol. IV (1998), A1, 36. Note, however, 37.
29. *Collection of Fragments* A2, 40.
30. *Collection of Fragments* A1, 44; A37–64. *Collection of Fragments* B189, etc.
31. *Collection of Fragments* A1, 44; A37–64.
32. *Collection of Fragments* A38.
33. *Collection of Fragments* B8.
34. *Collection of Fragments* B6.
35. *Collection of Fragments* B156.
36. Aristotle, *De generatione animalium* E8, 789b2–4 = A66.
37. Simplicius "On Aristotle's *Physics*" 327, 24 = A67; trans. from Japanese by Judy Wakabayashi.
38. Iwata, *Seiyō shisō* (Western thought), 111. Even if we do not mention the examples of Plato's *Phaedo* and Anaxagoras's "Nous," it was in fact common in Greece to take the discussion to this point. See Iwata, *Seiyō shisō* (Western thought), 110.
39. Stobaeus, *Eclogae* II, 7, 3i = B170, 171.
40. Stobaeus, *Florilegium* III, 1, 27 = B187.
41. *Florilegium* III, 1, 47 = B189.
42. *Florilegium* III, 1, 210 = B191.
43. *Florilegium* III, 7, 25 = B214.
44. *Florilegium* III, 18, 35 = B235.
45. *Florilegium* IV, 39, 17 = B286.
46. *Eclogae* II, 9, 3 = B174.
47. *Eclogae* II, 31, 59 = B181.
48. *Eclogae* II, 31, 56 = B178.
49. *Eclogae* II, 31, 57 = B179.
50. See *Collection of Fragments* B264.
51. H. Diels and W. Kranz, *Die Fragmente der Vorsokratiker*, vol. 2 (Berlin: Weidmann, 1951–52), 181.
52. *Collection of Fragments* B181.
53. *Collection of Fragments* B248.
54. *Collection of Fragments* B166.

CHAPTER 3

Socrates and Plato (1): Socrates, the Sophists, and Plato

1. Socrates

Socrates (470–399 BCE) himself did not leave a single written word behind. Nor is it entirely clear to what extent Plato (427–347 BCE), his disciple who penned twenty-seven dialogues featuring Socrates as the protagonist, used Socrates as a mouthpiece to air his own philosophical views. Nevertheless, by focusing on the early dialogues (particularly the *Apology of Socrates* and the *Crito*), which are thought to reproduce Socrates' words quite faithfully compared with Plato's middle and later dialogues, here I would like to isolate those ideas that are regarded as representing the core of Socrates' beliefs.

Although they cannot compare with those by Plato, other writings about Socrates include Xenophon's *Memories of Socrates*, Aristophanes' *Clouds*, and Aristotle's *Metaphysics*. What can be verified as historical fact from these works is that Socrates engaged in philosophical debate on the street corners of Athens, which led to him being sentenced to death in 399 BCE on charges of "corrupting the young, and . . . not believing in the gods in whom the city believes."[1] It is highly likely that the corresponding statements by Socrates in the above-mentioned dialogues convey Socrates' own views.

KNOWLEDGE OF IGNORANCE

According to the *Apology of Socrates*, a priestess at the Temple of Apollo in Delphi made the divine revelation that "no one is wiser"[2] than Socrates. On hearing of this oracle, Socrates was apparently "at a loss," because he himself was "aware that I am not at all wise," but nor could he believe that the god was "saying something false."[3] So he visited politicians, poets, and artisans who were regarded as wise by everyone, including themselves. After talking with these people, Socrates realized that "he supposes he knows something when he does not know, while I, just as I do not know, do not suppose I do. I *am* likely to be wiser than he in just this little something: that what I do not know, I do not suppose I know."[4] Socrates came to interpret this enigmatic oracle as follows: "That one of you, O human beings, is wisest, who, like Socrates, knows that in truth he is worth nothing with respect to wisdom."[5] Realizing that his divinely appointed task was to make people aware of this paradox of the "knowledge of ignorance," Socrates then went on to engage in dialogues with people who considered themselves wise. He devoted himself to disabusing them of this notion, with the result that "I have had no leisure worth speaking of, either to do any of the things of the city or any of my own things. Instead, I am in ten-thousandfold poverty"[6] and that he was exposed to the "hatreds" and "slanders" of those he had exposed as not being wise.[7]

   This is the origin and outcome of Socrates' dialogues as recounted in his speech of defense on being brought before the court in Athens. Having witnessed the whole proceedings from the public gallery, the young Plato made his record of the events public some time after Socrates had been put to death. This record is thought to be Plato's *Apology of Socrates*.

KNOWLEDGE OF GOOD

Yet despite his protestations of "not know[ing]," did not Socrates in fact know a great deal? Politicians presumably know about politics, poets about poetry, and artisans about the techniques of their craft. So what did Socrates mean when he said that people in general are ignorant? Ignorant of what?

   The answer is hinted at after a dialogue with a politician in the *Apology*, when Socrates says "neither of us is likely to know anything noble and good [*kalon kagathon*]."[8] Socrates was of the view that goodness is beautiful,[9] so from the perspective of ethical thought, this can be summed up as signifying that the main intent behind Socrates' entire dialogic activities was to learn about this goodness of which he was ignorant. He vowed not to give up "the love of knowledge [*philosophein*, i.e., philosophy]" even if he were to receive an offer of clemency in return for abandoning such activities.

> I will not stop philosophizing. . . . Best of men, you who are
> an Athenian, from the city that is greatest and best reputed for
> wisdom and strength, are you not ashamed that you care for
> having as much money as possible, and reputation, and honor,
> but that you neither care nor think about prudence, and truth,
> and how your soul will be the best possible?[10]

In other words, goodness entails taking steps to better one's soul, through dialogue aimed at learning something. This was the focus of Socrates' lifelong engagement with philosophy. And in pursuing this goal, he repeatedly carried out "cross-examining dialogues [*elenchi*]." The usual pattern was for Socrates to ask his partner in the dialogue what constitutes ethical goodness—that is, of what do virtues such as bravery, temperance, justice, and wisdom consist—and then to refute both their answer and his own, with the upshot that the dialogue would end still mired in the darkness of ignorance, with no resolution. Here the meaning of Socrates "not know[ing]" becomes clearer. In the final analysis, it means "not knowing the ultimate basis for fragmentary knowledge . . . relating to ethical truth."[11] In other words, through Socrates' "midwifery,"[12] his dialogue partners would deduce fragmentary knowledge about the nature of goodness but "fail to discern the relationships amongst these fragmentary pieces of knowledge or to systematize the whole."[13] In that sense, neither Socrates nor his sparring partners truly pinned down the essence of goodness. This, I believe, is why Socrates was forced to return repeatedly to the knowledge of ignorance.

DAIMONION

It is not difficult to imagine how such dialectical cross-examinations ended up in negative conclusions that overturned conventional wisdom and led to concern over how Socrates made "the weaker speech the stronger"[14] and "corrupt[ed] the young."[15] Subsequently, in fact, Plato rightly pointed out in book VII of the *Republic* and elsewhere that there is a danger attached to philosophy whereby the lack of a single ultimate answer to their repeated philosophical questions might lead young people to think they have also discredited the good traditions, to justify what amounts to a self-indulgent lifestyle, and to act as their whims take them.[16] So as far as the rationalist aspect of Socrates' philosophy is concerned, the accusation that he "corrupt[ed] the young" can be considered unfounded in the commonly accepted sense but partially legitimate in another sense. In any case, the complaints lodged against him were also directed at his mystic aspects, for "he does not believe in the gods of the State."[17] So what about this allegation?

Socrates interpreted this charge in the sense of "not believ[ing] in gods at all,"[18] though he had long "believe[d] in and [taught] *daimonia* [demigods]."[19] On the contrary, "we . . . believe that daimons are either gods or children of gods."[20] So it is completely unjustified, he argued, to claim that he did not acknowledge gods.[21] The expression *to daimonion* derives from *daimōn*, which expresses a supernatural, spiritual being, and it is a nominalization of the neuter form of the adjective *daimonios*, which means "*daimōn*-like." In this careful way, Socrates is referring to something divine, although he does not clarify its nature. He says, "This is something which began for me in childhood; a certain voice comes, and whenever it comes, it always turns me away from whatever I am about to do, but never urges me forward."[22]

Amazingly, though, not once in his trial did the *daimonion* stop Socrates,[23] so this is "likely to be good."[24] An unjust death is usually regarded as "the extreme of evils,"[25] but as throughout his whole life, so too at its end Socrates listened to this divine entity and sought to face death with equanimity. Socrates' philosophical activities, which were triggered by the oracle at Delphi, demonstrated their true value at the point where the vector of his questioning people about ethical goodness was matched against a vector that lent ear to the voice of the transcendent and worked out its meaning. Here lies a more direct transcendental experience, one that predates Plato's speculations about a theory of Ideas as the realization of universal concepts (see chapter 4).

ACHIEVING JUSTICE

This way of ending the *Apology*, underpinned by transcendental experience, sounds as if Socrates is "of good hope"[26] in relation to his own happiness (*eu-daimoniā*), and, if anything, it leaves the reader with an upbeat impression. By contrast, the *Crito*, where Socrates rejects his old friend Crito's proposal to escape from prison in the days between his death sentence and execution, conveys a different, austere aspect of Socrates whereby he tries to achieve justice according to human *logos*. This is impressive in a different fashion.

Here Socrates returns to the "principle" (*logos*)²⁷ that "We mustn't think the most important thing is living, but living well [*eu zēn*],"²⁸ and he affirms that "'well,' 'right,' and 'justly' all mean the same thing." On the other hand, he concludes that "injustice is evil," and "Whether the many admit it or not and whether we must suffer punishments milder or harsher than these, still committing injustice is evil and shameful under any circumstances for the one who commits it,"²⁹ so "we must never repay an injustice or do any evil to anyone."³⁰ In this way, the morality that Socrates pursued throughout his life is wonderfully achieved. Moreover, here he also displays an "amazing innovativeness"³¹ that overturns the traditional Greek view of justice,³² which deemed revenge to be good.

COMPARISON WITH NATURAL PHILOSOPHY

Let me comment further on the position of Socrates' ethical thought from his viewpoint, or rather that of Plato.³³ The *Phaedo*, one of Plato's middle dialogues, relates Socrates' last days from a different perspective, with Plato here having Socrates reflect on his own intellectual pilgrimage. In his youth, Socrates had become interested in the study of Nature and sought to delve into the cause of everything in the world coming into being, existing, and perishing. Socrates notes that, in an attempt to get to the bottom of what "placed each thing severally as it was best that it should be,"³⁴ he perused works by Anaxagoras. Socrates was greatly disappointed, however, because Anaxagoras did "not [make] it in any way responsible for the ordering of things, simply accounting mists and air and water and many other strange things causes."³⁵ Plato also has Socrates comment on other writers:

> And so one man encompasses the earth with a vortex, and claims that it is kept in its place by the heavens, while another puts the air underneath it as a support. . . . But they don't even look for the force that causes things to be now arranged in the best manner in which they possibly could be arranged, nor do they think that this force has any divine power; they think that they may at some time find an Atlas stronger than this one and more immortal and better able to hold all together, and do not suppose that that which is really good and "fitting" can fit or hold anything together.³⁶

As commentators have pointed out,³⁷ it is thought that "one man" refers to Empedocles and "another" to people such as Anaximenes, Anaxagoras, and Democritus. What Socrates is criticizing here is the fact that all of the natural philosophers in the sixth to fifth centuries BCE explained only the state of things, not the *"real* reasons" behind things.[38]

By contrast, the *"real* reason" into which Socrates was inquiring was why things are as they are. For instance, Socrates was sitting in prison about to swallow a draught of poison. Even if one were to explain his situation extrinsically as being due to the fact that he relaxed his tendons and bent his knees, this would not identify the true intrinsic cause. If anything, the reason Socrates was sitting in prison was that he believed it was good to obey the state's laws and submit to its ruling, so it is this that should be regarded as the *"real* reason."[39] The fact that Socrates steered the direction of inquiry not toward an explanation of the state of Nature but toward *"real* reasons"—particularly those relating to human goodness—can be regarded as his greatest achievement. As a result, philosophy was "fetch'd down . . . from Heaven and lodg'd . . . in Cities,"[40] and the philosophical mind, which until then had been bent on the world of Nature, came to gaze on man's inner self. This is how Socrates can be positioned in the history of philosophy.[41]

Of course, as was made apparent by our discussion in chapter 2, it is perhaps going too far to reject the Pre-Socratics so sweepingly. If we examine the role of these philosophers from the perspective of the history of ethical thought, then inasmuch as they inquired into ethics in relation to transcendency, they can be regarded as having bequeathed many achievements that paved the way for Socrates. By now there should be no need to go into the details of how even these philosophers "look[ed] for the force that causes things to be now arranged in the best manner in which they possibly could be arranged."[42] Admittedly, though, their discussions and interests did tend to focus mainly on Nature, as distinct from human ethics. Socrates' momentous significance in the history of ethical thought lay in the fact that he made ethics the sole preoccupation of philosophical interest.

2. The Sophists

It was Socrates' student Plato who inherited and developed this ethical concern, as well as the interest in transcendency that had existed ever since the natural philosophers; but before moving on to a discussion of Plato, we must first look at the Sophists (*sophistēs*). These were intellectuals—*sophistēs* is virtually synonymous with *sophos*, which refers to wise men with specialized knowledge (*sophiā*)—who were contemporaries of Socrates or overlapped with Plato, being active in Athens in the fifth to

fourth centuries BCE. They made it their vocation to travel around various cities and impart knowledge and expertise, including rhetoric (*rhētor-
ikē*), to young people. Protagoras (ca. 500–ca. 400 BCE), Gorgias (ca.
484–ca. 375 BCE), and Thrasymachus (fifth to fourth centuries BCE)
are three particularly well-known Sophists, all of whom made frequent
appearances in Plato's dialogues.[43] Here we will focus on Thrasymachus,
who engages Socrates in a debate on justice in the first volume of the
Republic, one of Plato's middle dialogues.

THRASYMACHUS'S VIEW OF JUSTICE AS THE
ADVANTAGE OF THE STRONGER

In the *Republic*, Thrasymachus argues that "the just is nothing else than
the advantage of the stronger."[44] This is because "each form of government enacts the laws with a view to its own advantage," and "by so
legislating they proclaim that the just for their subjects is that which is
for their—the rulers'—advantage and the man who deviates from this
law they chastise as a law-breaker and a wrongdoer."[45]

In the *Republic*, Socrates counters Thrasymachus's argument as follows. The arts benefit not the artisans but their subjects. For instance,
medicine does not benefit the physician but the sick. Likewise, surely
politics benefits not the ruling politicians but their subjects, that is, the
people.[46]

Thrasymachus's response was unexpected. "Tell me, Socrates, have
you got a nurse?" When Socrates failed to grasp his intent, Thrasymachus followed up by saying, "Because . . . she lets her little 'snotty' run
about driveling and doesn't wipe your face clean."[47] In other words,
Thrasymachus was of the view that Socrates' argument—which was akin
to a shepherd fattening his sheep not for his own gain but purely for the
sheep's own good—was nothing more than the hypocritical rhetoric of
a callow fool.[48] Thrasymachus argued that this is obvious if one considers
the case of tyrants, absolute rulers who commit the "most consummate
form of injustice"; they take "away what belongs to others . . . not little
by little but at one swoop."[49] Swindlers and thieves are punished if they
perpetrate just one such act, but dictators, who commit these acts whole-
sale, even earn acclaim from the very citizens they have enslaved. Hence,
Thrasymachus asserted again, justice is none other than the advantage of
plundering tyrants, that is, of the stronger.[50]

THE PERSUASIVE TECHNIQUES OF THE SOPHISTS

This argument was subsequently refuted in Socrates' *elenchi*, or cross-examinations, but we will forgo the details here. Instead, I would like to focus on the fact that this probably incorporates Plato's criticism of how in Thrasymachus' attempts to argue the other person down in an unpredictable manner—such as his "nurse" statement and his attitude in response to Socrates' comment that Thrasymachus was "telling us your real opinions about the truth," whereby Thrasymachus replied, "What difference does it make to you . . . whether I believe it or not? Why don't you test the argument?"[51]—Thrasymachus was not necessarily trying to probe the truth or to speak of what he himself believed to be true but simply trying to browbeat his opponent, which was a feature of the Sophists' art of persuasion.[52] Gorgias has left us marvelous examples of speeches and debates using these persuasive techniques,[53] and Protagoras's proposition that "Of all things the measure is man"[54] is a famous formulation of the value relativism that underpins such a belief in persuasion for the sake of persuasion. Today, when a relativistic attitude in relation to value judgments predominates, there is also a tendency to reevaluate the Sophists.[55] Here, however, I would like to return to the thrust of the argument put forward by Socrates (i.e., Plato)—who maintained that value standards reside not in human *nomos* (laws and customs) but in *physis* (Nature) and that these standards are absolute—to ascertain this trend.[56]

ISSUES RAISED BY GLAUCON

It is no easy matter, however, to develop this direction adequately in line with the concept of justice that constitutes the main theme of the *Republic*. So in an attempt to reexamine this issue, from book II onward Plato has his own elder brother, Glaucon, who although not a Sophist was quite a polemicist, elaborate on the Thrasymachian argument on justice. Glaucon feels "good will and encouragement"[57] toward Socrates and is an "aid"[58] who does not engage in superficial persuasion but pursues the truth, yet he sets out from the position that perhaps Thrasymachus's claim is accurate, citing the memorable tale about the ring of Gyges in doing so.

3. The Ring of Gyges

THE ORIGIN OF JUSTICE

Plato first has Glaucon present a variation on Thrasymachus's argument:

> By nature, they say, to commit injustice is a good and to suffer
> it is an evil, but that the excess of evil in being wronged is
> greater than the excess of good in doing wrong. So that when
> men do wrong and are wronged by one another and taste of
> both, those who lack the power to avoid the one and take the
> other determine that it is for their profit to make a compact
> with one another neither to commit nor to suffer injustice; and
> that this is the beginning of legislation and of covenants be-
> tween men, and that they name the commandment of the law
> the lawful and the just, and that this is the genesis and essential
> nature of justice.[59]

In fact, from the Athenian pretext for the Melos massacre in the Peloponnesian War as narrated by Thucydides[60] right up to the ethics of the
strong proposed by Kallikles, who in the *Gorgias* argues that it is
strength that constitutes justice,[61] arguments that regard precisely such a
world where the weak are victims of the strong as natural justice are so
commonplace that one's "ears are dinned."[62] (What also springs to mind
today is Nietzsche's reasoning surrounding the origins of good and evil
in *Zur Genealogie der Moral*, where he argues that slave-like *ressentiment*
on the part of Hebraism and Christianity reversed ancient aristocratic
value judgments of survival of the fittest.)[63] Yet Glaucon goes on to say
that the legitimacy of such a theory about the origin of justice is obvious
simply by giving someone the ring of Gyges.[64]

IF ONE WERE INVISIBLE

Gyges was a shepherd in the service of the king of Lydia, and one day
after an earthquake he found a body in a chasm that had opened up in
the earth. Gyges removed a gold ring from the corpse's finger and placed
it on his own hand. He realized that turning the ring one way made him
invisible, while turning it the other way made him visible again. So Gyges
became invisible and seduced the queen, slew the king, and took over the

kingdom. Glaucon used this tale to introduce the argument that anyone who put on this ring would, without exception, act in the following manner:

> No one could be found, it would seem, of such adamantine temper as to persevere in justice and endure to refrain his hands from the possessions of others and not touch them, though he might with impunity take what he wished even from the marketplace, and enter into houses and lie with whom he pleased, and slay and loose from bonds whomsoever he would, and in all other things conduct himself among mankind as the equal of a god. And in so acting he would do no differently from the other man, but both would pursue the same course.[65]

WHO IS HAPPIER: THE JUST OR THE UNJUST?

Glaucon claims that "the proponent of this theory" asserts this to be "a great proof" that the belief "that there is far more profit for him personally in injustice than in justice is what every man believes."[66] Glaucon is of the view that it is our task to scrutinize the validity of this argument. He suggests that in order to examine this issue, we must postulate an entirely unjust person and an entirely just person and ask who is the happier.[67] An entirely unjust person is one who commits injustices but acts so as not to be discovered, so that he is regarded as being just. By contrast, an entirely just person must lose his reputation as a just person, because such a reputation might result in him acting justly for the sake of receiving honor rather than for the sake of justice itself, so he could no longer be said to be purely just. Hence the entirely just person earns the reputation of being unjust even without committing a single unjust action and must resolutely tread the path of justice until death, even if this means having to "endure the lash, the rack, chains."[68] It is not difficult to imagine that in this portrayal of the entirely just man Plato had in mind Socrates, who was executed after an unjust trial.[69] The question raised here by Glaucon (i.e., Plato) is who is truly the happier of two such people.

So how does the *Republic* respond to this acute question? It goes on to raise various points, and these interact with the theory of state that constitutes the fundamental argument put forward in the *Republic*. Plato's line of reasoning is by no means easy to follow, but—most noticeably in book IX—his reply can be construed as being presented in the following three dimensions: (a) a reply based on an analogy with the ideal state system (book IX, chapters 4–6); (b) a reply based on the three levels of the functioning of the soul (book IX, chapters 7–8); and (c) a reply based on hedonics (book IX, chapters 12–13). Let us examine the broad outline of each of these replies in turn, referring also to related passages outside of book IX.

PLATO'S REPLY

(a) Plato's Reply in an Analogy to the State System

The epitome of an entirely unjust person is the dictator (tyrant, *tyrannos*), because despite using his authority to steal away everything he is even praised for his justness by the very people he oppresses. There are six different types of state systems: monarchy, aristocracy, timocracy, oligarchy, mob rule, and tyranny.[70] It is clear that the system leading to the most wretchedness and unhappiness is tyranny,[71] because the people are not free, living instead under oppression.[72] By analogy, then, dictators are the most wretched and unhappy individuals, because they are enslaved to ceaseless desires yet are constantly unfulfilled, and they are continually tormented by dread and distress out of fear of a rebellion.[73] By contrast, monarchies and aristocracies are bundled together here as a desirable form of government, representing the state systems that bring most happiness.[74] By analogy, in individuals too it is the most just person, in whom the best elements of the soul govern the worst and maddest appetitive parts,[75] who is the happiest.[76] This is the gist of Plato's response to the question above in terms of an analogy with the ideal state.

(b) Reply Based on the Three Parts of the Soul

The division of the soul into its most superior and inferior parts is premised on the tripartite theory of the soul that is set out in chapters 11–15 of book IV of the *Republic*.[77] According to this theory, the soul consists of three parts:

1) a *rational* part that contemplates the good of the soul;[78]
2) an *appetitive* part (hunger, sexual desire, etc.), which has nothing to do with considerations of what is good or bad;[79]
3) a *spirited* part (indignation, pride, shame, desire for honor, etc.),

which is based on beliefs about good and evil but does not depend on considerations of what is best for the soul.[80]

Plato's second reply follows this tripartite theory more clearly.

People in whom the rational part dominates the soul are lovers of wisdom, while those in whom the appetitive part prevails become enamored of gain, since their desires are fulfilled by money,[81] and people in whom the spirited part is predominant love honor.[82] Yet even lovers of wisdom must gain something in order to live, and if they strive hard they will naturally achieve honor, thereby experiencing the pleasures of both of the other two parts of the soul. These two parts, however, will be ignorant of the pleasures of acquiring wisdom. Hence the lover of wisdom is better off as far as experiencing pleasures is concerned. Furthermore, compared with people in whom the other parts of the soul dominate, the experiences of lovers of wisdom are more based on prudence and carried out more through discussion, and it is judgments based on experience, prudence, and discussion that are the truest. Hence it is most accurate to judge the lover of wisdom as having pleasure. The following reasoning is omitted from Plato's description, but as long as his reply in (b) is included among the "proofs" for the question above,[83] then it naturally has the following implications: it is true that wisdom is pleasurable, and just people who love wisdom are the happiest; conversely, unjust people who love gain are the unhappiest.

(c) Reply Based on Hedonics

Plato's third reply relates to hedonics. The opposite of pleasure is pain, but between the two lies a static state where the soul experiences neither pleasure nor pain.[84] When experiencing pain, this static state seems pleasurable, and in times of pleasure the static state seems painful when the pleasure ceases.[85] In this way, things that are in fact neither pleasurable nor painful take on the semblance of pleasure or pain. Moreover, although the act of becoming is a motion, by rights this should be a static state. In other words, this medium between pleasure and pain merely seems like pleasure or pain but does not include true pleasure or pain.[86]

On reaching the intermediate state between pleasure and pain as a result of satisfying their pangs of frustration, people in whom the appetitive part of the soul is dominant merely mistake this for pleasure. Since they have never "tasted stable and pure" rational pleasure, they "graz[e] and copulat[e]" under the impression that this constitutes pleasure.[87] These are mere "phantoms of true pleasure, illusions of scene-painting, so colored by contrary juxtaposition as to seem intense in either kind, and to beget mad loves of themselves in senseless souls, and to be fought for."[88] People in whom the spirited part of the soul dominates are swayed by a desire for honor, a craving for victory, and anger, and even if they gain pleasures that satisfy these desires of their spirited part, these are not true pleasures, but lead to mutual conflict.[89] By contrast, taking "only those pleasures which reason approves . . . will . . . enjoy the truest pleasures."[90] In this way it is the tyrant swayed by desires who leads the most repugnant life, while the philosopher–king in an aristocracy, in whom the rational part of the soul is dominant, leads the most pleasurable. Plato's third reply closes with the calculation that the pleasures enjoyed by the latter are 729 times those of the former.[91]

RECONSIDERING THE TALE OF GYGES

The figure of the utterly just person who is persecuted—a figure that Glaucon contrasts with the utterly unjust person—is not always maintained consistently in the tale related by Socrates (i.e., Plato) in book IX of the *Republic*, but that is not the key point. What is crucial here is whether this tale of Gyges really does portray the truth about human nature, that is, whether it is true that anyone would, on becoming invisible, touch "the possessions of others" and do as they please. The answer to this is surely obvious from the discussion above.

The most unjust tyrant is someone who pursues unchecked his nonrational desires for eros and power. A person who is obsessed by the desire for eros becomes, to borrow Socrates' figures of speech in the *Gorgias*, "like a leaky jar," and "he is forced to be always filling [it] day and night, or else he suffers the most extreme distresses."[92] He is "itching and wanting to scratch, with no restriction on scratching, and continuing to scratch all [his] life,"[93] and he is a kind of invalid in whom the appetitive part of the three divisions of the soul has become bloated, resulting in an imbalance. Moreover, since the tyrant has gained power unjustly, he will neither be trusted by nor will he trust others, as he will live in constant fear that in turn he, too, will be deposed by unjust means. Where is there any happiness in such a life full of confusion and insecurity, pain, and suspicion?

As Plato himself recognizes, it is true that "there exists in every one of us, even in some reputed most respectable, a terrible, fierce and lawless brood of desires, which it seems are revealed in our sleep."[94] Taming this nonrational monster of the soul through reason and through achieving balance and peace in the soul represents the lifestyle of the just philosopher; even if he were to obtain the ring of Gyges, why would he abandon his truly happy lot and stoop to become a slave to illicit desires? This is the nub of Plato's response to the tale of Gyges.

In this chapter we have moved from Socrates through to the Sophists and then naturally on to Plato's views, but where and how should the ideas of Socrates and Plato be properly separated? What specifically did Plato have in mind in relation to the "lifestyle of the just philosopher" mentioned at the end? And how is justice related to the other Greek virtues, such as bravery, temperance, and wisdom? In the following chapter I would like to explore these points further by focusing again on Plato and his dialogues and through them reexamine the scope of Plato's response to the issues raised by the tale of Gyges.

Notes

1. Plato, *Apology of Socrates* 24C; for an English translation, see *Plato's Apology of Socrates*, trans. T. G. West (Ithaca, NY: Cornell University Press, 1979).
2. *Apology of Socrates* 21A.
3. *Apology of Socrates* 21B.
4. *Apology of Socrates* 21D.
5. *Apology of Socrates* 23B.
6. *Apology of Socrates* 23B–C.
7. *Apology of Socrates* 22E–23A.
8. *Apology of Socrates* 21D. A footnote in Teruo Mishima's translation, *Sokuratesu no benmei* (The apology of Socrates) (Tokyo: Kōdansha Gakujutsu Bunko, 1988), accordingly points out the possibility of translating *kalon kagathon* along the lines of anything "fine" (p. 90, n. 30).
9. See 48B in the below-mentioned *Crito*.
10. *Apology of Socrates* 29D–E.
11. Yasuo Iwata, *Seiyō shisō no genryū* (The origins of Western thought) (Tokyo: Hōsō Daigaku Kyōiku Shinkōkai, 1997), 137.
12. Plato, *Theaetetus* 150A–C.
13. Iwata, *Seiyō shisō* (Western thought), 137.
14. *Apology of Socrates* 23D.
15. *Apology of Socrates* 24C.
16. Plato, *Republic* VII, 15–18, 535A–541B.
17. *Republic* VII, 15–18, 535A–541B.
18. *Apology of Socrates* 26C.
19. *Apology of Socrates* 27C.
20. *Apology of Socrates* 27D.

21. *Apology of Socrates* 27D–E.

22. *Apology of Socrates* 31D.

23. *Apology of Socrates* 40A–B.

24. *Apology of Socrates* 40C.

25. *Apology of Socrates* 40A.

26. *Apology of Socrates* 41C.

27. See also Plato, *Gorgias* 512D.

28. Plato, *Crito* 48B; for an English translation, see *The Apology and Crito of Plato and the Apology and Symposium of Xenophon*, trans. R. Larson (Lawrence, KS: Coronado, 1980).

29. *Crito* 49B.

30. *Crito* 49C.

31. Iwata, *Seiyō shisō* (Western thought), 142. Iwata states, "As far as I am aware . . . the only person other than Jesus who spoke of an ideology of overcoming . . . revenge was Socrates" (143). Yet, as we shall see in chapters 9, 10, and 14, the Old Testament also frequently mentions this idea in unexpected places (Lev 19:17–18; Prov 25:21–22; Isa 52:13–53:12). See also Seizō Sekine, *Kyūyaku seisho no shisō: 24 no danshō* (The thought of the Old Testament: 24 fragments) (Tokyo: Iwanami Shoten, 1998), 215–19.

32. See, for example, Plato, *Meno* 71E.

33. According to Shinrō Katō (*Girishia tetsugaku-shi* [A history of Greek philosophy] [Tokyo: University of Tokyo Press, 1996], 115–16) and prevailing theories, this represents Plato's criticism of natural philosophy, rather than Socrates' own words. See the beginning of chapter 4 for a discussion of the distinction between the views of Plato and Socrates.

34. Plato, *Phaedo* 97C; for an English translation, see *Phaedo: A Translation with Introd. Notes and Appendices*, trans. R. S. Bluck (London: Routledge & Kegan Paul, 1955).

35. *Phaedo* 98B–C.

36. *Phaedo* 99B–C.

37. See, for example, Mie Ikeda's translation of the *Phaedo* in *Sekai no meisho 6 Puraton I* (Great books of the world 6, Plato I) (Tokyo: Chūō Kōron, 1978), 557.

38. *Phaedo* 98E, 99B.

39. *Phaedo* 98E.

40. Cicero, *Tusculanae disputationes*, Vol. 5, 4 (10); translated as *The Five Days Debate at Cicero's House in Tusculum*, trans. Christopher Wase (London: Printed for Abel Swalle, 1683).

41. See, for instance, the outstanding discussion in Iwata, *Seiyō shisō* (Western thought), 135.

42. *Phaedo* 99B–C.

43. See, for example, *Protagoras*, *Gorgias*, *Theaetetus*, and the *Republic*.

44. *Republic* I, 338C. No such claim is particularly evident in the other fragments collated in *Sokuratesu izen tetsugakusha dampen-shū* (Collection of fragments from pre-Socratic philosophers), Part I, ed. Katsutoshi Uchiyama (Tokyo: Iwanami Shoten, 1996), Vol. 5, 115ff.

45. *Republic* I, 338E.
46. *Republic* I, 341A–342E.
47. *Republic* I, 343A.
48. *Republic* I, 336C, 343D.
49. *Republic* I, 344A.
50. *Republic* I, 344A–C.
51. *Republic* I, 349A.
52. In order to reveal such deceit on the part of the Sophists, Plato's later dialogue, the *Sophist*, pursues their fallacies and presents an exposé of their infinite Not-Being (*to mē on*: 256E). Thorleif Boman compares this expression with various words frequently used by the Hebrew prophets and in Psalms, such as "illusion" (*sheqer*) and "vanity" (*hevel*), focusing particularly on the features they have in common. In other words, this represents a nihility that has no substance and gives rise to no value. See Thorleif Boman, *Das hebräische Denken im Vergleich mit dem Griechischen*, 2nd ed. (Göttingen, Germany: Vandenhoeck & Ruprecht, 1954), 51.
53. *Collection of Fragments*, Vol. 5, 43ff.
54. *Collection of Fragments* B1.
55. G. B. Kerferd, *The Sophistic Movement* (Cambridge: Cambridge University Press, 1981).
56. For a broad overview of the whole history of Greek ethical thought and a survey of the issue of *nomos* versus *physis*, see Teruo Mishima's "Nomosu to pyushisu—sono rinriteki imi" (*Nomos* and *physis*—their ethical meaning), in *Kihan to imi: Sokuratesu to gendai* (Norms and meaning: Socrates and modern times) (Tokyo: Tōkai Daigaku Shuppan Kai, 2000), 3–33.
57. *Republic* V, 474A.
58. *Republic* V, 474B.
59. *Republic* II, 358E–359B.
60. Thucydides, *The History of the Peloponnesian War* V, 105.
61. *Gorgias*, particularly 482Cff.
62. *Republic* II, 358C.
63. The first essay, "Good and evil, good and bad," in F. W. Nietzsche, *Zur Genealogie der Moral* (Leipzig: Naumann, 1887).
64. *Republic* II, 359Dff.
65. *Republic* II, 360B–C.
66. *Republic* II, 360C–D.
67. *Republic* II, 361D–E.
68. *Republic* II, 362A.
69. See, for instance, Katō, *Girishia tetsugaku-shi* (A history of Greek philosophy), 139.
70. *Republic* VIII.
71. *Republic* IX, 576E.
72. *Republic* IX, 577C.
73. *Republic* IX, 577E–578A.
74. *Republic* IX, 576E.
75. *Republic* IX, 577D.

76. *Republic* IX, 580B–C.
77. *Republic* IV, 435B–441A, in particular, 439D.
78. *Republic* IV, 439D, 441C, 442B.
79. *Republic* IV, 439D.
80. *Republic* IV, 439E–441C.
81. *Republic* IX, 581A.
82. *Republic* IX, 581A–D.
83. *Republic* IX, 580C–D.
84. *Republic* IX, 583C.
85. *Republic* IX, 583D–E.
86. *Republic* IX, 584E.
87. *Republic* IX, 586A–B.
88. *Republic* IX, 586B–C.
89. *Republic* IX, 586C–D.
90. *Republic* IX, 586E–587A.
91. *Republic* IX, 587B–588A.
92. *Gorgias* 493E; for an English translation, see *Gorgias*, trans. Terence Irwin (Oxford: Clarendon, 1979).
93. *Gorgias* 494C.
94. *Republic* IX, 572B.

CHAPTER 4

Socrates and Plato (2): Focusing on Plato

1. Plato and His Dialogues

SKETCH OF PLATO'S CAREER

As we saw in the transition from section 3.1 to 3.2, Plato inherited and developed the interest in transcendence that had existed ever since the pre-Socratic natural philosophers, as well as Socrates' interest in ethics. Born in Athens in the early stages of the Peloponnesian War (431–404 BCE), Plato grew up during the war years. After the war he witnessed the tumultuous events of the oligarchy known as the Thirty Tyrants (404–403 BCE) and the execution of his teacher Socrates, then for the next dozen years he led the life of an itinerant. In about 387 BCE Plato founded his Academy in Athens, and he dedicated himself to the running of the school and the task of philosophy. Plato continued his untiring pursuit of knowledge until his death at the age of eighty, leaving behind twenty-seven dialogues that are divided into the Socratic dialogues, the middle dialogues, and the later dialogues. In this chapter, I would like to focus on Plato's views and ascertain his unique position in the history of ethical thought.

THE MIDDLE AND LATER DIALOGUES

Specifically, building on chapter 3, I would like to reconsider the discussions of justice and virtue found in the *Republic*, Plato's main work in his middle period. While referring also to the other middle dialogues (e.g., the *Phaedo*, *Phaedrus*, *Meno*,[1] *Symposium*) and his later dialogues (e.g., the *Theaetetus* and the *Philebus*), I will examine the essence of

Plato's views on *erōs*, his theory of Ideas, the immortality of the soul, and so on, as well as the relationships among these concepts, in an attempt to provide a bird's-eye view of Plato's entire ethical thought. Through this I would like to reexplore the validity of Plato's response to the tale of Gyges as mentioned at the end of chapter 3.

Although Socrates is usually the protagonist in these dialogues, it is thought that he is actually voicing Plato's own opinions, and these views often seem to conflict with those of the historical Socrates in the Socratic dialogues examined in section 3.1. No doubt Plato continued to use the figure of Socrates as protagonist because he believed that these dialogues expounded Socrates' key ideas. In fact, however, we can assume that in order to expound these ideas, Plato modified Socrates' opinions considerably, resulting in new ideas.[2]

2. Virtue and Happiness

VIRTUE AND HAPPINESS

Socrates was of the opinion that justice suffices for achieving happiness. Book I of the *Republic* contains traces of these views on the part of Socrates, but in books II to IX, which we examined in chapter 3, Plato focused only on the relative thesis that the just are happier *than the unjust*.[3] According to Plato's dispassionate perception of reality, justice does not necessarily entail the good reward of happiness in the usual sense of the word. If we rank justice leading to happiness above justice unaccompanied by such a good outcome, it would mean that justice not leading to a good outcome would be an imperfect and inferior goodness. Yet there is no such distinction between perfect and imperfect justice, and surely people should always act justly, regardless of any happiness that might result. This should leave Plato with no choice but to argue that one must act justly whether or not this leads to happiness in the usual sense and that the very act of behaving in this way leads to supreme happiness more so than does acting in an unjust manner.

At the root of this lies the principle of happiness (*eudaemonism*), which postulates that what all people desire is happiness (*eudaimoniā*). Plato inherited this view from Socrates. In order to defend virtue, then, Plato felt it necessary to demonstrate that the happiness of people who act virtuously is guaranteed in some way.

This, then, must be our conviction about the just man, that whether he fall into poverty or disease or any other supposed evil, for him all these things will finally prove good, both in life and in death. For by the gods assuredly that man will never be neglected who is willing and eager to be righteous, and by the practice of virtue to be likened unto god so far as that is possible for man.[4]

The problem is what is referred to here as "good," that is, the meaning of happiness. It seems, too, that this is not necessarily incompatible with what is usually regarded as "any other supposed evil," such as "poverty" or "disease." So what, then, is the supreme "happiness" referred to by Plato? In the *Republic* this is construed as harmony and peace of soul, with one's desires tamed by reason. But just what is the relationship between reason and desire? I would like to revisit this point, including a review of what was said in the previous chapter.

REASON AND DESIRES

In the *Protagoras*, one of the Socratic dialogues, Socrates states that people who think x is better than y would never choose y. Plato, however, gives no credence to this link between belief (*doxa*, opinion) and choice. For instance, even if one thinks it best to avoid alcohol for health reasons, one sometimes gives in to desire and has a drink. Plato also criticized Socrates for not taking into account the strength of desires that run counter to reason,[5] and he suggests the following terminology:

[Name] that in the soul whereby it reckons and reasons *the rational* [knows *logos*] and that with which it loves, hungers, thirsts, and feels the flutter and titillation of other desires, *the nonrational and appetitive*—companion of various repletions and pleasures.[6]

THE TRIPARTITE THEORY OF THE SOUL

Taking the views in these criticisms a step further, Plato is thought[7] to have arrived at the argument we saw in section 3.3, that is, the tripartite theory that divides the soul into a *rational* part,[8] an *appetitive* part,[9] and a *spirited* part.[10] Plato was of the view that Socrates' belief that virtue relates solely to knowledge was erroneous, as it failed to recognize the nonrational parts of the soul.

Plato discusses this tripartite theory of the soul in terms of an analogy with the tripartite functions of the State:

(a) the intellectual class that deliberates on policies,
(b) the appetitive class that deals with earning money, and
(c) the spirited class that assists the ruler.[11]

He argues that the State consists of classes engaged in these three duties.

THE NONRATIONAL ASPECTS OF VIRTUE

Plato also describes the Greek "cardinal virtues," that is, wisdom (*sophiā*), bravery (*andreiā*), temperance (*sōphrosynē*), and justice (*dikaiosynē*),[12] from the dual perspectives of the State and the individual:

(1) First, these are the virtues of a state (*polis*). Thus, they are fully realized in the ideal state portrayed in the *Republic*. Of these virtues, Plato equated wisdom, temperance, and bravery with the ideal state's three functions of reason, appetite, and spirit, and he regarded a just *polis* as one in which all three functioned together properly.[13]
(2) By analogy, these virtues also pertain to the individual. According to Plato, wisdom, temperance, and bravery are synonymous with the correct functioning of these three parts of an individual soul, and a person in whom they are in harmony is regarded as being just.[14]

This argument in book IV of the *Republic* is based on the hypothesis that the three parts of the soul are analogous to the three parts of the State. Plato often develops his argument in the *Republic* in the direction of his tripartite theory of the State, but since our theme here is the pursuit of ethical thought, we will omit this argument and focus instead on the relationship between virtue and the soul in individual ethics, elaborating further on Plato's views.

Together the cardinal virtues constitute optimal orderliness in the tripartite soul, with each individual virtue supporting a particular aspect of this orderliness. For instance, the virtue of *bravery* conserves "the conviction which the law has created by education about fearful things— what and what sort of things are to be feared"[15]—and it entails endurance. Yet when the spirited part of the soul fails to become rightly indignant because of unwarranted fear, it is protected through the virtue of bravery, and proper indignation becomes possible.[16] The virtue of *temperance* consists of "a continence of certain pleasures and appetites,"[17] and it imparts orderliness to the appetitive part of the soul.[18] The virtue of *wisdom* explores the proper desires of the spirited and appetitive parts and calls for appropriate knowledge in the rational part.[19] Finally, the virtue of *justice* demands that each part of the soul carry out its own task properly.[20]

In this way, when discussing the element of endurance in bravery or the element of orderliness in temperance, for instance, Plato focuses on the spirited and appetitive parts of the soul. Although Socrates does mention the nonrational elements of the virtues, he drops them from his argument,[21] whereas a feature of Plato is his reinstatement of these nonrational elements.

Nevertheless, Plato also paid ample attention to the importance of the rational element. Although one aim of moral education lies in fostering proper nonrational responses to pluck and desires,[22] the rational element is also regarded as vital at all such times. Since Plato viewed mental conflict as dangerous,[23] he argued that people need the habit of rationally choosing pleasure or suffering so as to avoid such conflict. He therefore advocated acquiring the art of correct rational judgment so that one naturally comes to act in accordance with such considerations.[24]

3. The Virtues and Justice

THE RECIPROCITY OF THE VIRTUES

Plato, who links the features of the rational and nonrational parts of the soul to different virtues, regards each virtue as the same as the knowledge of good and evil, so his views diverge from Socrates' straightforward notion that in the long run all the virtues boil down to wisdom.[25] Plato was of the opinion that the various virtues differ from each other and that they each demand their own distinct training and behavior.[26]

Nevertheless, Plato agreed with Socrates on the following point: it is not until people possess all the virtues that they can have any of them, and the virtues interact with each other.[27] Plato explains this based on a discussion of the fourth cardinal virtue, justice, which constitutes the "inner doings" of the "soul."[28] Let me restate Plato's argument here, distinguishing this from the ordinary kind of justice, which is expressed through actions. I will refer to the justice of the individual soul as "internal justice."[29]

Unlike the other virtues (i.e., wisdom, which relates mainly to the rational part of the soul; bravery, which relates to the spirited part; and temperance, which relates to the appetitive part), "internal justice" is a virtue that constitutes the inherent relationships between the rational and nonrational parts of the whole soul. In other words, guided by the wisdom of the rational part, it is the task of "internal justice" to exhort the different parts of the soul to fulfill their respective roles.[30] For instance, when the appetitive part of the soul tries to acquire excessive riches or to succumb to the pleasures of the flesh, the rational part judges this to be improper, and the spirited part then bravely obeys this judgment by the rational part, struggling so that the soul is not governed by such desires. In other words, the task of the soul's "internal justice" is to be mindful so that people will achieve orderliness in their soul and govern themselves and become balanced individuals.[31] In this sense the virtue of justice has the function of integrating the other virtues of wisdom, bravery, and temperance.

It is conceivable that we might, out of fear of punishment, for instance, act in a manner that is superficially brave or temperate, without "internal justice." In other words, it is possible to adopt just the trappings of "external justice." Nevertheless, the only time when such actions are legitimately desirable is when the parts of the soul are properly ordered. And "internal justice" is essential to achieving this orderliness. Conversely, as long as we have "internal justice" and proper order in the parts of the soul, the other virtues require nothing further to fulfill their mission.[32]

TWO UNRESOLVED ISSUES IN THE THEORY OF JUSTICE

Plato's supreme "happiness" was a state in which the soul had achieved harmony and peace—in other words, one in which "internal justice" of the soul had been realized. We know that the upshot of Plato's response to the tale of the ring of Gyges in section 3.3 was that it would be inconceivable for a just philosopher who has achieved true happiness in this sense, based on "internal justice," to indulge in the satisfaction of desires such as *erōs* and power that would noticeably disturb this harmony, that is, in outward impropriety.

Nevertheless, we need to reexamine this here. Ultimately, would not the "internally just" person who abandons happiness in the usual sense of the term, without fulfilling these various desires, be simply trampled underfoot by externally unjust people, thereby being disadvantaged? Can this truly be regarded as justice? This question was precisely what concerned the Sophist Thrasymachus, who engaged in dialogue with Socrates in book I of the *Republic*:[33]

> And you must look at the matter, my simple-minded Socrates, in this way: that the just man always comes out at a disadvantage in his relation with the unjust. To begin with, in their business dealings in any joint undertaking of the two you will never find that the just man has the advantage over the unjust at the dissolution of the partnership but that he always has the worst of it.[34]

This is a doubt cast on justice expressed through actions, that is, "external justice." In one sense, Plato's metaphysics and epistemology seem to adopt the matter-of-fact attitude that there is no need to respond to such questions. This is because he believed that philosophers come to know about Ideas, which are the fundamental object of knowledge, and immerse themselves wholly in their contemplation.[35] Nevertheless, if such contemplations degenerate into an excuse for shirking one's obligations to others, that is, for carrying out "external justice," they are no longer ethical. So Plato thought that "internally just" people would naturally act with "external justice."[36] Yet is that really so?

We cannot simply ignore these points. To sum up, then, first, is it not so that the justice of the "internally just" person is trampled underfoot by external injustice? Second, can we positively assert that an "internally just" person is truly someone who will act in an "externally just" manner? In other words, we must seek an explanation that delves further into the question of whether "internal justice" conflicts with "external justice." Plato seems to fail to supply an adequate response to this in the *Republic*. Instead, what seems to suggest an answer is the discussion of love (*erōs*) in the *Symposium*, which like the *Republic* is one of the middle dialogues. So here I would like to supplement our analysis by turning to Plato's discussion of *erōs*.

4. Love and Pleasure

THE THEORY OF LOVE

In the *Symposium*, Plato has the prophetess Diotima, Socrates' instructor in the art of love, raise the question of what is people's objective in pursuing love.[37] Her provisional reply is "the use of what is beautiful for the purpose of reproduction, whether physical or mental."[38] People wish to reproduce "[b]ecause begetting is, by human standards, something eternal and undying."[39] Diotima states that since procreation is a divine act that rides on the coattails of immortality, it turns away from ugliness toward beauty.[40]

By analogy, Plato applies this concept of procreation to the sameness of the individual.[41] People experience various transformations throughout their lifetime. Their disposition, character, memory, goals, and so forth all undergo change. Yet although themselves destined to die eventually, humans play a part in immortal sameness by renewing and preserving through their recollections the knowledge that tends to become lost in oblivion. We can construe this as meaning that even within the individual there exists a desire for immortality.

Nevertheless, this desire for immortality burns more strongly when directed toward others. Plato states that human beings have a physical desire to give birth to "human children"[42] and a "far stronger"[43] spiritual desire to conceive wisdom and virtue in general[44] and to bequeath this to someone with a fair and noble soul. In other words, the path of *erōs* "begin[s], as a young man, with the pursuit of physical beauty,"[45] and then one realizes that "the physical beauty of one body is akin to that of any other body,"[46] and "he will become less obsessive in his pursuit of his one former passion, as he realizes its unimportance,"[47] will come to "put a higher value on mental than on physical beauty,"[48] and will move on to love "a virtuous soul."[49] Next, he is "direct[ed] . . . to knowledge,"[50] and then, rather than beautiful individuals, "he directs his eyes to what is beautiful in general, as he turns to gaze upon the limitless ocean of beauty,"[51] and eventually "his attention is caught by that one special knowledge—the knowledge of a beauty" everywhere.[52]

> When a man has reached this point in his education in love, studying the different types of beauty in correct order, he will come to the final end and goal of this education. Then suddenly he will see a beauty of a *breathtaking* [*thaumastos*] nature.[53]

Here again Plato speaks of the "wonder" that permeates ancient ethical thought. This wondrous "beauty" is none other than the idea of a beauty that "exists for all time, by itself and with itself, unique";[54] "All other forms of beauty derive from it, but in such a way that their creation or destruction does not strengthen or weaken it, or affect it in any way at all."[55] Plato concludes as follows: "If a man progresses . . . from the lesser beauties, and begins to catch sight of this beauty, then he is within reach of the final revelation."[56]

FICINO'S COMMENTARY

What springs to mind in connection with this shift from physical love to spiritual love is the commentary by the famous Renaissance Platonist, Marsilio Ficino. Under the patronage of Cosimo de Medici, the humanist Ficino was the first to translate Plato's complete works into Latin and to introduce them to the Western world. In his commentary on Plato's theory of *erōs*, Ficino reports that love is a "bitter thing" and that a lover "is a soul dead in its own body."[57] This is a surprising claim, the meaning of which can be elaborated as follows. People in love can no longer bear to live alone, continually thinking, as they are, of their beloved. Yet spirits that are incapable of thinking independently are no longer autonomously alive—it is as if they were dead. Nevertheless, experiencing spiritual death makes people newly aware of the existence of the spirit, and those who have become spiritual in this way take on a spiritual alertness to things they had previously overlooked, and they are blessed with a keen sensitivity.[58] Ficino's understanding of *erōs* seems to have been that a spiritual orientation toward the idea of beauty was also a blessing bestowed in return for having experienced the dangers of spiritual death as a result of such physical love.

CONCLUSIONS FROM THE THEORY OF ERŌS

In any case, from the viewpoint of ethical thought I would like to focus on the following three points in particular as conclusions to be drawn from Plato's theory of *erōs*:[59]

1) This appraisal of love between particular individuals plays a vital role in Plato's ethical thought. The philosopher becomes aware of the Ideas of justice and beauty and, ultimately, the Idea of the Good.[60] It is this Idea of the Good that explains the other Ideas and the good in other good things. This awareness of various Ideas generates a desire to reproduce these Ideas not only in the philosopher's own life but also in the lives of others.[61] The philosopher is the "least eager to hold office,"[62] but because of this love for others he voluntarily seeks to become the ruler of the ideal state, instead of taking it upon himself

to remain in the pure state of "internal justice." Rather than an escape from "internal justice," this instead becomes the fulfillment of that justice.

2) The reason that the just of soul have a concern for others is presented through this view on love, that is, it is because they wish to reproduce their justness of soul in suitable people. Initially the "internal justice" of the just of soul consists of concern for their own future, and it benefits themselves. If they wish to replicate this "internal justice" in others, they will do their utmost for the benefit of other people. Since the just of soul have this concern for others, we can of course claim that they are also acting altruistically in the usual sense of the word. Hence Plato argues that his defense of "internal justice" also constitutes a defense of "external justice." Here we finally have a positive answer to the second unresolved question from the previous section as to whether a person of "internal justice" truly does manifest "external justice."

Naturally, actions expressed as "external justice" work to benefit the rational part of the soul, without giving in to the other person's nonrational or unjust desires. The beautiful youth Alcibiades who appears at the end of the *Symposium* approaches Socrates with physical desire in mind, but Socrates takes no action, instead inviting Alcibiades to the love of knowledge.[63] Aristotle, who will be discussed later (see chapter 15, in particular), expresses the rights and wrongs of giving in to such desires more explicitly, but it seems that in response to the first question—that is, Thrasymachian doubts such as that noted in section 4.3 as to whether the pursuit of "internal justice" might violate "external justice"—Plato replies that this is not necessarily so, because an "internally just" person would not simply give in meekly when subjected to an externally unjust action.

In this way, both doubts concerning the relationship between "internal justice" and "external justice" in the *Republic* are basically resolved in the *Symposium*.

3) In any case, we know that Plato's "ultimate goal" lay in the contemplation of Ideas, and above all the Idea of the Good. In the following section we will examine these Ideas comprehensively, including the problems entailed therein, but first I would like to take a fresh look at happiness from the perspective of hedonics.

PLEASURE AND HAPPINESS

As we saw in section 4.1, in book IX of the *Republic*, Plato, who argued that just people are happier than the unjust, also stated that just people experience the most pleasure.[64] Unlike Socrates in the Socratic dialogue *Protagoras*, however, Plato does not revert to a simple hedonism that regards pleasure as good.[65] According to Plato, the rational part of the soul has its own unique pleasures,[66] and the pleasures of this rational part are superior to those of the appetitive and spirited parts. The latter are false pleasures like shadow pictures and scene paintings made to look authentic,[67] whereas the former constitute "real" or "pure" pleasure.[68] The latter two pleasures are contaminated by misconceptions about pleasure or the nature of the object of pleasure, so they cannot contribute to true happiness.[69]

This analysis of pleasure is taken further in the later dialogue, the *Philebus*. The key arguments there can be summed up in the following three points:[70]

(1) A life that lacks reason and consists solely of pleasure is the life of a primitive creature, not that of a human being.[71] A life lacking the intrinsic elements of rational activity is not worth living for people as rational agents.

(2) Wisdom is needed for choosing worthwhile pleasures and avoiding other pleasures.[72] People who enjoy unworthy pleasures are worse off not because of the outcome but because of the very fact of enjoying such pleasures. Value judgments come into play in considering the act of pleasure itself, rather than in its outcome.[73]

(3) Plato criticizes several different types of pleasure because of their falsity. He argues that such pleasures are based on false beliefs, and these reduce the value of the pleasures.[74] Although x will not happen in reality, people sometimes enjoy x in anticipation of its pleasures.[75] At other times their error is more complex. Plato argues that people are sometimes convinced that a life that is neither congenial nor unpleasant is pleasurable, simply because it contains no suffering.[76] He goes into a lengthy discussion of false pleasures that can be summed up as follows—a life devoted to pleasure, without the guidance of wisdom, cannot result in a good life.

The main thrust of the argument in the *Philebus* lies in providing support for claims regarded as self-evident in the *Republic*. The *Philebus* attempts to demonstrate why the general criteria for the best life, that is, completeness and rational activity, regard a certain way of life as superior to others, and in particular why these criteria rule out a life devoted solely to the satisfaction of one's desires. In this sense the *Philebus* can be viewed as a forerunner of Aristotle, in that it poses abstract questions about the nature of goodness.[77]

5. The Soul and Ideas

SOUL AND BODY

As we saw in section 3.1, Socrates urged people to be concerned for their soul rather than for their body or possessions.[78] In advocating this, he stressed the importance of a virtuous nature, which is contrasted with external conditions. Inheriting this distinction between concern for one-self and concern for external matters, Plato sought to interpret this in terms of a dualistic concept of soul and body. According to Plato, human beings are characterized by their reason and capacity for thought, and since the intellect is immortal, humans are likewise immortal. Whereas the body is material, perceptible, and mortal, the soul is immaterial and immortal. It is capable of knowing Ideas in a nonsensory manner, and it delights in Ideas. The soul is neither perceptible nor mortal. Plato also argued that nonrational and physical impulses and desires should be gov-erned by the rational intellect of the soul.[79]

Plato was of the opinion that accepting this dualistic view of the self leads to two ethical conclusions:[80]

(1) When we cultivate the virtues and are liberated from the body, we reach the ideal state to which we ultimately aspire. For the sake of material gain, certain kinds of people act in a manner that is outwardly brave, temperate, or proper, but they merely have the "trappings" of virtue, that is, "external justice." By contrast, the philosopher acts virtuously without any such rewards, because he is indifferent to worldly losses incurred through acting virtuously. Plato argued that it is this that constitutes true virtue and "internal justice."[81]

(2) In response to the second of the doubts raised in section 4.3 concern-ing the relationship between "internal" and "external" justice in the *Republic*, in section 4.4 we reached a tentative reply based on the *Sym-posium*. That is, in relation to the question of whether the "internally just" are truly "externally just," the answer was that their concern to reproduce their "internal justice" naturally leads them to act with "external justice." Nevertheless, is it not the case that this concern involves taking "internal justice" for others into account, whereas,

strictly speaking, "external justice" surely involves more material and physical matters. The conclusion of the dualistic body–soul theory is, however, that philosophers have little interest in worldly matters, because they are focused on the contemplation of Ideas.[82] Does this not mean, then, that the intended balance between "internal justice" and "external justice" is destroyed after all?

QUESTIONS FOR PLATO

At this point we need to ask the following elementary question: Do people actually consist of a purely rational soul? This would mean equating people with their reason at the expense of their other faculties. Yet surely such a view of humanity leaves certain questions unresolved. Even if a rational nature that regulates nonrational impulses represents true human nature, this obviously cannot mean that humans consist solely of pure intellect devoid of impulses.[83] In an attempt to examine the appropriateness of Plato's replies to the issues raised by the tale of Gyges mentioned in chapter 3, we have broadened our discussion to encompass other texts and have explored the depth and scope of Platonic thought with its various orientations. By now, however, perhaps many readers are feeling uneasy at Plato's overly rigid body–soul dualism and his rejection of this world. Several such doubts are outlined below.

First, even if supreme happiness is the outcome of "internal justice," and it constitutes true pleasure and represents harmony in the rational soul, this is merely the ultimate aim. Can we ignore the fact that people have various subsidiary goals before reaching that point?

Moreover, Plato envisages only the extreme case of someone who is maximally unjust, such as a dictator, but if we look at less extreme instances, in terms of an ethics for the normal person on the street, can we reject and ignore outright as spurious pleasures those lesser aims that are pursued in the normal course of events and that, once achieved, are followed by the emergence of fresh desires?

Furthermore, can we be so sure, in the first place, that pleasure itself contains differing value levels? When we focus solely on pleasure and discuss its ethical value, there is room for Popperian criticism of totalitarian domination by the philosopher class.[84] Should not the ethical value of pleasure be determined in accordance with the ethical nature of the activities involved? For instance, should we not take the view that the pleasure of satisfying hunger is inherently neither good nor bad and that it is only when this pleasure is pursued to the point of stealing someone else's food that it should be condemned?

Does not a rationalism that regards only rational pleasures as constituting true pleasure end up in a biased view of humans that ultimately neglects the body? Or, in contrast to such a rigid asceticism renouncing this world and the flesh, is there not at least room for ethical thought that realistically perceives human beings in their spiritual and physical entirety, as creatures with no choice other than to live in this world in their physical form?

In the final analysis, does not a pursuit of Plato's ethical thought force readers not only to ask such questions but also to choose their own position? This is a choice among the options of abandoning lesser aims for the sake of an ultimate aim, concerning oneself with achieving minor goals without setting any ultimate goal, or seeking an appropriate balance of the two in an attempt to reconcile both aims.

In any case, it seems that Plato was himself implicitly and explicitly concerned with these questions and difficulties. In book X of the *Republic* he suggests that the soul has nonrational parts while the body is alive, but these are discarded at death.[85] With this suggestion Plato tries to link to a belief in immortality just the rational part among the three parts of the soul that he postulated in book IV (see sections 3.3 and 4.2). Moreover, in the *Phaedrus*, one of his middle dialogues, he takes the view that it is not the "perfect winged"[86] soul soaring above the earth toward Ideas that has nonrational desires but the soul that has "lost its wings," even though it is a soul.[87] In this way Plato himself seems to seek various explanations for the constitution of the immortal soul, testing out different solutions so as not to contradict observations of reality. In the final analysis, however, his stance of abstracting the physical things of this world for the sake of the ultimate aim of rational harmony through contemplation of the Idea of the immortal soul remains fundamentally unchanged.

At all events, there is no point in disallowing such a strict view rejecting this world simply because we cannot follow it. Whether or not we accept this view, in bringing this chapter to a close I would like to ascertain the direction in which such a sweeping line of thought takes us, as well as its positive aspects.

PLATO'S THEORY OF THE SOUL'S IMMORTALITY AND HIS THEORY OF IDEAS

Plato is attempting somehow to prove the soul's immortality, in which his teacher Socrates had believed. Plato's understanding of Ideas occupies an important position here. We have examined various aspects of Plato's ethical thought, but in closing I would like to bring together a discussion of the relationship between his theory of Ideas and his views on the immortality of the soul, which lie at the base of Plato's ethical thought, so as to reach an overall assessment of his views.

Plato's demonstration of the soul's immortality through an analogy with the theory of Ideas is set out in detail in the *Phaedo*, one of the middle dialogues. Let us first review the main points of his argument there.

Here Plato has Socrates utter the following statement: "a beautiful, itself by itself, is something, and so are a good and a large and all the rest. If you grant me that . . . I hope that from them I shall . . . find out that soul is immortal."[88] Here, "itself by itself" refers to the Idea. Socrates' partners in the dialogue concur with him, and he goes on to say that he holds "in a plain, artless, and possibly simple minded way" to the fact that "nothing else makes it beautiful except that beautiful itself; . . . it is by the beautiful that all beautiful things are beautiful."[89] This is how the discussion starts off. What Plato is questioning here is the difference between Ideas and the things of this world in which they are to be found. For instance, "whenever you say that Simmias is larger than Socrates but smaller than Phaedo, you mean then, don't you, that both things are in Simmias, largeness and smallness?"[90] In the same way, in relative terms beautiful things are sometimes ugly and good things sometimes bad. The things of this world are relative, in flux, contradictory. Yet if beauty constitutes ugliness at the same time it constitutes beauty, we can no longer describe it as Beauty itself. The same goes for the idea of Good, the idea of Largeness, and so on. In that case, what distinguishes Ideas from the things of this world is the fact that "an opposite will never be opposite to itself."[91]

Plato's ensuing argument is problematic,[92] but the main points are as follows. Snow has the quality of coldness, but "what is snow will never . . . admit the hot and still be what it was, namely snow, and also hot; but at the advance of the hot, it will either get out of the way or perish."[93] The same goes for the relationship between fire and coldness. In short, here Plato is arguing that even snow and fire, which are not Ideas, "will never be opposite to" themselves. Having put forward this argument, he finally moves on to demonstrate the immortality of the soul.

First, Plato argues that it is the appearance of the soul that renders a body alive (I will discuss the background to this argument later).[94] Now the soul, which shares the idea of Life, can never receive something opposite to life, that is, death.[95] In terms of the earlier analogy with snow, when death draws nigh, the soul will either "get out of the way or perish." It is impossible for it to perish, however, because the soul, which is the fundamental principle of life, is immortal.[96] When death approaches, the soul simply withdraws from this world, without perishing. Plato concludes that this demonstrates the imperishability of the soul.[97]

Plato makes three other attempts in the *Phaedo* to prove that the soul does not perish: (1) if we suppose that there is a movement from death to life that offsets the movement from life to death, then the soul must be imperishable; (2) if we suppose that knowledge depends on recollections, then the soul must be imperishable from previous existences; and (3) like perfect things, the soul is invisible, so like perfect things it must also be imperishable. The earlier proof in terms of an analogy with the theory of Ideas should perhaps be positioned merely as an attempt to complement these three approaches.

As scholars have pointed out, the fact that the soul is the fundamental principle of life corresponds to how the Greek word *psychē*, the Hebrew word *ruah*, and the Latin words *anima* and *spiritus* all originally signify "breath."[98] In other words, as long as "breathing" is a sign of "life," this accords with ancient views that naturally regarded the soul, that is, breath, as the fundamental principle of life.

Nevertheless, even if we recognize the implications of such an overall context and the fact that it is premised on a different conceptual framework from that of today, the following points alone seem sufficient to jeopardize the credibility of this argument. For instance, although Plato initially argues that only an Idea "will never be opposite to itself," he ends up by claiming that even snow and fire, which are things of this world, "will never be opposite to" themselves. Furthermore (although Plato does in fact stipulate several restrictions that have been omitted from the above summary), if one takes the immortality of the soul as one's premise, then it is an easy matter to conclude that it is imperishable, but the validity of this very premise has not been explored adequately.

DIFFICULTIES WITH THE THEORY OF IDEAS

Hence it seems that proof of the soul's immortality through an analogy with the theory of Ideas is not entirely successful, and this relates to the problematic nature of the actual theory of Ideas. The theory is unclear as to whether it is Ideas alone that are not "opposite to" themselves, but that is not the only point on which it is vague. Plato earlier spoke as if there are ideas of Beauty, Good, Largeness, "and so on," but are there also Ideas for negative values such as Ugliness and Evil? Does "and so on" encompass everything from natural objects such as "human beings" and "horses" to imperfect things such as "hairs" and "human waste"? Plato does not clarify this in any of his dialogues.[99]

There is also the question of the Third Man Argument. For example, when Socrates, Plato, and any other is referred to as a "man" (I), the idea of Man is posited as the form of Man common to them. This idea is also called Man (II). Then Man (III) is posited as an idea common to I and II, and this process continues on *ad infinitum*, with the ideas (IV), (V), and so on being common to all of these. So a problem arises whereby once an idea has been posited, the number of ideas increases infinitely.[100] This is reported as an argument used by Aristotle in *On Ideas*, but in fact Plato himself anticipated, considered, and struggled with this issue in the *Parmenides*, a transitional work leading into his later period,[101] as well as the question of whether ideas for "and so on" exist.

Even just in relation to ethical questions alone, Plato's theory of Ideas has been criticized by Aristotle in the *Nicomachean Ethics* from the following perspectives (see chapter 5 for details):

(1) Since "the good" is discussed in terms of various categories, such as its essence, relation, and location, it cannot be a universal Idea.
(2) Even if the Idea of the good did exist, it is not clear to what extent a knowledge of this would improve the techniques of the weaver or carpenter.

The second criticism is tenuous, but what Plato is probably trying to say is that people who are aware of Ideas become considerate of others, so they become able to use their own skills well at least. This can be regarded as an ethically important contention. By contrast, linking point (1) to the Third Man Argument would lead to criticism such as the view that the "idea of the good" is a universal concept, and it is wrong to give it substance. "Man" is a universal essence common to Socrates and Plato, but there is no reason this must exist separately from each individual man as Man "itself," and if we were to argue along those lines, then the idea of Man would have to multiply *ad infinitum*. When people say that "temperance is good" in relation to quantity and "opportunity is good" in relation to time, there is no need to postulate the idea of a common "Goodness," and doing so would merely lead to an infinite increase in the number of ideas of goodness. In contemporary terms, one would be criticized here for having committed the error of "substantiation of a universal concept."[102]

TRANSCENDENCE IN THE THEORY OF IDEAS

In the light of this, it should be clear what there is to criticize in the theory of Ideas. In the past there was a tendency to disparage it as the source of the *Zweiweltentheorie*, or dualism, that has since governed Western thought, that is, a world of Ideas and a world that shares in these Ideas, an invisible world grasped through reason and a visible world perceived through the senses.[103] We could also describe the former as the world of transcendental existence and the latter as the world of becoming and change. This theory was discussed in an analogy to body–soul dualism. Philosophers were exhorted to live lives in which they avoided being swayed by the senses and hovering in a state of becoming and change, and where they suppressed their physical desires as much as possible and focused purely on matters of the soul, aspiring to permanent transcendence.[104] This is why philosophy is described as "the cultivation of dying [*meletē thanatū*]."[105] In contrast to this strict and austere teaching that rejects the world and our bodies, in one respect Aristotle's *Nicomachean Ethics* offers an ethics that took the view that we have no choice but to live in the present world in our physical bodies and that proposes reinstating human beings in their true essence. Even so, in book X at the end of the *Nicomachean Ethics*, Aristotle does extol the contemplation of a transcendental good (god) beyond this world, so criticizing the transcendency in the theory of Ideas was not Aristotle's real intent. Instead, it seems more appropriate to view his criticism as targeting the substantiation of abstract universal concepts.[106]

As if to supplement his argument about the "cultivation of dying," which moves toward a rigorous negation of this world and the flesh, Plato himself also presented a beautiful variation on the theory of Ideas through his positive theory of "recollection" (*anamnēsis*), which is a love of Ideas.[107] Here the yearning and feeling for the transcendental that is also apparent in Aristotle is extolled in a highly poetic fashion. I would like to pinpoint the positive aspects of Plato's theory of Ideas by quoting here a section from the *Phaedrus* that seems to acknowledge the roots of the love of knowledge:

> [O]nly the mind of the philosopher has wings. In his memory, to the best of his ability, he is always close to those things whose closeness makes gods godlike. Only the man who makes good use of memories of this kind, and is fully initiated in perfect rites, can become truly perfect. Withdrawing from human interests, and coming close to what is divine, he is criti-

cized by the many; they say he is out of his mind. They do not realize, the many, that he is possessed by god.

. . . When a man sees beauty here, in this life, he is reminded of true beauty. He grows wings, and stands there fluttering them, eager to fly upwards, but unable to do so. Yet still he looks upwards, as birds do, and takes no notice of what is below; and so he is accused of being mad. . . . Of all forms of divine possession, this is the best. . . . [I]t is the nature of every human soul that it has seen the things that are [ta onta, or "true being, being"]. . . . But the task of recollecting what it saw there from what it now sees here is not an easy one for every soul, either for the ones which caught only a quick glimpse of what was up there, or for those which fell to earth and fared badly down here, being led into injustice by bad company of one sort or another, and so forgetting the holy things they saw up there.

There remain a few souls whose recollection is adequate. These, when they see some likeness of what is there, are dumbfounded [ekplēttō]; they are no longer masters of themselves, though their perception is unclear, and so they do not realize what is happening to them. In the day-to-day likenesses of justice and self-control, and the other things which are valuable to souls, there is little power to illumine; nevertheless, weak as our organs of perception are, it is possible—though hard and few achieve it—to approach these images, and detect the nature of the thing they are images of. Before, its beauty was plain to see; . . . we were . . . granted the final revelation, in the pure light of day, of those manifestations which are whole, uncompounded, unmoving and full of joy. Ourselves pure, we were not entombed [sēma] in this thing we now call our body [sōma].[108]

This is a lengthy passage, but it represents one of Plato's most moving utterances. His complex reasoning continues on, superimposing an account of a romantic attachment to a beautiful person with his argument that philosophy consists of an achingly crazy "love" (erōs) of noumena and ideas once seen but no longer visible.[109] This portrayal has the power to touch our modern-day minds, and also has a certain sense of nostalgia.[110]

WONDER

The above discussion highlights the need to distinguish between what is problematic in the theory of Ideas and the lessons to be drawn from it.

In other words, we must abandon the substantiation of universal concepts, yet retain the thoughts that yearn for such transcendence and that have even a little in common with the way of philosophy. Such a yearning for transcendence forms an undercurrent in ethical thought, from the pre-Socratics through Socrates and Plato on down to Aristotle. Prior to the passage cited earlier from the *Phaedo*, Plato has Socrates admit that

> I wonder [*thaumazō*] if, when they were apart from each other, each was one; . . . whereas when they came close to each other, this then became a reason for their coming to be two.[111]

This corresponds to the famous utterance in the *Theaetetus* that we mentioned in the introduction:

> [T]his is an experience which is characteristic of a philosopher, this *wondering* [*thaumazein*]: this is where philosophy [*philosophiā*] begins and nowhere else.[112]

It is also related to the above passage in the *Phaedrus* that discusses the recollection of Ideas seen in the previous world:

> There remain a few [who] . . . when they see some likeness of what is there, are dumbfounded [*ekplētō*].[113]

In other words, Plato leads Socrates to the remarkable conclusion that a heart of "wonder" is the starting point of philosophy and that being found guilty by the Athenians is "better" and "more just."[114] This is because it is "wonder" that shatters common beliefs about the "true reasons" of ethical deeds.[115] In this sense "wonder" also clearly exists as the origin of practical philosophy. In essence, this also boils down to wonder at transcendent Ideas (the "beauty of a *breathtaking* [*thaumastos*] nature" in Plato's *Symposium* 210E; emphasis added).

In the *Metaphysics*[116] Aristotle, too, pointed out such "wondering" (*thaumazein*) as the starting point for men who "began to philosophize [*philosophein*]," from the days of Thales right up to the present. So next we must move on to Aristotle, who criticized his teacher Plato's theory of Ideas and who, while trying to construct a system of ethics by analyzing the realities of this world, also entertained a keen interest in and sense of wonder at this transcendence. Plato's ethical thought is fragmentary, being scattered throughout works from various periods, and along with the question of how these works were created and changed in the light of each other and the question of their contexts and positioning, it has not been easy to give even an internal overview of Plato's ethical thought in its entirety or to ascertain where the problems lie. By contrast, despite remaining redactional problems, Aristotle's ethics basically constitute a superb system and can be regarded as an orderly compilation of Greek ethical thought. In line with Aristotle's systematic description, in the following chapters I would like to reorganize the problematic phenomena outlined in all their intricacy in this chapter and reconsider and develop them further.

Notes

1. The *Meno* is sometimes classified among the Socratic dialogues (e.g., Tadashi Inoue et al., *Seiyō tetsugaku-shi* [A history of Western philosophy] [Tokyo: University of Tokyo Press, 1965], 28, and Ninzui Saitō, *Puraton* [Plato] [Tokyo: Iwanami Shinsho, 1972], 188), but here I will follow such commentators as T. H. Irwin, "Plato," *Encyclopedia of Ethics*, II, ed. L. C. Becker (New York: Garland, 1992), 973, and Shinrō Katō, *Girishia tetsugaku-shi* (A history of Greek philosophy) (Tokyo: University of Tokyo Press, 1996), 67, and include the *Meno* among Plato's middle dialogues.

2. Key works that highlight the contrasts between Socrates and Plato from such a perspective are T. H. Irwin, *Plato's Moral Theory* (Oxford: Clarendon, 1977), and Irwin's "Plato," 970–78, which is a synopsis of *Plato's Moral Theory*. According to p. 971 of "Plato," the views of Socrates and Plato differ particularly with respect to the following points: (1) Socrates thought that virtue was sufficient for happiness and that the virtuous person would not suffer any real harm. By contrast, Plato was of the opinion that virtue does not necessarily lead to happiness in the normal sense, and he believed only in the comparative hypothesis that virtue results in greater happiness *than* not being virtuous. (2) According to Plato, virtue was itself the goal, not a means toward happiness. Socrates, however, made no such explicit claim. (3) Socrates equated virtue with knowledge and criticized ignorance and lack of self-restraint, but Plato did not subscribe to this criticism. For Plato, virtue consists of more than knowledge. He also disagreed with the idea of the unity of virtue, arguing that there are sundry virtues and vices corresponding to the various nonrational desires. (4) Since Plato rejected Socrates' argument equating virtue with happiness, the defense of justice put forward in the *Republic*, one of Plato's middle dialogues, differs in several key respects from the argument in the *Gorgias*, one of the Socratic dialogues. In the middle dialogues, particularly in the *Symposium*, Plato takes his advocacy of love a step further, arguing that a rational concern for one's own welfare leads to a concern for the good of others. (5) In book IX of the *Republic* and in the *Philebus*, one of the later dialogues, Plato develops and refines Socrates' ideas on pleasure and goodness in the Socratic dialogues the *Protagoras* and the *Gorgias*, ending up by rejecting both hedonism and extreme antihedonism. (6) Socrates believed in the immortality of the soul but failed to prove this. Inheriting Socrates' interest in this subject, Plato attempts a philo-

sophical proof of the soul's immortality in one of his middle dialogues, the *Phaedo*. Similarly, in the *Phaedrus*, another middle dialogue, he argues that the focus of ethical concerns is the indestructibility of the soul. Plato contrasts this indestructibility of the soul with nonrational desires and physical appetites.

Shinrō Katō's *Shoki Puraton tetsugaku* (Early Platonian philosophy) (Tokyo: University of Tokyo Press, 1988) is a leading study that argues that a simple equation of the views expressed in Plato's Socratic dialogues with Socrates' own views is inadequate and that the Socratic dialogues also contain rich seeds of Plato's later thought.

3. *Republic* I, 347E, 352E.

4. *Republic* X, 613A–B.

5. *Republic* IV, 438A–439D.

6. *Republic* IV, 439D; emphasis added.

7. *Republic* IV, 435B–441A. In particular, 439Dff.

8. *Republic* IV, 439D, 441C, 442B.

9. *Republic* IV, 439D.

10. *Republic* IV, 439E–441C.

11. *Republic* IV, 427Eff. See in particular the summary in 441A, for instance.

12. *Republic* IV, 427E.

13. This classification is possible based on passages such as the *Republic* IV, 434C and 441Aff., but Plato's account also contains certain elements where he does not simply match up the three virtues other than justice with the three parts of the soul on a one-to-one basis. See, for instance, 442Bff. Focusing on this, Irwin ("Plato," 974) stresses that "Plato . . . identifies bravery with a particular relation between the spirited and the rational parts, but identifies temperance with a relation between the rational and the appetitive parts."

14. See note 11.

15. *Republic* IV, 429C.

16. *Republic* IV, 429A–430C, 441E.

17. *Republic* IV, 430E.

18. *Republic* IV, 430D–432A, 442D.

19. *Republic* IV, 428A–429A, 442C.

20. *Republic* IV, 441D–442B.

21. See the Socratic dialogues *Laches* 192B–E, 194C–D, and *Charmides* 159B. Also see the *Gorgias* 507A–B, another early work.

22. *Republic* II–III.

23. Cf. T. H. Irwin, "Plato," 973.

24. *Republic* III, 401E–402A. Plato follows Socrates in regarding knowledge as indispensable to virtue. Socrates distinguished between knowledge and beliefs (*Gorgias* 454D–E, 465A, 508E–509A), taking the view that it is knowledge that is a virtue. He did not, however, explain why virtue requires knowledge beyond mere belief. By contrast, in the *Meno*, one of his middle dialogues, Plato distinguishes between belief and knowledge from the following two perspectives, and he discusses their relationship on this basis: (1) unlike belief, knowledge is permanent; (2) knowledge can be explained theoretically, so it is reliable (97E–98A). In connection with these two points, Plato suggests in book IV of the *Republic*

that certain persons—in particular, the subordinate classes in the ideal state—do not fulfill the criterion of reliability in (2), but to some extent they do fulfill that of permanence in (1). Since moral education inculcates solid and proper beliefs and ensures that people are not swayed by selfish and nonrational desires, they become capable of actions similar to those based on permanent knowledge. Yet if we seek to choose virtue itself, then the second aspect is also important. When people who have been properly trained but lack knowledge deem a certain action to be proper, it is simply their spirited part responding automatically, with no other motivation beyond that. To choose justice itself, we must select it for the distinctive properties that constitute justice. Without knowledge of what these are, we cannot consciously elect a proper course of action. This is an outline of Plato's explanation (*Republic* IV, 442C) of why virtue requires not just belief but also knowledge in the rational part of the soul.

25. There are also counterarguments to the accepted view of Socrates as an advocate of such a rational ethics. For details, see Katō, *Shoki Puraton tetsugaku* (Early Platonian philosophy), 158ff.

26. The specific training and behavior are particularly emphasized in Plato's later dialogue, *The Statesman* 306A–308B.

27. *Protagoras* 329E. Cf. T. H. Irwin, "Plato," 974ff.

28. *Republic* IV, 443C–444A.

29. An excellent discussion of this point can be found in Yūji Matsunaga, "Uchinaru seigi" (Internal justice), ch. 9 in his book *Chi to fuchi—Puraton tetsugaku kenkyū josetsu* (Knowledge and ignorance: An introduction to the study of Plato's philosophy) (Tokyo: University of Tokyo Press, 1993).

30. *Republic* IV, 441D–444A.

31. *Republic* IV, 443D–E.

32. In this way the cardinal virtues constitute the aspects of a well-ordered soul. Proper judgments by the rational part of the soul make us wise (*wisdom*). When we subjugate our nonrational desires to our rational desires we are temperate (*temperance*) and become brave (*bravery*). "Internal *justice*" arises when each part of the soul maintains a proper relationship with the other parts and fulfills its own mission. Thus the various virtues derive from a rational and thoughtful soul.

33. *Republic* I, 343C; II, 367C.

34. *Republic* I, 343D.

35. *Republic* VII, 519B–C.

36. *Republic* IV, 442D–443B.

37. Plato, *Symposium* 206B.

38. *Symposium* 206B; for an English translation, see Plato, *Symposium and Phaedrus*, trans. Tom Griffith (New York: Knopf, 2000).

39. *Symposium* 206E–207A.

40. *Symposium* 206C–D. Ninzui Saitō adds the following subtle commentary on how Plato thus cites this desire for "immortality" as the grounds for the joys of erotic love: "The desire for 'immortality' seems to be the factor most lacking in the views of contemporary sex theorists. Perhaps today we have become overly sophisticated in the rational sense and have lost the honesty and

courage to talk about such factors. We should regard Plato as being far more down-to-earth and wholesome, as well as serious, in this respect." Plato, 75.

41. *Symposium* 207D–208B.
42. *Symposium* 209C.
43. *Symposium* 209C.
44. *Symposium* 209A–B.
45. *Symposium* 210A.
46. *Symposium* 210A–B.
47. *Symposium* 210B.
48. *Symposium* 210B.
49. *Symposium* 210C.
50. *Symposium* 210C.
51. *Symposium* 210D.
52. *Symposium* 210D.
53. *Symposium* 210E; emphasis added.
54. *Symposium* 211A–B.
55. *Symposium* 211B.
56. *Symposium* 211B.
57. M. Ficino, *Commentarium*, Oratio Secunda VIII; see M. Ficino, *Commentary on Plato's Symposium on Love*, trans. Sears Jayne (Dallas, TX: Spring, 1985), 55.
58. See Saitō, *Puraton* (Plato), 81ff.
59. See also Plato, *Phaedrus* 250E–256D. Cf. Irwin, "Plato," 976.
60. *Republic* VI, 504E–506B.
61. *Republic* VI, 500A–C.
62. *Republic* VII, 520D.
63. *Symposium* 212Cff.
64. See section 3.3 (c).
65. The hedonism in *Protagoras* 354C and elsewhere in that dialogue, whereby pain is bad and pleasure good, is firmly rejected by Socrates in the other dialogues (*Gorgias* 495Eff.; although it is one of the middle dialogues, see also the *Republic* VI, 509A). Hence, quite a few scholars do not regard Socrates' argument in the *Protagoras* as sincere or serious (J. Adam and A. M. Adam, *Platonis Protagoras* [Cambridge: Cambridge University Press, 1893], xxxi). Yet as long as the subject of discussion is not mere hedonism but the virtues of measuring and enjoying pleasure in moderation through knowledge, then it seems that this too could be regarded as an idea specific to Socrates, in the sense that it constitutes a rational hedonism (see the commentary on p. 199 of Norio Fujisawa's translation, *Purotagorasu* [Protagoras] [Tokyo: Iwanami bunko, 1988]). In any case, the perspective evident in the *Republic*, which discusses the pleasures unique to the rational part of the soul, is not yet apparent in the *Protagoras*.
66. *Republic* IX, 580D–E.
67. *Republic* IX, 583B, 586B.
68. *Republic* IX, 583B, 586B.
69. *Republic* IX, 583C–586C.

70. Cf. Irwin, "Plato," 976f.
71. Plato, *Philebus* 21C.
72. *Philebus* 12C–13D, 28C–31A.
73. Needless to say, this view conflicts with the right to folly (the freedom to do anything whatsoever on the basis of personal choice, as long as it does not hurt others) recognized by contemporary liberalist individualism. Furthermore, as will be discussed in detail in section 7.2, in Aristotle's view, the hedonics proposed by Plato and others merely discusses the rights and wrongs of pleasure itself without realizing that pleasure depends on the ethical nature of the actions concerned. The contemporary advocate of communitarianism, Alasdair MacIntyre, who proposes rehabilitating an Aristotelian theory of virtue, states that "the Aristotelian tradition can be restated in a way that restores intelligibility and rationality to our moral and social attitudes and commitments." MacIntyre ventures the criticism that "we still, in spite of the efforts of three centuries of moral philosophy and one of sociology, lack any coherent rationally defensible statement of a liberal individualist point of view" (A. MacIntyre, *After Virtue: A Study in Moral Theory* [Notre Dame, IN: University of Notre Dame Press, 1981], 259). For a straightforward summary of the opposition between liberalism (libertarianism), which views humans as atomic entities, and communitarianism, which regards them as belonging to a community, see Hisatake Katō, *Gendai rinrigaku nyūmon* (An introduction to contemporary ethics) (Tokyo: Kōdansha gakujutsu bunko, 1997), 179–88.
74. *Philebus* 32B–50E.
75. *Philebus* 32B–40E.
76. *Philebus* 42C–44A; *Republic* 583B–584C.
77. Cf. Irwin, "Plato," 977. Under the rule of the Wise, people should move toward choosing rational pleasures of true value. What springs to mind here, however, is the criticism of Plato by Carl Popper, the great modern-day social and political philosopher. In the face of the Nazi threat, Popper penned *The Open Society and Its Enemies* (London: Routledge & Sons, 1945), in which he criticized Plato's political ideals as embodying a call for domination by a ruling class of totalitarians who govern even the nature of pleasure. Plato scholars have put forward various counterarguments that are more firmly grounded in Plato (e.g., R. Bambrough, *Plato, Popper and Politics: Some Contributions to a Modern Controversy* [Cambridge: Heffer, 1967]; Saitō, *Puraton* [Plato], 110ff.; Takeshi Sasaki, *Puraton no jubaku* [Plato's spell] [Tokyo: Kōdansha, 1998], 185ff.), but we cannot explore these here. I would, however, like to note just one fact: although Popper defends liberalism and democratic politics, his skepticism about democratic politics itself is also apparent in Plato's underlying tenor.

For instance, democratic politics glorifies the freedom of the people and promotes dissipative desires, calling "modesty" silliness and "temperance" a lack of bravery, and twisting things so that "moderation and thriftiness" are regarded as vulgarity and meanness and are cast out (*Republic* VIII, 560D). Conversely, democratic politics mistakes "insolence" for good breeding and misconstrues "anarchy" as liberty, applauding "waste" as magnanimity and "impudence" as bravery (*Republic* VIII, 560E). Young people brought up in this way spend their lives indulging their passing whims. At times they become intoxicated, while at other times they drink nothing but water and exercise in an attempt to lose weight. Or they remain idle, or pretend to immerse themselves in philosophy. One moment they are dabbling in politics and sounding off about their views; the next they are envying warriors and businessmen and trying their hand at that. Hence their whole lives lack order and certainty (*Republic* VIII, 561C–D). Such a climate gives rise to a state of anarchy, and fathers fear their children, while children have no respect for their fathers. Teachers pander to their students out of fear, while students despise their teachers. Older people ingratiate themselves with the young and try to please everyone. This, too, is an attempt to avoid being regarded as uninteresting or authoritarian (*Republic* VIII, 563A–B). People become overly sensitive, and when subjected to even the slightest repression they cannot take it and lose their temper. They no longer care even about the laws, determined as they are to have no master (*Republic* VIII, 563D). Once things reach this state, excessive freedom leads to a yearning for barbaric enslavement, and the situation can easily degenerate into a tyrannical dictatorship (*Republic* VIII, 563E–564B).

This is a glimpse into Plato's portrayal of the evils of democratic politics. Here the sharp observations of reality on the part of Plato, who grew up witnessing the confusion of democratic politics in post-Periclean Athens, are reported with a lively touch. These observations are perhaps equally valid as an accurate diagnosis of contemporary democratic politics.

78. Plato, *The Apology of Socrates* 29D–E, and *Crito* 47E (both Socratic dialogues).

79. Plato, *Phaedo* 94C–E; *Republic* 441B–C.

80. Cf. Irwin, "Plato," 976f.

81. *Phaedo* 67E–69E; Plotinus, *Enneads* I.2.2–4.

82. Plato, *Theaetetus* 173C–177A; Plotinus, *Enneads* I.2.5–7.

83. Irwin, "Plato," 978.

84. See note 77.

85. *Republic* X, 611B–612A.

86. *Phaedrus* 246B; for an English translation, see Plato, *Symposium and Phaedrus*.

87. *Phaedrus* 246A–B.

88. *Phaedo* 100B; for an English translation, see Plato, *Phaedo*, trans. David Gallop (Oxford: Oxford University Press, 1988).

89. *Phaedo* 100D.

90. *Phaedo* 102B.

91. *Phaedo* 103C.

92. This has been pointed out, for example, by Yasuo Iwata in *Seiyō shisō no genryū* (The origins of Western thought) (Tokyo: Hōsō Daigaku Kyōiku Shinkōkai, 1997), 153.

93. *Phaedo* 103D.

94. *Phaedo* 105C.

95. *Phaedo* 105D.

96. *Phaedo* 106B.

97. *Phaedo* 106C–D.

98. Iwata, *Seiyō shisō* (Western thought), 154, cites only the Greek and Latin words, but a similar idea is also found in Hebrew and other languages.

99. Katō, *Shoki Puraton tetsugaku* (Early Platonian philosophy), 81.

100. Katō, *Shoki Puraton tetsugaku* (Early Platonian philosophy), 81–82.

101. Plato, *Parmenides* 2–7, 127D–135C.

102. Katō, *Shoki Puraton tetsugaku* (Early Platonian philosophy), 82; Yasuo Iwata, *Arisutoteresu no rinri shisō* (The ethical thought of Aristotle) (Tokyo: Iwanami Shoten, 1985), 49, n. 42.

103. Katō, *Shoki Puraton tetsugaku* (Early Platonian philosophy), 79.

104. *Phaedo* 64A–81E.

105. *Phaedo* 81A.

106. Iwata, *Aristoteresu no rinri shisō* (The ethical thought of Aristotle), 49, n. 42.

107. *Phaedo* 75E–76D; *Phaedrus* 249B–252C.

108. *Phaedrus* 249C–250C.

109. *Phaedrus* 250Dff.

110. The following words by Maimonides (1135–1204) come to mind as a corresponding expression in the tradition of Hebraism: "Do not imagine that these great mysteries are completely and thoroughly known to any of us. By no means: sometimes truth flashes up before us with daylight brightness, but soon it is obscured by the limitations of our material nature and social habits, and we fall back into a darkness almost as black as that in which we were before. We are thus like a person whose surroundings are from time to time lit up by lightning, while in the intervals he is plunged into pitch-dark night." (Introduction in *More Nebuchim*, ed. J. Ibn Shmuel [Jerusalem, 1947], 6). A. J. Heschel (*God in Search of Man: A Philosophy of Judaism* [New York: Farrar, Straus & Cudahy, 1955], 139f. and 143, n. 6), who cites this in comparison with passages such as Plato's *Epistles* VII, 341, contrasts such "ultimate insights" with "conceptual thinking," pointing out that whereas the latter is always clear and evident, ultimate insights are "events; . . . what is clear at one moment may subsequently be obscured." Heschel stresses "loyalty" to such events, as a matter of "faith" (131–32).

111. *Phaedo* 97A.

112. *Theaetetus* 155D; trans. M. Burnyeat (Indianapolis: Hackett, 1990); emphasis added.

113. *Phaedrus* 250A.

114. *Phaedo* 98E.

115. *Phaedo* 98E, 99B. See section 3.1.

116. Aristotle, *Metaphysics* I, 2, 982b12.

CHAPTER 5

Aristotle (1): Happiness and Ethical Excellence

Aristotle (384–322 B.C.E.) was born in Macedonia in northern Greece. At the age of seventeen he entered Plato's Academy, where he became recognized as the most outstanding student and also gave some lectures. When Plato died, Aristotle left Athens, and after working in such positions as tutor to the young Alexander the Great, Aristotle returned to Athens at the age of forty-nine and founded a school in the Lyceum. In line with the tradition since Plato, the students at the academy would debate with each other as they strolled around, so they are known as the Peripatetic School (*peripatetikoi*). Aristotle's writings cover a wide range, from philosophy, theology, natural philosophy, logic, politics, and the arts, right through to ethics. As the "father of learning," Aristotle was a giant figure who synthesized earlier Greek philosophy and laid the foundation of all subsequent Western thought. He did likewise in the field of ethics, where he constructed the first systematic ethics and where his influence has been immense, right down to the present day.[1]

1. The Status and Composition of the *Nicomachean Ethics*

STATUS

Three ethical treatises are attributed to Aristotle—the *Magna Moralia*, the *Eudemian Ethics*, and the *Nicomachean Ethics*. *Magna Moralia* diverges from Aristotle's fundamental ideas in certain respects—for instance, it does not acknowledge morality in the activity of the *logos*—and today it is generally regarded as the work of a later Aristotelian. *Eude-*

mian Ethics has heavy religious overtones that are uncharacteristic of Aristotle, and so for this and other reasons it has sometimes been regarded as having been written or largely revised by his disciple Eudemus, although scholars nowadays generally accept that it represents the ethics of the young Aristotle and was indeed written by him. In any case, the work that expresses Aristotle's most mature ethical system is the *Nicomachean Ethics*, which is thought to have been edited by his illegitimate son, Nichomachus. As with Aristotle's other works, this consists of his lecture notes, and it was not published. The numerous digressions and duplications are thought to result from the editor's attempts to include all of the revisions and notes added when Aristotle revised his lectures each year. On the whole, however, each book is similar in length, and the *Nicomachean Ethics* can be regarded as a comprehensive overview of Aristotle's ethical thought, with the whole volume having an orderly structure. This structure, which consists of ten books, is described below.

STRUCTURE

Book I: Preface and discussion of happiness
Book II: General observations on ethical excellence (virtue) (focusing on the mean)
Book III: Further general observations on ethical excellence (virtue) and a discussion of specific virtues—bravery and temperance
Book IV: Further discussion of individual ethical excellences (virtues)—liberality, magnificence, high-mindedness, ambition and its mean, mild-temperedness, agreeableness, sincerity, wittiness (modesty)[2]
Book V: Further discussion of individual ethical excellences (virtues)—justice
Book VI: General observations on and individual discussions of intellectual excellences (learning, art, practical wisdom, intuition, wisdom) and various problems
Book VII: Self-restraint and lack of self-restraint, and an excursus on pleasure (part A)
Book VIII: A discussion of friendship
Book IX: Further discussion of friendship
Book X: Excursus on pleasure (part B) and a discussion of happiness, as the overall conclusion

2. Differences from Plato's Ethics, with Particular Focus on Criticism of the Idea of the Good

DIFFERENCES FROM PLATONIC ETHICS

Methodological differences from Plato's ethics are evident in the prefatory remarks in book I of the *Nicomachean Ethics*. The key points can be summarized as follows:[3]

(1) Plato demanded of ethics the same strict proof and certainty as found in mathematics, for instance. By contrast, Aristotle believed that it is wrong to expect such exactitude in ethics, and that it is sufficient to achieve the degree of precision allowed by this particular subject.

(2) On questions such as ethical virtue, Plato was of the opinion that we should follow the views of philosophers who have been trained in awareness of the world of Ideas. Aristotle, however, respected the common ethical beliefs (*endoxa*) of ordinary people and thought their beliefs warranted investigation. He adopted the method of setting out from what is given incoherently in the experiences of ordinary people and inducing universal judgments from this.

(3) Ethical discussions have two aspects: on one hand, they prescribe what people should do and exhort them to do so, and on the other hand, they describe how people actually act and analyze this dispassionately. The first approach is more apparent in Plato, while the latter is more evident in Aristotle. Nevertheless, the discussion of happiness in book X, for instance, does set forth Aristotle's ideal of how people should behave.

In relation to the second point, Aristotle's criticisms of the theory of Ideas have already been mentioned in chapter 4, but since this is an important point at issue in the *Nicomachean Ethics*, let us revisit it in a little more detail.

CRITICISMS OF THE IDEA OF THE GOOD

Aristotle makes the following statement:

> [S]ince the term "good" has as many senses as the term "being" (for it is predicated of whatness [essence], as in the

case of God and of the intellect, and of a quality, as in the case
of the virtues, and of a quantity, as in the case of the right
amount, and of a relation, as in the case of the useful, and of
time, as in the case of right time, and of place, as in the case of
the right location, and similarly with the other categories),
clearly it cannot be a universal which is common and one, for
it would not have been used in all the categories but only in
one.[4]

In other words, since "good" is predicated in various categories such as
essence, quality, quantity, relation, time, and place, it cannot constitute a
universal Idea. This is obvious if considered in an analogy to the copula.
The word "is" (whatness) is also predicated in every category, so we have
expressions such as "he is seventy kilograms in weight" (quantity) or "he
is brave" (quality). Obviously, however, there is no shared universality
between "seventy kilograms" and "brave," which belong to different categories. It is simply that the same predicate, "is," is used as an attribute
of the same entity, "he."[5] Similarly, there is no shared universality or
Idea between the good of "the useful" and the good of "place"; it is
simply that they are united by the word "good" when predicated as
depending on a certain "thing." This is the first criticism of the Idea of
the Good in the *Nicomachean Ethics*.

Aristotle also criticizes the theory of Ideas from another perspective:

Furthermore, one does not see how a weaver or a carpenter
will benefit in the practice of his art by knowing *Good Itself*,
or how one will be a better doctor or a better general by having
contemplated that Idea [the *Good*]; for it appears that what a
doctor examines is not health in this manner at all, but the
health of man, or perhaps rather the health of an individual
man, since what he cures is an individual.[6]

As we saw in chapter 4, if we follow Plato's view of Ideas it is problematic
whether we really can categorically declare that doctors do not in fact
study sickness or health themselves, abstracting the symptoms common
to each patient and delving into the general cause, and whether a doctor
or general who has "contemplated that Idea" really would not be "a
better doctor or a better general" by having done so. Nevertheless, "to
Aristotle the Idea of the Good is a universal concept that is one and the
same in all particular goodnesses, but by adopting such a universal concept as the basis of goodness, the particulars lose their particularity, are
indiscriminately homogenized, and lose substance, and the ultimate basis
unifying all the various particulars as goodness (human reason) is also

lost sight of.''[7] This is why Aristotle presumes to criticize the views of his teacher Plato, noting that "such an inquiry is made with reluctance because those who introduced the Forms [*eidos*; i.e., Ideas] are friends. Yet . . . it is sacred to honor truth above friendship.''[8] Here we can already perceive the fundamental stance of Aristotelian ethics, with its strong tendency toward describing individual facts.[9]

3. Theory of Happiness

WHAT IS GOODNESS, WHAT IS HAPPINESS?

"Every art and every *inquiry*, and similarly, every *action* and every intention is thought to aim at some good.''[10] This is the opening sentence in the *Nicomachean Ethics*. Good is "that at which all things aim," and the subject of ethics is also "the good for mankind" (*tanthrōpinon agathon*),[11] that is, as much good as humans can seek and achieve. Chapter 6 in book I of the *Nicomachean Ethics* revisits this topic and asks, "What is the highest of all goods achievable by *action*?''[12] It states that there is general agreement on the answer to this: it is "happiness" (*eudaimoniā*). "But there is disagreement as to what happiness is, and the account of it given by ordinary people is not similar to that given by the wise." In other words, ordinary people cite "something obvious or apparent, such as pleasure, or wealth or honor." Moreover, different people have different opinions, and even the same person will give different answers on different occasions. When ill, for instance, people say that happiness lies in good health, and when poor they say it lies in wealth. By contrast, wise people argue that there is something intrinsically good and that it causes these particulars to be good. On this basis, then, Aristotle argued that "there are three kinds of life which stand out most": the life of pleasure (*apolaustikos bios*), the political life (*politicos bios*), and the contemplative life (*theōrētikos bios*).[13] Aristotle observes that these lifestyles aim at pleasure, honor, and contemplation, respectively. He also mentions the life of money making (*chrēmatitēs bios*) but rules that out.[14]

Aristotle's subsequent argument tends to be convoluted and unclear, no doubt because the supplementary digressions complicate matters and also because he was trying not to reveal in advance the overall conclusion reached in book X. Nevertheless, here I will preemptively summarize

Aristotle's main points and the conclusions that can naturally be anticipated on the basis of this.[15]

WHAT CONSTITUTES THE HIGHEST GOOD?

To gain a deeper understanding of what constitutes the highest good, we
need to consider human beings' functions (*ergon*). We share with animals
the functions of nutrition and growth. Animals, too, have sensations. So
the function unique to humans must be the *"actions [praktikē]* of the
soul *[psychē]* with reason *[logos]*," that is, the function of reason (*nūs*).
Let us suppose now that there is a lyre player who has a family. No
matter how good a husband or father he might be, unless he can play the
lyre well he cannot be regarded as a good lyrist. What ultimately makes
a lyre player a good lyrist is the unique function of playing the lyre well.
Humans, too, have various functions, but what ultimately makes them
good human beings, then, is that function unique to humans, that is,
reason. This means it is the functioning of reason that is the ultimate
"highest good" (*to ariston*) for human beings and constitutes true happiness. Supreme bliss is thought to consist of the reason-based contemplative life of the wise man or philosopher that was mentioned earlier.

What ethics should have pursued was "the good for mankind." Although this good consisted of happiness, out of all the different possible
interpretations of happiness it is the functioning of good reason that
constitutes the greatest happiness. This is the ultimate goal that ethics
should pursue. In the long run, however, an ultimate goal is simply that.
While keeping this ultimate end in sight, we need to delve further into
the particulars that precede achievement of this supreme goal.

Aristotle does not take his discussion this far in book I, but if we
examine the overall structure of the *Nicomachean Ethics* and foreshadow
its conclusion and reveal its perspective, then his views can be summed
up along these lines.

4. Ethical Excellences (Virtues)

ETHICAL EXCELLENCES AND INTELLECTUAL
EXCELLENCES

Let us take a look at the following famous passage:

> [T]he good for a man turns out to be an activity of the soul
> according to virtue [excellence; *aretē*], and if the virtues are

many, then according to the best and most complete virtue. And we should add "in a complete life," for one swallow does not make a spring, nor does one day; and so too one day or a short time does not make a man blessed or happy.[16]

Books II to VI are devoted to a consideration of such excellences. Aristotle divides excellences into ethical *excellences* (depending on the context, the word *aretē* is sometimes translated as "virtue"; see chapter 6), such as bravery and temperance, and intellectual excellences, such as wisdom and practical wisdom. He maintains that whereas wisdom is acquired through "teaching," practical wisdom is obtained through "habituation."[17]

HABIT

> [A]n ethical virtue [*ēthikē aretē*] is acquired by habituation, as is indicated by the name "ethical" [*ēthikē*], which varies slightly from the name "ethos" [habit].[18]

The word *ēthikē* (ethical) is the adjectival form of the feminine singular noun *ēthos*, which expresses "ethics or character," and *ēthos* is said to derive from *ethos* (customs or mores). Regardless of the etymological validity of this purported origin,[19] the neuter plural form of *ēthikē*— *ēthika*—is part of the title *Ēthika Nikomakheia* (the *Nicomachean Ethics*), and this was transliterated directly into Latin as *ethica*. From this word derive the modern European terms for "ethics"—*ethics* (English), *Ethik* (German), and *éthique* (French)—so this is a classic passage that is often cited as an explanation of the original meaning of "ethics." In any case, Aristotle stressed that ethical excellences are acquired through habit, and he continued on as follows:

> [N]o thing which exists by nature can be changed into something else by habituation; e.g., no stone, which moves downwards by nature, can be changed by being habituated to move upwards. . . . Hence virtues arise in us neither by nature nor contrary to nature; but by our nature we can receive them and perfect them by habituation.[20]

Here something along the lines of "Since it is true that various ethical excellences arise in us" is probably omitted before the "Hence" in this quote. This might be easier to grasp if, instead of the falling of a stone, we were to substitute a physiological characteristic such as hunger or thirst. No matter how many times one might fast, one's physiology—the fact that failure to eat will lead to starvation—cannot be fundamentally changed. By contrast, one can acquire the virtue of bravery through performing brave deeds repeatedly, thereby altering one's innately cowardly nature. Aristotle argues that ethical excellences, or virtues, unlike physiological characteristics, are a latent disposition that can be brought out through habituation.

Yet how can people who are lacking in bravery perform brave deeds in the first place?[21] Aristotle's response to this rudimentary question seems to be along the following lines.

BRAVE PEOPLE AND BRAVE DEEDS

Even though there are cowardly people in the world, there are none who lack even a single shred of courage. Nobody is in a perpetual state of fearfulness, in the way that a stone falls down. Instead, "it is by our actions in dangerous situations in which we are in the process of acquiring the habit of being courageous or afraid that we become brave or cowardly, respectively."[22] Aristotle seems to regard the above question as flawed, in that it is based on the unrealistic assumption of someone who is entirely "lacking in bravery." Aristotle's attitude also means that habituated training from childhood is important.

It should be noted, however, that Aristotle is using the expression "brave" in two different senses: one in relation to people and the other in relation to their actions. It is the former sense that represents the primary use of this word. That is why Aristotle says "it is by *similar* activities [*energeia*] that habits [*hexis*] are developed in men."[23] In contrast to modern-day ethics, which tends to focus solely on a discussion of actions, this ancient ethics is characterized by its examination of the good and bad in humans themselves, the agents of these actions. Just because someone has carried out a "brave" deed does not necessarily mean that person is truly "brave." Aristotle's "standard of moral virtue is . . . a high one."[24] What kind of person, then, is regarded as "brave" according to Aristotle's high standards? First, he must "know" what he does,[25] "otherwise animals would be called brave, and this Aristotle was not prepared to allow."[26] Second, he must "[intend] to do what he does and [intend] to do it for its own sake."[27] Third, he must act "with certainty and firmness."[28] Those people performing "brave" deeds in a manner that meets these three criteria deserve to be called "brave" in the true sense of the word.

FEELINGS, FACULTIES, HABITS

Naturally, then, it also obvious which of the following three functions of the soul constitutes ethical excellence—neither (1) feelings (*pathos*) nor (2) faculties (*dynamis*), but (3) habits (*hexis*).[29] Feelings include such emotions as desire, anger, fear, love, and hatred and generally entail pleasure or pain. Faculties refer to the capacity to feel these emotions. By contrast, habits are the disposition whereby one decides which feeling to feel and to what extent. For instance, some people feel anger strongly from birth, whereas others feel it weakly. This is an inherent attribute. The former are regarded as hot tempered and the latter as lacking in spirit (weak spirited).[30] Those who are quick-tempered must be schooled in self-control, while timid people must be trained to show some guts in situations calling for anger. Repeated, such training will result in even-tempered people who are neither excessively irascible nor excessively timid. It is this that can be regarded as ethical excellence (virtue). This includes the element of choice, so one is praised on choosing well and criticized for choosing poorly.

These examples suggest that what Aristotle regarded as virtue lies between excess and deficiency, but I will reserve discussion of that for the next chapter.

Notes

1. For a detailed discussion of Aristotle's wide-ranging impact on the views of philosophers such as Alberti, Locke, Kant, and Hegel in relation to the family and moral systems, as well as on the value theories of Scheler and Meinong or on Husserl's *Intersubjektivität*, for instance, see Yukiyoshi Ogura, "Arisutote-resu to gendai rinrigaku" (Aristotle and modern-day ethics) in *Arisutoteresu* (Aristotle), ed. Japanese Society for Ethics (Tokyo: Keiō tsūshin, 1986), 129–61.

2. "Modesty" is discussed in book IV of the *Nicomachean Ethics*, but the conclusion is that it should not be included among the "ethical excellences."

3. See G. E. R. Lloyd, *Aristotle: The Growth and Structure of His Thought* (London: Cambridge University Press, 1968), 204–8.

4. *Nicomachean Ethics* I, 6, 1096a23–29. Unless otherwise noted, English translations are from Aristotle, *The Nicomachean Ethics*, trans. H. G. Apostle (Dordrecht, Netherlands: Reidel, 1975). Hereafter, the *Nicomachean Ethics* is abbreviated as *NE*.

5. Aristotle, *Metaphysics* IV, 2, 1003a33–b1. See also IV, 3.

6. *NE* I, 6, 1097a8–13.

7. Yasuo Iwata, *Arisutoteresu no rinri shisō* (The ethical thought of Aristotle) (Tokyo: Iwanami Shoten, 1985), 29.

8. *NE* I, 4, 1096a12–15.

9. Aristotle raises many other issues in his criticism of the theory of Ideas in chapter 4 of book I of the *Nicomachean Ethics*. See the detailed note 42 in Iwata, *Arisutoteresu no rinri shisō* (The ethical thought of Aristotle), 47–49, for an introduction to and evaluation of this.

10. *NE* I, 1, 1094a1–2.

11. *NE* I, 2, 1094b7.

12. The following quotations are from *NE* I, 4, 1095a15–17.

13. *NE* I, 5, 1095a17ff.

14. *NE* I, 5, 1096a5–10.

15. The following is from *NE* I, 7, 1097b22–1098a20.

16. *NE* I, 7, 1098a16–20.

17. *NE* II, 1, 1103a17.

18. *NE* II, 1, 1103a17–18.

19. See, for example, Iwata, *Arisutoteresu no rinri shisō* (The ethical thought of Aristotle), 139, and Aristotle, *Nikomakosu rinrigaku* (Nicomachean Ethics), *Arisutoteresu zenshū* (Complete works of Aristotle), trans. Shinrō Katō, vol. 13 (Tokyo: Iwanami Shoten, 1973), 378, n. 3.

20. *NE* II, 1, 1103a19–26.

21. Lloyd, *Aristotle*, 215.

22. *NE* II, 1, 1103b16–17.

23. *NE* II, 1, 1103b21–22.

24. Lloyd, *Aristotle*, 215.

25. *NE* II, 4, 1105a31.

26. Lloyd, *Aristotle*, 215–16. As a source in the *Nicomachean Ethics*, we could cite, for instance, book III, 8, 1116b23–1117a5.

27. *NE* II, 4, 1105a31–32.

28. *NE* II, 4, 1105a32–33.

29. *NE* II, 5, 1106a10–12.

30. *NE* II, 7, 1108a4–9.

CHAPTER 6

Aristotle (2): The Doctrine of the Mean and the Doctrine of Virtue

1. The Doctrine of the Mean

Aristotle's doctrine advocating the "mean" (*mesotēs*), which constitutes the core of his theory of ethical virtue, can already be inferred from the examples in the previous chapter. As with his theory of "practical wisdom" (*phronēsis*), this doctrine, which distinguishes between virtue and vice, is characteristic of Aristotle. (When contrasting intellectual *aretē* with ethical *aretē*, *aretē* should be translated as "excellence," but when referring only to ethical excellence it is more comprehensible if translated as "virtue." In chapters 5 and 7, a contrast is made with "intellectual excellence," so there we have no choice but to use the expression "ethical excellence"; but in this chapter, *aretē* will usually be rendered as "virtue.") Of course, the doctrine of the mean is thought to have had forerunners in the proverb "Nothing in excess," which is said to have been engraved on the temple at Delphi, and in folk medical and physiological theories that regarded health as an intermediate state in which one is neither too hot nor too cold.[1] It is to Aristotle, however, that the unique achievement of having the insight to place this idea of the mean at the heart of ethics can be attributed, as can having the acumen to analyze individual cases in detail using this as a criterion for dealing appropriately with various virtues and vices.

ANALOGIES TO EXERCISE, EATING AND DRINKING, AND WORKS OF ART

Aristotle starts out with an explanation of the origins of his focus:

> [B]oth excess and deficiency in exercise destroy strength; and similarly, when too much or too little drink or food is taken,

it destroys health, but when the amount is proportionate, it produces or increases or preserves health. Such is the case also with temperance and bravery and the other [ethical] virtues; for a man who flees from and fears everything and never stands his ground becomes a coward, but he who fears nothing at all but proceeds against all dangers becomes rash, and, similarly, a man who indulges in all [bodily] pleasures and abstains from none becomes intemperate, but he who avoids them all, like a boor, becomes a sort of insensible man; for temperance and bravery are destroyed by excess as well as by deficiency, but they are preserved by moderation (or the mean) [mesotēs].[2]

In addition to these analogies with exercise and eating and drinking, Aristotle proffers an analogy to fine works of art: the reason people speak highly of the exquisite objects produced by artisans, saying "nothing can be subtracted or added," is that these works strike a beautiful balance between excess and deficiency. Based on an analogy with such works of art, Aristotle infers that the mean is likewise important in ethics.[3]

THE MEAN IN ETHICS

[E]thical virtue . . . is concerned with feelings and *actions*, in which there is excess, deficiency, and moderation. For example, we may have the feelings of fear, bravery, *desire*, anger, pity, and any pleasure or pain in general either more or less than we should, and in both cases this is not a good thing; but to have these feelings at the right times and for the right things and towards the right men and for the right purpose and in the right manner, this is the mean and the best, and it is precisely this which belongs to virtue. . . . Virtue, then, is a kind of moderation [mesotēs], at least having the mean [meson] as its aim.[4]

This amounts to defining virtue in terms of the mean. Aristotle also expresses this in the following terms:

[Ethical] virtue, then, is a habit [hexis], disposed toward *action* by deliberate choice, being at the mean relative to us, and defined by reason [logos] and as a prudent man would define it.[5]

CHOOSING THE MEAN

How, then, can people choose this "mean" between excess and deficiency? What immediately springs to mind here is the method of calculating the arithmetic mean, for example, "if ten [*minae*] is many and two is few, . . . then six is taken as the mean."[6] Aristotle comments, however, that perhaps "for Milo it is too little, but for a beginner in athletics it is too much." The *mina* is a unit of weight, roughly equivalent to what in modern-day nutritional terms we would refer to as 1,000 kilocalories, and Milo was a great athlete in the sixth century BCE who was known for his voracious appetite, having devoured a calf in a day after killing it with a blow from his fist. Therefore, even food intake varies from person to person and cannot be determined simply by calculating the mean. All the more so for the ethical mean, which for each individual must be the "mean *for me*." How, then, does one choose this mean?

If we recall the examples cited in the previous chapter, the median virtue in relation to the two extreme vices of irascibility and timidity was "even-temperedness." The mean between "cowardice" and "rashness" was "bravery," and that between "profligacy" and "insensibility" was "temperance." Vices are excessive or deficient in relation to the virtues, but it should be noted that in some cases the more antithetical element differs more greatly from the virtue. Specifically, what is more antithetical to "bravery" is not "rashness" but the deficiency known as "cowardice," and what is more antithetical to "temperance" is not "insensibility" but the excess known as "profligacy."[7] Aristotle does not mention "even-temperedness," but it is likely that what would be more antithetical to this would be excess in the form of "irascibility." Aristotle points out that there are two principles involved here: (1) one of the extremes is closer to the mean, and (2) people are naturally drawn toward one of the extremes.[8] In the light of the first reason, we could consider "rashness" as closer to "bravery," "insensibility" to "temperance," and "timidity" to "even-temperedness." The second reason refers more specifically to our inclination to avoid pain and to tend toward pleasure. In other words, people are easily drawn toward the pleasures of profligacy, so it is easier for this vice to be more antithetical to the virtue of "temperance."[9] Since "rashness" entails danger and pain, people usually avoid it and tend toward "cowardice," so the vice that is more antithetical to "bravery" would be "cowardice." Similarly, if we assume that venting one's "anger" is pleasurable, then people will be liable to become angry easily, and the vice that is more antithetical to the virtue of "even-temperedness" will be "irascibility."

No doubt, of course, there are people who find anger instinctively unpleasant and avoid it as much as possible, preferring a state of "timidity," just as there are those who revel in countless different adventures and regard "rashness" as pleasurable. If these exceptions are also taken into account, then the *"mean for me"* can differ for each individual. Nevertheless, Aristotle generally recommends that people seek their own mean in line with these two principles.

One other point that must be noted when choosing a "mean" is that it is futile to seek a "mean" for any and all actions and feelings. For instance, there is no virtue of the "mean" in such actions as adultery, stealing, or murder, or in such feelings as malice, shamelessness, or envy. These are outright vices, and it does not mean that if one commits "adultery with the right woman, at the right time, in the right manner"[10] then the vice will turn into a virtue. Likewise, no "mean" exists for "cowardice" and "rashness" themselves. These vices are the two extremes constituting an excess or a deficiency, but it does not mean that within excess and deficiency themselves there exist further stages of excess, the mean and a deficiency, and that there is virtue among these vices. Instead, in the case of an excess, we need to look at the opposite deficiency, and in the case of a deficiency, at the excess, seeking on each occasion the mean between the two.

2. Evaluation of the Doctrine of the Mean

Here I have outlined Aristotle's argument about the mean and how to determine it. There have, however, long been various criticisms of this doctrine. Let us touch briefly here on the main criticisms and their validity.

1. First, it has often been claimed that Aristotle adopts a dogmatic position that regards the doctrine of the mean as an absolute rule, and that he seems to view this standard as determining virtue and vice in every case.[11] As we have already seen, however, Aristotle recognizes that this doctrine does not apply to cases such as adultery, murder, or envy, and he repeatedly points out that finding the mean virtue as an intermediate point between the two extremes of vice and virtue is no easy task in specific instances.[12] Instead, he is merely *advocating* that people who tend toward cowardice, for example, look toward its opposite, rashness, and reform themselves into someone possessing the intermediate quality of bravery.[13]

2. Some critics have latched on to this exhortation (*parainesis*) and argued that, although there is hope for happiness here, it does not pre-

sent a model of goodness that could constitute the core of ethics.[14] In fact, however, Aristotle also repeatedly discusses "what one should do [*dei*]" in relation to the mean,[15] and in his view happiness is linked to goodness right from the outset.[16]

3. Other critics argue that Aristotle has substituted the quantitative issue of the mean and excess or deficiency for the qualitative issue of good and evil. Kant was a leading critic in this vein.[17] Yet when making ethical judgments, we do in fact use expressions such as "suffers from excessive ambition" or "lacks sufficient pride."[18] As long as virtues and vices both have to do with the life of flesh-and-blood human beings, surely we cannot deny the quantitative aspects.[19] It seems that we could in turn criticize Kant for an overly hasty judgment of the doctrine of the mean based on his own perspective, which regarded the categorical imperative as the sole principle of virtue.[20]

4. Finally, one might point out that the doctrine of the mean falls into self-contradiction if overly stressed as a doctrine. In other words, if the intermediate between excess and deficiency consists of the goodness of the mean, then one commits the error of deviating from the mean if the principle of the mean is itself argued to excess. Since Aristotle also applied the virtue of the mean to "truthfulness" and regarded the "truth" between "boastfulness" and "self-depreciation" as a "virtue,"[21] then this criticism is by no means unfounded. We could, however, defend Aristotle by saying that here, too, he exhibits caution. As we saw with the first criticism, he makes no excessive claim or boast that everything can be explained in terms of this principle; instead, he relativizes it and turns his attention to a balance with *other elements*.

What, then, are the "other elements" distinct from Aristotle's doctrine of the mean? Next, I would like to consider the case of the three virtues of "bravery," "justice," and "love" and demonstrate that, far from advocating the mean as the sole guiding doctrine, Aristotle gave ample consideration to many diverse aspects.

3. The Doctrine of Virtue: Bravery, Justice, and Love

BRAVERY

Bravery is discussed in chapters 6 to 9 of book III in the *Nicomachean Ethics*. The positioning of "bravery" as the mean between "cowardice"

and "rashness" that we saw earlier is merely one tiny aspect of Aristotle's
wide-ranging discussion of bravery. For instance, he cites a bad reputation or an insult to one's wife and children as things that even a brave
person should fear, and he points out that just because someone has no
fear of poverty or disease it does not signify bravery on their part.[22]
Aristotle considers the truly brave person to be someone who does not
fear a noble death, as epitomized by death in war.[23] Suicide is criticized
as a cowardly escape from poverty or rejected love.[24] Aristotle goes on
to list five phenomena that resemble bravery but in fact differ from it: (1)
actions taken out of fear of legal penalties or criticism; (2) the attitude of
professional soldiers who attack boldly only when the odds are in their
favor; (3) the uncivilized reaction of rushing at another person like a wild
beast, out of a sense of rage; (4) calmness in the face of danger merely
because one is drunk and feeling daring or because of inherent optimism;
and (5) a carefree attitude stemming from ignorance and misconceptions,
where one fails to sense a hidden danger.[25]

Finally, Aristotle points out that "bravery" has more to do with
"cowardice" than with "rashness," because the brave person is someone
who does not lose his nerve and run away when faced with something
frightening but is able to deal with it properly. Aristotle brings his discussion of bravery to a close with the following portrayal of a brave
person:

> [D]eath and wounds will be painful to a brave man or to a man
> who does not want them; but he faces them, since it is noble
> to do so or disgraceful not to do so.[26]

JUSTICE

From the latter part of book III, the *Nicomachean Ethics* moves on to a
discussion of different ethical virtues, discussing twelve virtues such as
bravery and love through to book V, which is devoted solely to an overall
account of "justice." This is indicative of the importance of this particular virtue, and in a sense we could say that justice constitutes "complete
virtue" and "the best of the virtues," and that "in justice is included
every virtue."[27] Aristotle's comments, however, are detailed and wide-
ranging, and along with redactional problems this has led to debate over
how to interpret his remarks.[28] Since we cannot enter into a specialized
debate on the history of how his comments have been construed, I would

like to sum up just the key points, analyzed in my own way as much as possible.[29]

Aristotle classifies justice into general justice and special justice (book V, chapters 1 and 2), with the latter being further subdivided into distributive justice (chapter 3), corrective justice (chapter 4), and reciprocal justice (justice in exchange; chapter 5). He states that " 'the just' means that which is lawful or that which is fair."[30] General justice is concerned with legality, and special justice with fairness. My earlier statement that "in a sense we could say that justice constitutes 'complete virtue' " was intended in the sense of legal, general justice. Here "virtue and this kind of justice . . . are the same, but their essences are not the same. Insofar as the disposition is defined in relation to something else, it is justice, but insofar as it is such-and-such a disposition [hexis], it is a virtue without qualification."[31] The law regulates our behavior toward others in society, and obeying the law is what constitutes general justice.

From chapter 3 onward, book V of the *Nicomachean Ethics* is devoted to a detailed discussion of special justice, which relates to fairness, and "the enduring contribution of Aristotle's theory of justice lies in how it revealed the nature" of justice.[32] We will now examine each of these three forms of justice in turn.

Distributive Justice

"Distributive justice" "concerns itself with the distributions of honor or property or the other things which are to be shared by the members of the state."[33] Here justice lies not in all people receiving the same distribution but in each person receiving an amount in proportion to each person's value.[34] This is Aristotle's claim of distributive justice. How, then, is each person's value to be measured? Aristotle admits that opinions will differ on this. He notes that a person's value is measured variously by, for instance, such yardsticks as "high lineage," "wealth," "virtue," or "freedom"[35] (he seems to view the extent of freedom as differing depending on one's social status).[36] Nowadays one's "abilities in the broad sense"[37] would probably be regarded as the basis for distribution, rather than these criteria, but I would suggest that the actual principle of basing distribution on values of some kind or other is acknowledged as an unchanging truth right up to the present.

Corrective Justice

Next, Aristotle discusses "corrective justice," which is the principle of taking remedial action when unfairness has occurred as a result of an injustice involving exchanges between people.[38] We could conceive of cases where something was initially purchased or lent voluntarily and then a violation of the agreement occurred, or cases where one party suffered involuntary damage such as theft or assassination.[39] Restoring fairness on such occasions should not involve considering each person's value, as happened with distributive justice. In this respect, each individual is equal before the law, and no matter what value the thief might have, it is the judge's duty to ensure that what was stolen is returned to the person from whom it was taken. Although Aristotle argues that justice is restored correctively in this way, there are at least two unresolved issues here. There are problems that Aristotle himself was aware of[40] but does not seem to have resolved: (1) Even if the unfairness resulting from theft can be remedied, how should cases of injury or assassination be handled? (2) Even with cases of theft, is it sufficient simply to return the stolen goods, with no further penalty? In relation to this second question in particular, writers such as the compiler of *Magna Moralia*[41] have argued that the perpetrators should suffer a penalty more severe than their own deeds, and they have quite rightly corrected Aristotle's view.[42]

Reciprocal Justice (Justice in Exchange)

Aristotle makes it clear that distributive justice and corrective justice fall under the category of special justice,[43] but it is uncertain to which category the third type of justice, "reciprocal justice (justice in exchange)," belongs.[44] In terms of content it has similarities to distributive justice, which relates to the distribution of common property, but it particularly concerns exchanges of individually owned property, so it can be construed as a special justice.[45] In other words, the members of a community exchange the fruits of their individual labors in accordance with demand, but a principle of equivalent exchange needs to be operating in this process. This is none other than reciprocal justice (justice in exchange).

For instance, when a house built by a carpenter is exchanged for shoes made by a shoemaker, it is necessary to calculate how many pairs of shoes one house is worth. If in view of market demand the value of the house is deemed equivalent to one thousand pairs of shoes, then a craftsman producing one house and another craftsman producing a thousand pairs of shoes would be equivalent in value. And if it would take a carpenter one year and a shoemaker two years to produce these products, then the value of a carpenter would be twice that of a shoemaker. Here Aristotle is working on the assumption of differing values for people according to their merits, and he takes the view that justice consists of products being exchanged and assets being acquired in line with these merits.

In this way Aristotle regards justice as "complete virtue," and he devotes the bulk of his discussion of virtue to this topic, examining it from many angles. Yet he places even greater emphasis on love, as something transcending justice. In his discussion of virtues Aristotle mentions love only briefly in chapter 6 of book IV and leaves a detailed discussion for later, in books VIII and IX. Let us now refer to these passages to grasp the essence of Aristotle's thinking on love.

LOVE

The fact that Aristotle regarded love (*philiā*) as more important than justice is already apparent in the following passage:

> Friendship [i.e., love] seems to hold a state together, too, and lawgivers seem to pay more attention to friendship than to justice. . . . And when men are friends, they have no need of justice at all, but when they are just, they still need friendship; and a thing which is most just is thought to be done in a friendly way.[46]

According to Aristotle, love is directed at three objects, that is, the lovable consists of "the good or the pleasant or the useful."[47] Aristotle argues that love exists when two people are "well-disposed towards each other and wish each other's good without being unaware of this."[48] For instance, even if a great wine is "pleasant," it is not an object of love. It would be ridiculous to "wish wine well," because this is merely a matter of taste preferences. Aristotle also notes that even if one feels affection for another, unless that person returns the "affection" this is a one-sided feeling, not love. And even if people who have never met entertain warm feelings toward each other as being "good" or "useful" on the basis of that person's reputation, one cannot describe the relationship as one of love unless the other person is "aware of this."[49]

Love Resulting from Pleasure or Usefulness

In line with the three kinds of "lovable things," there are also three forms of love: love because something is "good," love because something is "pleasant," and love because something is "useful." Of these, the latter two cannot be regarded as proper love. For instance, loving a witty person does not mean loving his "character" (*ēthos*) but loving him because his wit is pleasurable and useful to oneself. This is an "easily dissolved" love, because this person might not always possess the attribute of wit. Whereas the elderly tend to seek out love that is "beneficial," young people tend to succumb to love that is "pleasant": "for the greater part of amorous friendship occurs by passion and for the sake of pleasure; and it is in view of this that they become friendly and soon end that friendship, and often do these the same day."[50]

Love Arising from Goodness

> Perfect friendship exists between men who are good and are alike with respect to virtue; for, insofar as they are good, it is in a similar manner that they wish each other's goods, and such men are good in themselves.[51]

This perfect love proper "requires time and familiarity,"[52] and good people are few and far between,[53] so such relationships are "rare."[54] Yet once such love has developed, one loves not the other person's changing outward qualities but their very essence, so it becomes a love that "lasts as long as they are good."[55] What then, does it mean for a person with such a love to "wish the other's good"? Do such people not desire their own good?

Is Self-Love Bad?

To answer the question posed at the end of the previous section, we first need to consider whether self-love should be condemned. Aristotle tackles this question head-on in chapter 8 of book IX. It is common to refer derogatorily to people with a strong sense of self-love as egoists (*philautoi*; people who love themselves), but although correct in one sense, in another sense this is wrong. In other words, if such a person tends to take more than his fair share of "property or of honours or of bodily pleasures" in line with his "*desires* and, in general, [his] passions and the nonrational part of [his] soul [*alogos*]"—as most people do—then as long as he loves such self-desires, this will lead to ugly competition with others, which should be deplored and rejected.[56] But if such a person lives "according to reason [*logos*]" and "his intellect [*nūs*] rules," and if he "is always earnest to do, above all things, what is just or temperate or any other thing according to virtue and, in general, if he [is] always earnest to safeguard for himself what is noble," then rather than reproach, self-love of this kind merits praise.[57] To put it another way, the self-love of

"bad men" who "aim to gratify their *desires* and, in general, their passions" should be rejected, while the self-love of "good men" who desire
"what is noble" in line with "reason" (*logos*) is acceptable.

Good for One's Friends and Good for Oneself

In that case, a person who "wishes good" for others may also wish well
for himself, and as long as he acts in accord with *logos* then in fact he
"should love himself most of all."[58] This also clarifies the meaning of
"insofar as they are good, it is in a similar manner that they wish each
other's goods, and such men are good in themselves." This does not
mean deferring to a friend's egoism and affording him the pleasures bad
men desire in accordance with their passions but taking care to enhance
his virtue in line with *logos*. In this way, it is not contradictory to wish
well for one's friends and also to wish well for oneself. Rather, as long as
"it is equality [*isotēs*] and likeness [*homoiotēs*] that is more conducive to
friendship [*philotēs*], and especially likeness in virtue,"[59] then the two
acts complement each other. Aristotle observes that the five characteristics that make for friendly relations are also directly applicable to one's
relationship with oneself: (1) wanting and doing what is good for that
person; (2) wanting that person to exist and live; (3) spending time with
that person; (4) choosing the same things as that person; and (5) sharing
that person's joys and sorrows. Here one could equally well substitute
"one's friend" or "oneself" for "that person."[60] (As far as oneself is
concerned, the third characteristic can be construed as meaning that
one's memories of the past are pleasant and one's hopes for the future
are positive, so there is no need to escape from oneself or kill time. Points
(4) and (5) mean not suffering from self-dissociation.)

Following just the gist of Aristotle's discussion of the essence of love
in this way might leave one with the strong impression that he portrays
the pre-established harmony of fraternity in a positive and one-sided
fashion, but in fact Aristotle develops a multifaceted discussion of love,
including, for example, an analysis of the lack of self-love, love between
husband and wife and parent and child, an analogy between this and the
state system, the need for happy people to have friends, and limits to the
number of friends. These matters are, however, beyond the scope of the
present chapter.

Notes

1. G. E. R. Lloyd, *Aristotle: The Growth and Structure of His Thought*
(London: Cambridge University Press, 1968), 217.

2. Aristotle, *Nicomachean Ethics* II, 2, 1104a15–27. Unless otherwise noted, English translations are from Aristotle, *The Nicomachean Ethics*, trans. H. G. Apostle (Dordrecht, Netherlands: Reidel, 1975). Hereafter, the *Nicomachean Ethics* is abbreviated as *NE*.

3. *NE* II, 6, 1106b9–14.
4. *NE* II, 2, 1106b16–28.
5. *NE* II, 6, 1106b36–1107a2.
6. *NE* II, 6, 1106a36–b2.
7. *NE* II, 8, 1109a2–5.
8. *NE* II, 8, 1109a5ff.
9. *NE* II, 8, 1109a14–19.
10. *NE* II, 6, 1107a15–16.
11. See Lloyd, *Aristotle*, 221.
12. *NE* II, 9, 1109a24–30, 1109b14, etc.
13. *NE* II, 8, 1108b35–1109b26. See also Lloyd, *Aristotle*, 221.
14. See V. Brochard, *Études de philosophie ancienne et de philosophie moderne* (Paris: Alcan, 1912), 489–503; Yasuo Iwata, *Arisutoteresu no rinri shisō* (The ethical thought of Aristotle) (Tokyo: Iwanami Shoten, 1985), 216.
15. *NE* II, 6, 1106b21–23, 1107a16; III, 12, 1119b16–17, etc. See also Iwata, *Arisutoteresu no rinri shisō* (Ethical thought of Aristotle), 217 and 231, n. 35.
16. *NE* I, 4, 1095a14–20.
17. I. Kant, *Metaphysik der Sitten* (Hamburg: Meiner, 1986), 404ff.
18. See Lloyd, *Aristotle*, 222.
19. Iwata, *Arisutoteresu no rinri shisō* (Ethical thought of Aristotle), 217.
20. For a more detailed rebuttal of Kant's criticism, see Iwata, *Arisutoteresu no rinri shisō* (Ethical thought of Aristotle), 218–22.
21. *NE* II, 7, 1108a19–22.
22. *NE* III, 6, 1115a10–24.
23. *NE* III, 6, 1115a24–34.
24. *NE* III, 7, 1116a12–15.
25. *NE* III, 8, 1116a15–1117a28.
26. *NE* III, 9, 1117b7–9.
27. *NE* V, 1, 1129b25–26, 27–28, 29–30.
28. Iwata, *Arisutoteresu no rinri shisō* (Ethical thought of Aristotle), 271, n. 1.
29. For further details, see chapter 7 in Iwata, *Arisutoteresu no rinri shisō* (Ethical thought of Aristotle), where Iwata considers this question in an outstanding and specialized manner, referring also to *Politics* and *Magna Moralia*.
30. *NE* V, 1, 1129a34.
31. *NE* V, 1, 1130a12–13.
32. Iwata, *Arisutoteresu no rinri shisō* (Ethical thought of Aristotle), 252.
33. *NE* V, 2, 1130b31–32.
34. *NE* V, 3, 1131b3–12.
35. *NE* V, 3, 1131a24–29.
36. Iwata, *Arisutoteresu no rinri shisō* (Ethical thought of Aristotle), 283, n. 90.
37. Iwata, *Arisutoteresu no rinri shisō* (Ethical thought of Aristotle), 259.

38. *NE* V, 4, 1131b25–26.
39. *NE* V, 2, 1131a2–9.
40. *NE* V, 4, 1132a10–14; V, 5, 1132b28–31.
41. *Magna Moralia* I, 34, 1194a37–b3.
42. Iwata, *Arisutoteresu no rinri shisō* (Ethical thought of Aristotle), 264.
43. *NE* V, 2, 1130b30–1131a1.
44. The original *antipeponthos* is often translated as "retributive," but since this rendition has strong religious and penal overtones I will translate it as "reciprocal," in the sense of an equivalent exchange, or as "reciprocating," in line with Iwata (*Arisutoteresu no rinri shisō* [Ethical thought of Aristotle], 264 and 285, n. 109).
45. Here I will follow Iwata (*Arisutoteresu no rinri shisō* [Ethical thought of Aristotle], 264–71), who provides a lucid analysis of this issue, including an interpretation of problematic expressions such as "proportionate reciprocity" and "diagonal combination." See also the translator's notes in Aristotle, *Nikomakosu rinrigaku* (Nicomachean Ethics), Arisutoteresu zenshū (Complete works of Aristotle), trans. Shinrō Katō, vol. 13 (Tokyo: Iwanami Shoten, 1973), 403–4.
46. *NE* VIII, 1, 1155a22–28.
47. *NE* VIII, 2, 1155b19.
48. *NE* VIII, 2, 1156a3–4.
49. *NE* VIII, 2, 1155b29–1156a3.
50. *NE* VIII, 3, 1156b2–4.
51. *NE* VIII, 3, 1156b7–9.
52. *NE* VIII, 3, 1156b26.
53. *NE* VIII, 3, 1156b25.
54. *NE* VIII, 3, 1156b24.
55. *NE* VIII, 3, 1156b11–12.
56. *NE* IX, 8, 1168b15–23.
57. *NE* IX, 8, 1168b25–1169a6.
58. *NE* IX, 8, 1168b10.
59. *NE* VIII, 8, 1159b2–4.
60. *NE* IX, 4, 1166a1ff.

CHAPTER 7

Aristotle (3): Intellectual Excellence and Contemplation

1. Intellectual Excellence

After discussing ethical excellence (virtue) from book II through to book V of the *Nicomachean Ethics*, in book VI Aristotle then moves on to another kind of excellence—intellectual excellence (*dianoētikē aretē*). In chapter 6 we skipped ahead to the discussion of love in books VIII and IX so as to supplement the discussion of the doctrine of virtue, but in this chapter we shall start out by returning to the description in book VI and considering intellectual excellence.

ART, KNOWLEDGE, INTUITIVE REASON, PRACTICAL WISDOM, AND PHILOSOPHIC WISDOM

Intellectual excellence refers to "the things by which the soul possesses truth,"[1] and it is divided into five types: artistry (*technē*), (scientific) knowledge (*epistēme*), intuitive reason (*nūs*), practical wisdom (*phronēsis*), and philosophic wisdom (*sophiā*).

(1) Artistry is related to production (*poiēsis*) rather than behavior (*praxis*), but since it includes an intellectual consideration of how things are produced, it is counted as one type of intellectual excellence.[2]

(2) Knowledge (sometimes translated as "learning," "academic knowledge," etc.) relates to an awareness of timeless matters that are not subject to variation and that cannot be other than they are, and it

consists of a demonstration (*apodeixis*) of the relationships among such matters.[3]

(3) Intuitive reason (intuition, nous, reasoning power) is used here in the sense of the faculty that affirms the guiding principle that acts as the starting point for the demonstration of these relationships.[4]

(4) Practical wisdom (practical knowledge, prudence) differs from knowledge in that it relates to transitory matters that are subject to variation and can exist in a form different from their current state. More particularly, it could be described as the ability to use rational principles (*logos*) to choose from among various behavioral possibilities a course of action that will constitute the optimum means for achieving the goal of "living well" (*eu zēn*).[5]

(5) Philosophic wisdom (wisdom) integrates knowledge and intuitive reason, and is said to be the form of knowledge that deals with the most honorable matters.[6]

Of these five intellectual excellences, only practical wisdom, intuitive reason, and philosophic wisdom play key roles in the *Nicomachean Ethics*. Intuitive reason and philosophic wisdom are referred to in particular in the last book, book X, when the supreme life, that is, the contemplative life, is discussed. So here I will examine only the attributes of practical wisdom in further detail.

Phronēsis (*Practical Wisdom*)

The example cited by Aristotle in chapter 7 of book VI of the *Nicomachean Ethics* relates to good health.[7] Good health is desirable, and so everyone has this as a goal. One must, however, possess the general knowledge necessary to achieve this goal—for example, the knowledge that light meats are healthy. One also requires specific knowledge about which meats are light meats. On reflection, one then chooses chicken from among the various types of meat. Such knowledge and deliberation as a means of achieving a goal constitute practical wisdom.

The nuances of Aristotle's argument in chapter 12 of book VI,[8] however, differ slightly. Here the concept of practical wisdom as a type of intellectual excellence is linked closely only with ethical excellence. Let us recall Aristotle's two major statements about ethical excellence, that is, the essence of virtue:

> [Ethical] virtue, then, is a habit [*hexis*], disposed toward *action* by deliberate choice, being at the mean relative to us, and de-

fined by reason and as a prudent man [*phronimos*] would define it.⁹

[E]thical virtue . . . is concerned with feelings and *actions*, in which there is excess, deficiency, and moderation. For example, we may have the feelings of fear, courage, *desire*, anger, pity, and any pleasure or pain in general either more or less than we should, and in both cases this is not a good thing; but to have these feelings at the right times and for the right things and towards the right men and for the right purpose and in the right manner, this is the mean and the best, and it is precisely this which belongs to virtue.¹⁰

Based on this viewpoint, in chapter 12 of book VI Aristotle again states that ethical excellence is a state of character that leads one to choose the mean, and that guidance toward appropriate choices is the primary task of the intellectual excellence known as "practical wisdom." Ethical excellence and intellectual excellence, virtue and practical wisdom—these go hand in hand. Without virtue, practical wisdom is mere shrewdness or unscrupulousness,¹¹ while virtue without practical wisdom is no more than a natural disposition (*physikē aretē*) that even animals and children possess.¹² So, as a means of achieving the goal of virtue, practical wisdom has to be exercised in a way that is closely linked to virtue. At that time various knowledges and considerations come together to result in proper behavior.

BEHAVIOR AND RESPONSIBILITY

Aristotle's view that virtue and practical wisdom are interrelated is connected to his ideas on behavior and responsibility.

In the past Aristotle's theory of action has been severely criticized on the grounds that it overlooks the element of the will.¹³ We can, however, defend Aristotle against this criticism from two directions.

First, we could argue that "however much the debate between free will and determinism may be an issue in theology, it seems safe to say that it is of little practical relevance to questions of behaviour."¹⁴ In other words, both advocates of free will and advocates of determinism act in the belief that it is possible to choose certain actions freely. They differ on the question of whether this belief is an illusion, yet both sides agree that even if one has acted in a particular manner on the basis of an illusion, the doer of that action should be held accountable for its outcome. What concerns Aristotle is not the theological level but the level of legal responsibility in civil society. Hence even if he does not enter into the debate over free will, this does not constitute a flaw in his theory of action.

Second, Aristotle does not completely ignore the question of intention. His famous argument about the "voluntariness" and "involuntariness" of actions is in fact an elaborate analysis of how the locus of responsibility differs depending on whether the action was in line with the doer's intentions. In the first part of chapter 1 of book III of the *Nicomachean Ethics*, Aristotle classifies behavior (*praxis*) into two types: (1) "what is voluntary [intentional, autonomous; *to hekūsion*]," and (2) "what is involuntary [unintentional, nonspontaneous; *to akūsion*]."[15] The second category is further subdivided into (2a) actions done by force (*biā*) and (2b) actions resulting from ignorance (*agnoia*).[16]

In the latter part of chapter 1 of book III, Aristotle classifies actions into three types.[17] He divides the actions in (2b) into those that will cause subsequent pain and regret and those that will not, and he classifies only the former as involuntary, while the latter—that is, actions committed out of ignorance but that are later not felt to be unintended—are collated as (3) "nonvoluntary" (*to ūk hekūsion*), along with actions committed unconsciously when one is drunk or enraged, for example. Nonvoluntary behavior is easily confused with "involuntary actions," and it falls outside of the original dichotomy,[18] but it seems best to set it apart as a separate kind of behavior.[19]

The voluntary actions in (1) are motivated by the doer himself, who is aware of the circumstances behind the act. The involuntary actions as a result of force in (2a) are motivated not by the doer but by another person, such as when one is forced to do something wrong by a tyrant. By contrast, involuntary actions resulting from ignorance are instances such as when, failing to realize that the tip of a spear is uncovered, someone stabs another to death, in which case there is an intention to stab someone but no intention to kill. The final category, (3) nonvoluntary actions, includes cases such as when a drunken person unconsciously acts in an offensive manner. How then should the locus of responsibility for each of these acts be regarded?

The voluntary acts in (1) are committed even by animals and children, and ethical responsibility is not in question in such cases. It is in actions taken by adults after due deliberation that ethical responsibility becomes an issue. Here the concept of "choice" (*proairesis*), which is "the key to Aristotle's conception of ethical responsibility,"[20] makes its appearance.[21] In the case of enforced actions there is virtually no room for choice, so in most cases the person's ethical responsibility is not called into question. Nevertheless, Aristotle does cite certain actions, such as matricide, as actions that must never be chosen no matter what coercion might be involved. One can also pardon or feel pity in relation to actions based on ignorance of individual phenomena, such as in (2b).[22] Yet universal ignorance is criticized even in relation to acts committed out of ignorance.[23] Legal violations committed out of an ignorance of laws of which one should rightly be aware are to be punished.[24] Even the disgraceful conduct of drunken people in (3) is not without responsibility—as long as these people can choose not to become drunk but do not make this choice, they are accountable for their actions.[25]

DISSIPATION AND LACK OF SELF-RESTRAINT

Aristotle is generally of the view that dissolute people who are addicted to debauchery are responsible for their own dissipation, because their personality is the outcome of repeated acts of voluntary dissipation. Since this is a kind of habit (*hexis*), however, it does not follow that a dissolute person can immediately exercise temperance simply by so desiring.[26] That is why it is all the more important to build up ethically good habits.

Here Aristotle is thought to be arguing against the sophistic concept of the "apparent good," whereby everyone aspires to what seems good for themselves, and even if that act is wrong in objective terms they cannot be blamed because it seems good to them.[27] In other words, the Sophists claimed that people are accountable in terms of their views on what appears to be good.

Even so, why is it that people still indulge in dissipation despite knowing it is wrong? According to Aristotle, this is because of a lack of self-restraint, or uninhibition (*akrasiā*), which consists of poor judgment.[28] For instance, Aristotle cites the example of a liking for sweet things.[29] Although people are aware of the principle that "sweets are bad for the health," they also know that "sweets taste good." Faced with a sweet in front of them, people feel desire (*epithymiā*) because it tastes good, and even if they decide "this is bad for the health, so it should be avoided," they ignore this conclusion. They might possess knowledge, but their judgment fails. In this way people succumb to their desires and indulge in things that are not good. From this, Aristotle concludes that Socrates' paradoxical argument whereby it is inconceivable to lose control when one possesses knowledge[30] is in a sense correct. This is because the knowledge on the part of people who lose control is not the true knowledge that "sweets are bad for the health," but the false knowledge that "sweet things are pleasant," whereby they succumb to the desire for pleasure.[31]

Aristotle adds that naturally this does not mean that all dissolute people know in their hearts that their actions are wrong but still give in to their desires and indulge in debauchery; rather, it is customary to believe that one should pursue the pleasures at hand and to actually do so.[32] Hence we need to think further about pleasure.

2. Pleasure

Aristotle discusses pleasure in two places in the *Nicomachean Ethics*—chapters 11 to 14 in book VII and chapters 1 to 5 in book X. In book VII, he examines the following three views on pleasure: (1) no pleasures whatsoever are good; (2) some pleasures are good, but most are bad; and (3) even if some pleasures are good, it is impossible for pleasure to constitute the highest good. Some scholars believe that each of these views relates to contemporaneous debates in the Academy,[33] but the advocates of these views cannot be historically identified. It is thought that the first view was put forward by Speusippus, but the few extant fragments of his writing contain no such argument. The second view appears as Socrates' own opinion in Plato's *Philebus*,[34] but we cannot be certain that Aristotle did not draw on other sources as well. The third view also appears in the *Philebus*,[35] but there is no clear indication of whose opinion it represents. Hence there is no way to determine whether the debates of the day lie behind these views or whether Aristotle categorized all of the reasonably conceivable arguments.[36] In either case, in book VII Aristotle discusses the weaknesses of each of these views, but he makes no clear statement as to his own position.

Instead, the part that clarifies Aristotle's views lies in book X. Here, too, he starts out by examining arguments such as that put forward by Eudoxus, who proposed that as long as all things under the sun seek pleasure, then surely pleasure is desirable and good.[37] Aristotle goes on to argue that "there is pleasure with respect to every faculty of sensation, and likewise with *thought* and contemplation [*theōria*]."[38] Through such considerations he reaches the conclusion that "the pleasure proper to a good activity is *good*, while that proper to a bad activity is evil."[39] On the question of whether pleasure is good, bad, or neutral, Aristotle is of the opinion that pleasure depends on the ethicality of the particular activity. Compared with earlier arguments that single out pleasure by itself and debate whether it is good or bad, this conclusion can be applauded as a completely innovative view.[40]

Aristotle adds a further point, asserting that those who determine whether pleasure is truly good or truly pleasant must be of high caliber.[41] Just as "Donkeys prefer chaff to gold"[42] and the sick sometimes prefer things that to healthy people are unpalatable, those who are corrupt and perverted sometimes take pleasure in things that are simply abhorrent to a good person.

> [I]f . . . the measure of each thing is virtue or a good man as such [i.e., as virtuous], those things, too, will be pleasures which appear to him to be pleasures and those things will be pleasurable which a good man enjoys.[43]

3. Contemplation as Happiness

CONTEMPLATION

When discussing the "theory of happiness" in chapter 5.3, I anticipated the overall conclusion reached on this topic in the *Nicomachean Ethics*. This was because this conclusion is, I believe, implied by the thrust of the theory of happiness as outlined in book I of the *Nicomachean Ethics*, and it was advisable to verify this from the outset so as to gain an overview of the entire framework. In any case, this conclusion is set forth in detail in chapters 6 to 8 of book X. I would like to conclude now by exploring its problematic points so as to reaffirm this in greater detail.

In book I, Aristotle stated that "the good for a man turns out to be an activity of the soul according to virtue, and if the virtues are many, then according to the best and most complete virtue."[44] This good is happiness, and in chapter 7 of book X Aristotle goes on to say:

> Since happiness is an activity according to virtue, it is reasonable that it should be an activity according to the highest virtue; and this would be an activity of the best part of man. So whether this be intellect or something else . . . being itself divine . . . its activity according to its proper virtue would be perfect happiness. That this activity is contemplative has already been mentioned.[45]

Complete happiness and the best life for human beings, who possess the unique faculty of reason, lie in none other than the contemplative life (*bios theōrētikos*). This can also be described as the life of a wise man (*ho sophos*), which Aristotle says is the most agreeable and self-sufficient life.[46] Other lifestyles require another person. For instance, in order to be just, just people need somebody toward whom they can act justly, but wise people can carry on their activities alone. Other practical activities are aimed at gaining leisure (*scholē*), but the purpose of the activities of the wise lies in the activity itself.

> [W]e toil for the sake of leisurely activity, and we are at war for the sake of peaceful activity. . . . So if political and military *actions* among virtuous *actions* stand out in fineness and greatness, and, being toilsome, are aimed at some other end but are not chosen for their own sake, whereas the activity of the intellect [*nūs*], being theoretical, is thought to be superior in seriousness and to aim at no other end besides itself but to have its own pleasure . . . then also self-sufficiency and leisure and freedom from weariness (as much as are possible for man) and all the other things which are attributed to a blessed man appear to exist in this activity. This, then, would be the perfect happiness for man.[47]

DIVINE THINGS

Aristotle adds a further point in comparison with divine things:

> So since the intellect is divine relative to a man, the life according to this intellect, too, will be divine relative to human life. . . . [W]e should try as far as possible to partake of immortality and to make every effort to live according to the best part of the soul in us.[48]

This famous passage demonstrates that "for all Aristotle's frequent references to, and obvious respect for, the commonsense point of view, when it comes to expressing his ideas concerning happiness, he is capable of highly idealistic sentiments."[49] We should not forget, however, that even these comments are based on Aristotle's commonsensical observations about the hierarchy among plants, animals, and human beings. In other words, plants possess only nutritive and reproductive faculties, whereas animals have the additional faculties of sensation, motion, desire, and imagination, and human beings possess not only these lower-order faculties but also reason, an attribute shared with the gods.

COMPARISON WITH THE *METAPHYSICS*

The fact that the activity of the gods consists of contemplation was also the conclusion reached by Aristotle in the *Metaphysics*. His reasoning there, however, differs from that in the *Nicomachean Ethics*. Book XII of the *Metaphysics* advocates the need for an immovable mover because of the conditions of change. In other words, there Aristotle states that by existing as an object of love, the immovable mover constitutes a pure actuality (*energeia*) that moves other things, and since in the activity of contemplation there are no movements or changes whatsoever, contemplation is a befitting activity for this actuality.[50] By contrast, in the *Nicomachean Ethics* Aristotle argues that worthy activity on the part of the gods consists not of justice, bravery, or production, but solely of contemplation. In other words, just activities, such as making contracts and returning things in their keeping, would not suit the gods, and intrepid gods who undertook adventures and overcame crises would be absurd.[51] Nevertheless, it is also true that the gods are living and carrying out various activities. This means that their actions do not consist of deeds or production but can conceivably consist only of the activity of contemplation.[52] So although the reasoning differs, the *Metaphysics* and the *Nicomachean Ethics* agree that the activity of a god lies in contemplation.

COMPARISON WITH PLATO

As did Plato, Aristotle regarded human beings as complex entities, part divine and part animal. Their views of human beings diverged, however, on the following point. In book VII of the *Republic*, Plato talks as if it is somewhat of a comedown how after philosophy encountered the Idea of the Good it then descended again to the arena of political conflict.[53] By contrast, Aristotle gives weight to practical activities in the political and social arenas as typical human activities. In fact, chapter 9 of book X, the last book in the *Nicomachean Ethics*, concludes by opening up a perspective for a path from ethics to politics.

FROM ETHICS TO POLITICS

The *Nicomachean Ethics* discussed the domains of practice and behavior, but in the final chapter of the whole work (chapter 9, book X), Aristotle stresses that the ultimate goal in such areas lies not in merely contemplating and knowing matters, but in putting them into practice. He speaks skeptically of the impact of speech on actual behavior.

> They cannot exhort ordinary men to do good and noble deeds, for it is the nature of these men to obey not a sense of shame but fear, and to abstain from what is bad not because this is disgraceful but because of the penalties which they would receive, since by leading a life of passion such men pursue the corresponding pleasures and the means to them but avoid the opposite pains, having no conception of what is noble and truly pleasant as they have never tasted it.[54]

Nor does Aristotle, who is thus scathing in his assessment of the ethical standards of the general public, have any illusions about the effectiveness of his own arguments. So what should be done then?

> In view of this, some think that legislators (a) should urge men to pursue virtue and should exhort them to act for the sake of what is noble, expecting those who are well on their way in their habits of acting well to follow the advice, (b) should impose punishments and penalties on those who disobey and are of inferior nature, and (c) should banish permanently those who are incurable.[55]

The "some" mentioned here probably refers to people such as those typified by Plato.[56] Aristotle concurs, taking the view that with "a bad man who desires [just bodily] pleasures" there is no choice but to advocate the pain of punishment by law so as to have him abandon his evil ways. Hence the study of ethics aims at and is linked to an examination of politics, which is the study of human society, including its laws, customs, and social and political organization. In this way Aristotle concludes in a manner that opens out his own ethics.

RECONSIDERING ARISTOTLE'S "CONTEMPLATION" OF "DIVINE THINGS"

The practical ethics of ancient Greece that we have surveyed over the past seven chapters of part I of this book set out from the Milesians and was encapsulated in Aristotle's *Nicomachean Ethics*. We have noted the perspective of "wonder" at that which transcends human beings and nature as constituting the ubiquitous source of ethical thought. In his wonderment, Thales cited "water" as the fundamental principle transcending nature, while Anaximander interpreted this as the Infinite. Aristotle, who mentioned Thales in connection with "wonder" and positioned him as the "founder of this school of philosophy," regarded metaphysics, which he viewed as "the primary philosophy" for pursuing the "first principle" (*archē*), as "divine . . . in a double sense" and as the science "more worthy of honour."[57] The reason Aristotle refers to metaphysics as "divine . . . in a double sense" is that it is "a science which God would most appropriately have," and it is one "whose object is divine." The object of Aristotle's "wonder" seems to reach its apogee in "divine things." Although still in line with the *Metaphysics*, the final chapter of the *Nicomachean Ethics* narrows the focus down to "divine things" and their "contemplation." Since Aristotle is focusing on "divine things" that transcend us, it is natural to regard "wonder" as underpinning this work, too, even though he does not discuss it openly.

Nevertheless, the mention of these "divine things" does initially seem rather abrupt, and it resembles the Platonic view of God,[58] so there is a strong argument that the whole theory of "contemplation" in the *Nicomachean Ethics* is a piece written during Aristotle's early phase, when he was strongly influenced by Plato.[59] All the same, since "'the religious fervor of being possessed by God' . . . is one of the unchanging constants in Aristotle's thought"[60] in places other than book XII of the *Metaphysics*—from fragments 11–13 of his early work, *Exhortation to Philosophy*, through to book III of his late work, *On the Soul*, albeit in a restricted sense that will be mentioned later—and since even in the *Nicomachean Ethics* Aristotle foreshadows "contemplation," for example, in chapter 7 of book I and chapter 13 of book VI,[61] it seems appropriate to regard his theory of "contemplation" as having constituted the conclusion to the framework of the *Nicomachean Ethics* right from the outset.

How, then, are this conclusion and the preceding parts linked? More specifically, what is the relationship between contemplation and the ethical virtues? Again opinions diverge,[62] but here I would like to side with Yasuo Iwata in taking the view that the connection "does not exist . . . internally, but . . . [exists] externally."[63] In other words, since "man is by nature political,"[64] practicing the ethical virtues in one's relationships with others is essential for human beings. Compared, however, with the supreme virtue (excellence) of contemplation through reason, inasmuch as Aristotle himself asserts that "the life according to the other kind of virtue [excellence] is happy in a secondary way,"[65] then it is also clear that an ethical life is not in itself considered to be the primary supreme life. We can construe Aristotle's intent here as signifying that the ethical life and the life of contemplation are not unconnected: "The contemplative philosopher is an ethical citizen who at the same time pays attention to his health and carries out contracts and participates in politics. In this case, however, an ethical life constitutes the underlying foundation of human happiness, and a contemplative life is the fruit that flowers on this basis."[66]

CONTEMPT FOR ORDINARY PEOPLE

We also need to question, however, whether ordinary people who cannot possibly attain the philosopher's contemplative state are destined to a pitiful "secondary" life whereby they cannot enjoy the supreme life. Aristotle would probably answer in the affirmative. In the past, criticism has focused on Aristotle's discriminatory views supporting slavery, where he comments that "no one would attribute happiness to a man with a slavish nature."[67] If we are to criticize Aristotle, however, perhaps the scope of our criticism should be broadened to include his contempt for "ordinary men" who have "no conception of what is noble and truly pleasant as they have never tasted it."[68]

The reason for such discrimination and contempt stems from Aristotle's view of human beings, whose true essence he believed to be reason. As long as one views people in this light, there is no option but to abandon those who lack superior reason and to cast them out from what Aristotle calls the primarily happy life. Yet does reason really constitute human beings' true essence? This claim is being fundamentally questioned today. Ever since the end of the modern period, the definition of human beings as *homo sapiens* (wise one) has been relativized by various other views of humans, such as *homo faber* (maker of tools), *homo ludens* (people at play), *animal symbolicum* (symbolic animal), and *homo absconditus* (the hidden person). Scheler's comment in the early twentieth century that "we no longer have any agreement in our views of man's nature"[69] seems to be even more appropriate in the twenty-first century.[70]

This question concerns not just the essence of human beings but also the essence of God. As stated earlier, as if inheriting and developing Xenophanes' criticism of anthropomorphic views of God, Aristotle regarded the act of attributing justice, bravery, and the act of production to God as risible. Nevertheless, Xenophanes' original point of departure was, as we also saw earlier, doubts about the unethicality of the gods of Homer and Hesiod. If God is just and brave and generally ethical, is there any need to deny anthropomorphic views of God out of hand? Aristotle, however, rejects these as well. "Aristotle has absolutely no intention of becoming involved with cultic religion in the usual sense in which people believe. So religious contemplation in the sense of a mysterious union with a personal God in prayer is nowhere to be found in Aristotle."[71] In other words, he rejects the general public's conception of God because it is a naïve view that personifies God.

DEFENSE OF AN ANTHROPOMORPHIC VIEW OF GOD

On reflection, however, surely Aristotle's perception of God as reason is impossible other than in an analogy with human reason, and people cannot in principle rise above a view of God personified. Moreover, is it really acceptable to look down on "ordinary men" as being so naïve and stupid? Perhaps few possess a rational view of God in the sense used by philosophers, but as long as the only way for people in this world to encounter God is through some personified symbol of this world, then does not the realization that an ethical personal God is an adequate symbol constitute a healthy point of departure for them whether they are aware of it or not? To put it in contemporary theological terms,[72] God has aspects of both unconditionality and concreteness, and even if it is necessary to inquire philosophically into this unconditionality, if we unnecessarily abstract the religious concreteness, then surely the God of human beings will inevitably be emasculated. In his rational radicalization of the concept of God, is not Aristotle overly hasty in dismissing the folk wisdom of those who cling to this duality?

TOWARD A HEBRAIC-LIKE ETHICS FOR SLAVES AND CAPTIVES

A consideration of such doubts makes it obvious that, while learning from the generally rational Hellenic concept of God, our perspective needs to be broadened to encompass a Hebraic-like understanding of God that pays great attention to people in the realm of concrete ethics. Surely this thought prompts us to seek a Hebraic-like ethics for slaves and captives that, unlike the Hellenic ethics for the nobility and free citizens, also tries to encompass the hopelessly ignorant masses. With this perspective in mind, we will develop our investigation further in part II.

Notes

1. Aristotle, *Nicomachean Ethics* VI, 3, 1139b15. Unless otherwise noted, English translations are from Aristotle, *The Nicomachean Ethics*, trans. H. G. Apostle (Dordrecht, Netherlands: Reidel, 1975). Hereafter, the *Nicomachean Ethics* is abbreviated as *NE*.

2. *NE* VI, 4.

3. *NE* VI, 3.

4. *NE* VI, 6.

5. *NE* VI, 5.

6. *NE* VI, 7.

7. *NE* VI, 7, 1141b18–21.

8. *NE* VI, 12, 1144a1ff.

9. *NE* II, 6, 1106b36–1107a2.

10. *NE* II, 6, 1106b16–28.

11. *NE* VI, 12, 1144a23–28.

12. *NE* VI, 13, 1144b1–17.

13. G. E. R. Lloyd, *Aristotle: The Growth and Structure of His Thought* (London: Cambridge University Press, 1968), 227.

14. Lloyd, *Aristotle*, 228.

15. *NE* III, 1, 1109b30–35.

16. *NE* III, 1, 1109b35–1110a1.

17. *NE* III, 1, 1110b18–27.

18. *NE* III, 1, 1109b30–35.

19. Lloyd, *Aristotle*, 229, adopts the four categories of "voluntary," "nonvoluntary," "unwilling," and "compulsory" actions, but this diverges even further from Aristotle's initial classification, so this approach will not be adopted here.

20. Lloyd, *Aristotle*, 231.

21. *NE* III, 2.

22. *NE* III, 1, 1110b33–111a2.

23. *NE* III, 1, 1110b32–33.

24. *NE* III, 5, 1113b33–1114a2.

25. *NE* III, 5, 1113b32–33.

26. *NE* III, 5, 1114a3–21.

27. *NE* III, 5, 114a31–b25. See Lloyd, *Aristotle*, 231.

28. *NE* VII, 2, 1145b21–22.

29. *NE* VII, 3, 1147a31–1147b3. See also Aristotle, *Nikomakosu rinrigaku* (Nicomachean Ethics), *Arisutoteresu zenshū* (Complete works of Aristotle), trans. Shinrō Katō, vol. 13 (Tokyo: Iwanami Shoten, 1973), 426, n. 7.

30. *NE* VII, 2, 1145b22–27.

31. *NE* VII, 3, 1147b9–17. There is debate over the interpretation of this

point, but here I will follow the interpretations put forward by Katō in *Nikoma-kosu rinrigaku* (Nicomachean Ethics), 426, n. 7, and by Hiroyuki Ogino, *Kodai Girishia no chie to kotoba* (The wisdom and language of ancient Greece), vol. 2 (Tokyo: Nippon Hōsō Shuppan Kyōkai, 1997), 190–200.

32. *NE* VII, 3, 1146b22–23.

33. Lloyd, *Aristotle*, 235.

34. Plato, *Philebus* 13B.

35. *Philebus* 66C.

36. Aristotle, *Nikomakosu rinrigaku* (Nicomachean ethics), trans. Saburō Ta-kada, vol. 2 (Tokyo: Iwanami Bunko, 1973), 203, n. 89.

37. *NE* X, 2, 1172b9–15.

38. *NE* X, 4, 1174b20–21.

39. *NE* X, 5, 1175b27–28.

40. Lloyd, *Aristotle*, 237.

41. *NE* X, 5, 1176a15–24.

42. Heraclitus, in *Ancilla to the Pre-Socratic Philosophers*, trans. Kathleen Freeman (Oxford: Blackwell, 1952), 25. See H. Diels and W. Kranz, *Die Fragmente der Vorsokratiker*, vol. 1 (Berlin: Weidmann, 1951), and a work based on this by Katsutoshi Uchiyama, ed., *Sokuratesu izen tetsugakusha dampen-shū* (Collection of fragments from pre-Socratic philosophers), part I (Tokyo: Iwanami Shoten, 1996), B9. See also B13 and 37.

43. *NE* X, 5, 1176a17–19. For a detailed comparison of the view that pleasure is a private matter and there are no general "measures" for evaluating this, and the contrasting argument about the Aristotelian criterion of a "good person," see Hiroyuki Ogino, "Zen to kai—Arisutoteresu rinrigaku no ichi danmen" (Goodness and pleasure: one aspect of Aristotelian ethics), *Arisutoteresu* (Aristotle), ed. Nihon rinri gakkai (Tokyo: Keiō tsūshin, 1986), 17ff.

44. *NE* I, 7, 1098a16–18.

45. *NE* X, 7, 1177a12–18. In a footnote to his aforementioned translation of the *Nicomachean Ethics*, Takada comments that the word *nūs* seems to be introduced here with a certain hesitancy (225, n. 42). In fact, when Aristotle discusses the five types of intellectual excellences in book VI, he gives greater weight to *sophiā* (philosophic wisdom), and there *nūs* is no more than intuitive reason. It is noteworthy, however, that in book X *sophiā* is simply mentioned in connection with *philosophia* (philosophy; chapter 7, 1177a, etc.), whereas *nūs* is described as if it epitomizes wisdom. Moreover, since what has "already been mentioned" at the end of the quotation above is in fact not mentioned anywhere, this suggests differences in the time of the lectures and in their editing, as some commentators have pointed out. See notes in the translations by Takada (225, n. 43) and Katō (442, n. 1).

46. *NE* X, 7, 1177a22–b1.

47. *NE* X, 7, 1177b4–26.

48. *NE* X, 7, 1177b30–34.

49. Lloyd, *Aristotle*, 239.

50. Aristotle, *Metaphysics* XII, 7, 1072b1–30.

51. This view shares something in common with Xenophanes' criticism of the anthropomorphic views of the gods that we saw in chapter 1.

52. *NE* X, 8, 1178b7–23.

53. Plato, *Republic* VII, 519Cff.

54. *NE* X, 9, 1179b10–16.

55. *NE* X, 9, 1180a5–10.

56. Plato, *Laws* 722Dff.; *Protagoras* 325A.

57. *Metaphysics* I, 3, 983a5–11.

58. This brings to mind such phrases as "God is the measure of all things" (*Laws* IV, 716C) and the saying that the ideal of human beings involves "becoming as like God as possible" (Plato, *Theaetetus*, trans. Myles Burnyeat and rev. Myles Burnyeat [Indianapolis: Hackett, 1990], 176B).

59. For an overview and brilliant refutation of this argument, see Yasuo Iwata, *Arisutoteresu no rinri shisō* (The ethical thought of Aristotle) (Tokyo: Iwanami Shoten, 1985), 385ff.

60. Iwata, *Arisutoteresu no rinri shisō* (Ethical thought of Aristotle), 396.

61. See Iwata, *Arisutoteresu no rinri shisō* (Ethical thought of Aristotle), 381–2, for a discussion of these instances and their interpretation.

62. See Iwata, *Arisutoteresu no rinri shisō* (Ethical thought of Aristotle), 397ff, 415ff.

63. Iwata, *Arisutoteresu no rinri shisō* (Ethical thought of Aristotle), 415.

64. *NE* I, 7, 1097b11.

65. *NE* X, 8, 1178a9–10.

66. Iwata, *Arisutoteresu no rinri shisō* (Ethical thought of Aristotle), 417.

67. *NE* X, 6, 1177a8–9. For instance, see Haruo Kaneko, *Rinrigaku kōgi* (Lectures on ethics) (Tokyo: Sōbunsha, 1987), 51. Although incomplete, one noteworthy refutation of such critiques from a wide-ranging perspective that remains grounded in Aristotle is Ichirō Mori's "Dorei-sei mondai no shōsoku: 'Tekunoroji no keifugaku' ni yosete (Jō) (Chū)" (The fate of the slave issue: on the occasion of "the genealogy of technology"; parts I and II), *Tōkyō Joshi Daigaku Kiyō "Ronshū"* ("Ronshū," Bulletin of Tokyo Woman's Christian University) 47 (1997) and 48 (1998).

68. *NE* X, 9, 1179b15–16.

69. M. Scheler, *Philosophische weltanschauung* (Bonn: Cohen, 1929). The quotation is from Scheler's 1926 article, "Man and History," reproduced in *Philosophical Perspectives*, trans. Oscar A. Haac (Boston: Beacon, 1958), 69.

70. For an excellent overview of these changes in how human beings have been regarded, see Yoshiaki Utsunomiya, *Rinrigaku nyūmon* (An introduction to ethics) (Tokyo: Hōsō Daigaku Kyōiku Shinkōkai, 1977), 16ff.

71. Iwata, *Arisutoteresu no rinri shisō* (Ethical thought of Aristotle), 396.

72. P. Tillich, "Wesen und Wandel des Glaubens," in *Gesammelte Werke*, Vol. VIII (Stuttgart: Evangelisches Verlagswerk, 1970), 142f.

Part II

THE RELIGIOUS ETHICS OF THE ANCIENT HEBREWS

Ancient Hebrew Chronology

I.   Patriarchal period (first to second half of the second millennium BCE)
     Abraham, Isaac, Jacob (Joseph)
II. The Exodus and wandering in the wilderness (thirteenth century BCE)
     Moses
III. The Invasion and conquest of Canaan (twelfth–eleventh centuries BCE)
     Joshua, Judges
IV. United kingdom period (1012–926 BCE)
     King Saul, King David, King Solomon, Yahwist source
V.   Divided kingdom period (926–722 BCE)
     First half of the ninth century BCE: The Omri Dynasty of the northern king-
     dom (Israel) and Elijah
     Latter half of the ninth century BCE: Jehu Dynasty in the north and Elijah
     First half of the eighth century BCE: Elohist source in the north
     Mid-eighth century BCE onward: Amos and Hosea in the north, Micah and
     Isaiah in the southern kingdom of Judah
VI. Single kingdom period (722–587 BCE)
     622 BCE: King Josiah's religious reforms
     Latter seventh century BCE onward: Zephaniah, Jeremiah, Habakkuk
     First half of the sixth century BCE: Ezekiel
VII. Period of Babylonian captivity (587–538 BCE)
     First half of the sixth century BCE: The Holiness Code, the Priestly source,
     Lamentations, the Deuteronomistic History, Deutero-Isaiah
VIII. Persian period (538–333 BCE)
     Latter sixth century BCE onward: Deutero-Isaiah, Trito-Isaiah, Haggai,
     Zechariah
     515 BCE: Building of the second temple
     Fifth century BCE: Ezra and Nehemiah's reforms, Book of Daniel
IX. Hellenistic period (333–63 BCE)
     First half of the third century BCE: Book of Esther, Proverbs, Book of Job,
     Qohelet
     Second half of the third century BCE: Chronicles, Book of Ezra, Book of
     Nehemiah
X.   Roman period/New Testament period (63 BCE–)

Preface to Part II

Our main source for Hebrew thought is the Old Testament. In Judaism this is called the "Scriptures," but in order to distinguish the Hebrew Bible from what is known as the New Testament in Christianity, here we will use the term "Old Testament."

The Old Testament consists of three parts—the "Law," the "Prophets," and the "Writings." The part that constitutes the core foundation in terms of ethical thought is the "Law." Within this, over the next three chapters I would like to examine the Ten Commandments, which constitute the principles, and the legal codes, where the lines between religious ethics and secular law are blurred. Then I would like to discuss the "Wisdom Literature" from the "Writings," devoting each of chapters 11 and 12 of part II and chapter 13 of part III to texts that represent important embodiments of ethical thought. Chapter 14 will focus on two books that constitute the core of the "Prophets."

This approach requires a certain degree of care. The Greek ethical thought studied in part I basically focused on a dialectic account that appealed to universal reason as a practical philosophy. By contrast, Hebraic ethics constitute a religious ethics, and it is usual for the existence of a personal God to be taken for granted and to be spoken of using the symbolic language of faith. Analyzing this and restructuring it in terms of the *discipline* of ethics will require certain scholarly procedures. Particularly in the first several chapters, the discussion is even more hermeneutical than that relating to Greek ethics. In places I will consciously devote space to drawing parallels with philosophical thought right up to contemporary times, perhaps thereby giving an impression of circuitousness, but I would like readers to be aware from the outset that this is an intentional step aimed at gaining a scholarly understanding of the unique ethics of the Hebrew people.

CHAPTER 8

The Ten Commandments (1): Focusing on the Sixth to Ninth Commandments

1. Overview of the Ten Commandments

THE LAW (TORAH) AND CASUISTIC AND APODICTIC LAW

The first part of the Old Testament—the Pentateuch, from Genesis to Deuteronomy—is known as the Law (*Torah*). However, the ethical, legal, and ritual "teachings"—the Ten Commandments,[1] the Book of the Covenant,[2] the Deuteronomic Code,[3] the Holiness Code,[4] sacrificial laws,[5] cleanliness laws,[6] and so on—are sometimes referred to more narrowly as "law."

The work that divided these laws in the narrow sense into two main types was the classic study by Alt, who grouped them into "casuistic law" (*kasuistisches Recht*) and "apodictic law" (*apodiktisches Recht*).[7] The former sets up cases (*Kasus*) along the lines of "if someone does such and such" and stipulates punitive provisions for each scenario, while the latter gives straight-out commands, such as: "Whoever strikes a person mortally shall be put to death";[8] "Cursed be anyone who dishonors father or mother";[9] and "You shall not murder."[10] Casuistic law assumes the existence of courts, and it has many counterparts in ancient Near Eastern law, so it was probably inherited by Israel from the Canaanites after the Israelite invasion of Canaan. By contrast, apodictic law is of pure Israelite origin, having its roots in the period in the desert before the invasion of Canaan. This was the gist of Alt's line of reasoning.

THE POSITIONING OF THE TEN COMMANDMENTS

After Alt's death, his argument came in for criticism from two main directions. One was to the effect that the term "apodictic law" in its pure sense is applicable only to the Ten Commandments.[11] The other criticism questioned whether, in light of the series of discoveries of similar apodictic laws as a result of the development of ancient Near Eastern studies, these can in fact be regarded as of purely Israelite origin.[12] As far as the first criticism is concerned, it is true that in terms of content, the *mot yumat* dictum, which states that whoever kills someone shall be put to death, and the *'arur* dictum, which states that anyone who dishonors his father or mother shall be cursed, can instead be regarded as casuistic laws, so they are best excluded from apodictic law. If, however, apodictic law is regarded as consisting solely of the Ten Commandments, then this collection of fundamental laws that lay down norms without explaining their legal effect at all—centering on the first and second commandments, which prohibit foreign gods and graven images—has no parallel in other ancient Near Eastern codes,[13] so it is appropriate to regard apodictic law as being of Israelite origin, despite the second criticism. On the other hand, the sixth to ninth commandments—"You shall not murder," "You shall not commit adultery," "You shall not steal," and "You shall not bear false witness," all of which revolve around interpersonal relationships—share similarities in content not only with the ancient Near East but also with the five Buddhist precepts, for instance, and these commandments are primarily regarded as universal laws for when human beings live together in society.[14] The Ten Commandments have both these aspects of particularity and universality, and it should be possible to position them properly as a distillation of Hebraic ethics that incorporates both of these facets.

THE ORIGINAL FORM OF THE TEN COMMANDMENTS

The so-called ethical Decalogue[15] appears in two places in the Old Testament—Exod 20:1–17 and Deut 5:6–21—with slight differences in wording but agreement in substance. Their original form can be restated as follows:

First commandment: I am YHWH. You must have no other gods in my presence.
Second commandment: You must not make a graven image for yourself.

Third commandment: You must not take the name of YHWH your God in vain.
Fourth commandment: Remember the Sabbath day, and keep it holy.
Fifth commandment: Honor your father and your mother.
Sixth commandment: You shall not kill.
Seventh commandment: You shall not commit adultery.
Eighth commandment: You shall not steal.
Ninth commandment: You shall not bear false witness against your neighbor.
Tenth commandment: Do not covet your neighbor's house.[16]

The first to the fourth commandments can be characterized as relating to God, and the fifth to tenth commandments as relating to human beings. As long as ethics is understood as the order underlying human relations,[17] which is what is meant by the characters representing the word "ethics" in Japanese, then it is appropriate for the time being to exclude the first four commandments from a consideration of ethics. Of the remaining six, there is dispute over the interpretation of the fifth and tenth commandments, so for now I would like to unravel the meanings of the sixth to ninth commandments in turn, as these have much in common with the five Buddhist precepts and present fundamental guidelines for human relations.[18]

2. A Discussion of the Individual Commandments, Focusing on the Sixth to Ninth Commandments

THE SIXTH COMMANDMENT: YOU SHALL NOT MURDER (EXOD 20:13 = DEUT 5:17)

The Hebrew word rendered here as "murder" is *ratsah*. It appears less frequently (47 times) than its synonyms *harag* (165 occurrences) and *hemit* (201 occurrences), and it is regarded as having somewhat special nuances. An investigation into when this word is not used shows that there are no instances of it being used to refer to capital punishment, the killing of Gentiles during war, or the slaughter of animals.[19] In that case, the meaning of the sixth commandment would be something along the lines of "Slaughtering of animals, capital punishment, and killing in battle are permitted, but you shall not gratuitously murder innocent members of the Israelite community." In ancient Israel it was customary to eat meat[20] and to make animal sacrifices,[21] the death penalty was applied for various crimes,[22] and the massacre of Gentiles in the name of holy war and holy destruction was taken for granted,[23] so this interpretation can be regarded as commensurate with the overall context of the Old Testament.

Restricting the sixth commandment to such a specific interpretation might, however, lead to the charge that this is an abuse of scholarship in a mere pretense of exactitude, and that it unnecessarily narrows down the scope of the broad sense of this commandment. This narrow interpretation is by no means fundamentally sound, and various questions remain. For instance, is it acceptable to establish the original connotations of this word simply on the grounds that the limited number of occurrences of *ratsah* include no examples of it being used in these other ways? If this view is to be accepted, then the other synonym, *qatal*, which occurs even less frequently (a mere three instances!), would have the same meaning, so the deliberate use of *ratsah* here could not be explained. Moreover, the occurrences in Num 35:30[24] can be construed as referring to capital punishment, so they potentially disprove this view. Critics who raise such questions might prefer to interpret the sixth commandment broadly rather than narrowly. They might construe it to mean that since the prohibition on the taking of life is not restricted to the killing of Israelites or even to human beings in general, it should be interpreted as encompassing all living creatures, and that the act of killing should not be confined to the taking of physical life but should also be understood as including the inflicting of physical and even mental harm.[25] In this way, the sixth commandment gives rise to beliefs such as nonviolence, humanitarianism, pacifism, opposition to the death penalty, the prevention of cruelty to animals, and vegetarianism.

Within this expanded interpretation, we must at least set right the question of to what the prohibition on killing applies. Critics claim that it smuggles in a Buddhist view of life and that it runs counter to the Hebraic perspective on life. They argue that a natural distinction is drawn between the value of an animal's life and that of a human being,[26] and since other words (e.g., *tabah* and *shahat*) exist to describe the slaughter of animals, it is unreasonable to go so far as to read into the sixth commandment an argument for vegetarianism or the prevention of cruelty to animals.

Well, then, what about extending the prohibition on killing to include all human beings? Obviously this does not accord with the intent outlined above, which approves of the massacre of Gentiles by the chosen people. Yet if we take the view that the whole Old Testament cannot be dealt with synchronically as a single entity, and that later prophets came to desire peace among nations,[27] there was increased advocacy of universal salvation,[28] and the ethnic intolerance of the past was overcome, then we could also argue that pacifism, for instance, is in fact in line with the real intent of the sixth commandment and that it frees this command-ment from the confines of its time. Moreover, in connection with the debate over the meaning of "to murder," a similar emotional-ethical analysis can be found in Jesus's interpretation of the law in the New Testament,[29] and this carries an authority that cannot be dismissed out of hand.

Here I have pursued the exegetical possibilities surrounding the sixth commandment while taking both the broad and narrow perspectives into account. Since we have only this short imperative as a basis, I will refrain for now from reaching any hasty conclusions as to which interpretation is correct. The answer will no doubt emerge of its own accord as we question the grounds for the Decalogue and query the sixth command-ment's relationship with the other commandments. Let us now move on to the seventh commandment, leaving the interpretation of the sixth commandment open for the time being.

THE SEVENTH COMMANDMENT: YOU SHALL NOT COMMIT ADULTERY (EXOD 20:14 = DEUT 5:18)

The original *na'af* that is rendered here as to commit "adultery" does not seem to allow such a polysemous reading as did *ratsah*. Its sole mean-ing is of sexual relations between a man and a married woman.[30] Hence this commandment does not particularly prohibit sexual relations be-tween a married man and an unmarried woman, and far less is it a warn-ing against sexual debauchery in general. Whether this is interpreted as a reflection of the low status of women in ancient Israel, where monogamy was not obligatory, or as the influence of the social function of marriage at that time, which lay in distinguishing the legitimate descendants of a family or a people, the main purport of the seventh commandment can by and large be understood as prohibiting a man from violating someone else's marriage or as prohibiting a woman from violating her own mar-riage.

Again, though, matters are not so simple. The word *zanah*, a syn-onym for *na'af*, has a broad coverage that refers not only to adultery,[31] but also to obscenity involving pagan cults,[32] immoral behavior before marriage,[33] prostitution,[34] and indecent behavior in general,[35] and occurrences such as in Ezek 23:43–45 can be regarded as putting *zanah* on the same footing as *na'af*, thereby generalizing the seventh commandment's range of application. Taking this interpretation a step further would mean that this commandment also prohibits[36] such acts as rape,[37] incest,[38] homosexuality,[39] bestiality,[40] and masturbation.[41] Again, Jesus's interpretation of the law in the New Testament is thoroughgoing, taking the investigation of this matter to its limits in emotional and ethical terms.[42]

Hence we can conclude that with the seventh commandment, too, at least when examined diachronically, already there is a shifting within the Bible between the original meaning based on its specific background and the general meaning, which becomes apparent when this background is removed. Again, however, we will leave a discussion of which of these two meanings to adopt until later.

THE EIGHTH COMMANDMENT: YOU SHALL NOT STEAL (EXOD 20:15 = DEUT 5:19)

According to Alt, the word *ganab*, which I have rendered here as "steal," should be translated along the lines of "to abduct someone," and the eighth commandment prohibits the kidnapping of a free Israelite man.[43] This is a well-known claim, but analysis shows that it is problematic in various ways.[44] To state only the conclusion here, the Old Testament does indeed contain examples of *ganab* that can be construed in the sense of kidnapping someone, but in the eighth commandment the object is omitted, and it is thought that various potential objects are instead suggested in general terms. Hence it is appropriate to interpret the eighth commandment as a general prohibition on "stealing" that involves depriving others of their possessions.

Adopting this approach allows the broader scope of this commandment to emerge. In other words, we could also take the view that even if the Old Testament occurrences of *ganab* only concern making off with individual members of the Israelite community or their possessions, the spirit of the eighth commandment prohibits depredation not only at the level of the individual, but also at the levels of society, the nation, and even humankind as a whole. In addition to theft and robbery, it is not beyond bounds to read into the eighth commandment a prohibition on such acts as fraudulent amassing of wealth from the weak by the upper classes, the invasion of other countries in the name of foreign policy, and the destruction of nature, which is a divine creation.[45] Again leaving open the possibility of both the broad and narrow interpretations, let us move on to a consideration of the ninth commandment.

THE NINTH COMMANDMENT: YOU SHALL NOT BEAR FALSE WITNESS AGAINST YOUR NEIGHBOR (EXOD 20:16 = DEUT 5:20)

The word given here as "false" is rendered in Exodus as "untruthful" (*sheqer*) and in Deuteronomy as "empty" (*shav'*), but there is no great difference between these meanings. Note that the act of "bearing witness" ('*ed* + '*anah*) is originally a legal term,[46] and bearing false witness refers specifically to making a false statement during a court trial. The ninth commandment forbids perjury, which "threatens the rights, honor, and life of one's neighbor and is an issue that is very grave and severe, as well as very specific and frequent."[47] The frequency with which perjury could become an issue in ancient Israel is evident not only from the stories of innocent victims killed[48] or nearly killed[49] as a result, but also from the many accounts that try to prevent this by forbidding perjury,[50] providing retaliatory regulations,[51] and setting up multiple witnesses.[52] This derives from the fact that trials in ancient times attached great importance to witness statements, as well as to divine decisions and confessions. Moreover, trials were a fundamental facet of social life, with free Israelites being obliged to participate in trials as well as in ritual practices and war, and it was only natural that trials should be mentioned in the group of commandments (from the sixth commandment onward) that laid down precepts for social life in the Israelite community.

Does this, then, refute the interpretation of the ninth commandment that has prevailed among commentators ever since Luther and that regards this commandment as a warning against lying and as forbidding libel or slander?[53] In view of the above legal terminology and the position occupied by trials in social life, we must recognize the primary meaning of the ninth commandment as consisting of a prohibition on perjury during trials. The question is, however, whether this excludes what Luther refers to as the expanded interpretation. In my view, it does not necessarily rule out such an interpretation. Surely this is self-evident if we discount the conditions characteristic of Israel at that time—such as the special position occupied by trials in social life and the form of lawsuits, which placed particular emphasis on statements by witnesses—and if we seek to extract the general spirit for which this commandment is striving. In other words, the spirit of this commandment was particularly manifest in the case of perjury, but in more general terms it was none other than an attempt to prevent "the rights, honor, and life of one's neighbor" from being jeopardized. Hence this commandment would naturally also cover and prohibit infringing a neighbor's rights by lying, sullying his honor through libel or slander, and trying to marginalize him through social ostracism. Hence the conclusion by some commentators that the Decalogue does not include any prohibition whatsoever on lying has, in its excessive fidelity to the original meaning of the words, perhaps lost sight of their spirit.[54]

Again I would like to close this section with a reminder that the interpretation of each commandment is linked to that of the other commandments, as well as to questions concerning the original grounds on which the commandments were issued.

3. An Attempt at Finding Ethical Grounds for the Sixth to Ninth Commandments

The previous section explored the meaning of the sixth to ninth commandments from both a particular and a general viewpoint in light of the overall context of the Old Testament and the history of philological exegesis. The interpretation of each commandment seemed, however, to be linked to the basis on which the commandment was handed down in the first place. In this section, I would like to move away from Old Testament studies for the time being and consider from the viewpoint of ethics this general question of the grounds for the commandments.

KANT'S CATEGORICAL IMPERATIVE

What immediately springs to mind in the history of ethics concerning this issue of the basis for the Ten Commandments is the second of Kant's four illustrations in relation to the categorical imperative. The above classification of Old Testament laws into casuistic and apodictic laws calls to mind Kant's classic distinction between hypothetical imperatives and categorical imperatives,[55] and since the categorical imperatives are a formularization of what we usually regard as the grounds for ethics, it is by no means inappropriate to start our examination with them. Although Kant does not say so directly, I believe he was presenting one classic possibility as a basis for the eighth and ninth commandments in the broad sense ascertained above.

Kant's second example of the application of the first formula derived from his categorical imperative—"Act only on that maxim which you can at the same time will to be a universal law"—concerned whether it is acceptable for a destitute person to defraud someone else of money, making a deceitful promise to repay the money by the deadline (although there is no prospect of doing so), and whether this violates that person's ethical obligations.[56] Faced with such a situation, all that is necessary is to apply the above formula derived from the categorical imperative. If the private maxim of making a false promise when one is destitute were to become a universal law, nobody would believe promises any longer. This would constitute a self-contradiction of promises and would mean that promises themselves would no longer have meaning. If we suppose that "in this case both promises and the intent of such promises become impossible, so the law invalidates itself, and far from being willed as a natural law, it would not even be regarded as a natural law," then this maxim cannot become a universal law, and it is obvious that stealing money by deceit violates one's ethical obligations. This is the gist of Kant's argument.[57] If, as we discussed in the previous section, appropriating another person's possessions constitutes theft, and perjury is regarded in a broad sense as encompassing false promises, then Kant is presenting here theoretical grounds underlying both the eighth and ninth commandments. Yet is his argument really valid? This point calls for further investigation.

CRITICISMS AND DEFENSE OF THE CATEGORICAL IMPERATIVE

Kant is frequently criticized on the grounds that, although claiming to be a deontologist, he is inconsistent in adopting a utilitarian stance here. This criticism, however, is based on a misreading of Kant.[58] He is not arguing that it is wrong to make deceitful promises because if everyone else is doing so you, too, will eventually lose by being swindled out of your money. Instead, he is saying that if everyone were to make false promises, nobody would believe promises any longer, and their very purpose would disintegrate; in other words, the maxim would negate itself, so it cannot constitute a universal law.

A second criticism ever since Hegel is that Kant's argument does not fully account for conflicts among different duties.[59] For instance, Frankena criticizes Kant for not taking into account "cases where in order to keep a promise sometimes it is no longer possible to help someone who is destitute" and for talking "as if he can show that promises ought never to be broken" under any circumstances whatsoever.[60] Certainly it is conceivable that in real life a situation might occur where in order to help a friend in trouble—this itself is the fourth duty that Kant regarded as being derived from the application of the categorical imperative—one might be driven to make a false promise and borrow money. In this situation, the problem is deciding which of two conflicting duties should be given priority—the duty not to make false promises or the duty to help one's friends. Discussing such specific situations in real life was not, however, Kant's aim in this work. Hence this second criticism represents an unreasonable demand; it is only natural that Kant, who aimed at formulating general principles, does not go into individual detailed scenarios. This criticism must also be refuted on the grounds that it has no connection with the actual debate over the duty not to make false promises.

There are various other criticisms of the categorical imperative,[61] but here we do not have space to explore these. In any case, it seems that we can side with Kant in refuting most of these criticisms of the categorical imperative. Yet the very existence of such criticisms in various quarters perhaps stems from the fact that Kant's argument is unconvincing in certain respects. In my opinion, the critique that most clearly exposes exactly where Kant's weaknesses lie is that by Tetsurō Watsuji.[62] Finally, then, let us turn to Watsuji's argument.

TETSURŌ WATSUJI'S CRITICISM OF THE CATEGORICAL IMPERATIVE

Watsuji asks the penetrating question, "What if we make a false promise while supposing all the while that this promise will turn out to be impossible?"[63] In this case, the maxim of the act would be as follows: "I want to have a society in which no promises are made; I engage myself in a false promise, insofar as there are persons who are involved in false promising, and I look forward to the time when the phenomenon of promising is extinguished." Even if this maxim were to become a universal law, it would not lead to self-contradiction. Rather, if everyone made false promises and nobody believed promises any more, so that a promiseless society eventuated, this person's maxim would be fulfilled. In terms of Kant's formula, this would mean that such a maxim would not be self-contradictory, so it would be compatible with moral duty. Yet if we follow conventional wisdom, we cannot conclude that "a false promise is an act in accordance with duty. Consequently, it is not the case that the self-contradiction inherent in making false promises is a decisive element to condemn it as anti-obligatory." But what is a promise? According to Watsuji, it consists of taking on the existing trust between people and forming a future relationship of trust. By contrast, a false promise consists of acting on the assumption of such a relationship of trust and pretending that something is a genuine promise, while all along intending to betray this trust. The reason that a false promise is contrary to duty lies not in its self-contradictoriness, but in the very fact that it betrays a trust. This is the gist of Watsuji's highly persuasive criticism of Kant.

Watsuji does not confine himself to criticizing the categorical imperative. As the perspective from which to attack Kant, he presents a proposition that is "simple"[64] yet one of the unalterable fundamental propositions of Watsuji's ethics. This is none other than the moral principle that among people "an act that responds to trust is good and an act that revolts against it is bad."[65] The reason I discussed Kant at some length was the prospect that his example of making a false promise and robbing someone of their money might present one possible basis for the eighth and ninth commandments, which are our main focus here. My conclusion was that his reasoning was flawed, and that instead it is the argument put forward by Watsuji as a critique of Kant that hits the mark. In other words, my conclusion is that what provides the grounds for these moral prohibitions is not the categorical imperative but the betrayal of trust. We have not yet answered the question raised in the previous section as to why the sixth to ninth commandments were handed down, but now we should be able to expect this fundamental concept in Watsuji's ethics to provide a comprehensive explanation. And, in fact, Watsuji did write a vivid discussion of the Decalogue, focusing particularly on the sixth to ninth commandments.

WATSUJI'S GROUNDS FOR THE TEN COMMANDMENTS

In response to doubts concerning the relativity of ethical value judgments, that is, doubts suggesting that there could conceivably be a time and society in which the commandment "You shall not murder" would not hold true, Watsuji states that it would be unthinkable in any period or society to approve of homicide and regard it as proper conduct, and that the only difference would be the limits of the circumstances under which actions would be regarded as homicide. These limits would coincide with the relationship of trust among people.[66]

For instance, even if at one time murder in revenge was not regarded as a crime, it would only be because in a society where vengeance has significance as the materialization of justice there is no relationship of trust between bitter enemies, and so taking revenge would not constitute murder. This is similar to the situation between headhunters and people outside their tribe, and also between priests and human sacrifices. Even in today's civilized society, killing an enemy in war is not regarded as murder. According to Watsuji, however, killing someone who has surrendered or is wounded—in other words, someone who is no longer an enemy—or someone who has reverted to a relationship of trust and is pleading for help clearly constitutes murder.

Naturally, the scope of the crime of murder will differ depending on where the relationship of trust is established. From the viewpoint of universal brotherhood, such as in Christianity, both war and the death penalty can constitute murder, while in Buddhism the relationship of trust is broadened to include all living creatures, so that any act that destroys life is forbidden. In this way, argues Watsuji, the scope of the crime of murder varies with the breadth of the relationship of trust, yet in no way does this alter the fact that murder itself is wrong.

By now the answer to the question of why it is wrong to kill is obvious. It is precisely because it betrays a relationship of trust. According to Watsuji, the trust that people have in others forms the very foundation of human existence,[67] and the act of killing, of erasing a human existence, "revolts most conspicuously against this and fundamentally betrays human trust."[68] Hence the thrust of the imperative "you shall not murder" lay precisely in prohibiting such betrayals of a relationship of trust.

Since Watsuji also discusses the seventh commandment onward from a similar viewpoint,[69] let us briefly examine his views here.

Even if promiscuity existed in certain circumstances in a primitive society, this would not mean a sanctioning of adultery. As long as men and women do not expect to be faithful to each other in this situation, it does not constitute adultery. Even in such societies, however, when there is a strict code governing marriage, then intimacy with a different member of the other sex constitutes adultery and is strictly punished, in line with the seventh commandment. In other words, where there is a relationship of trust, betraying this trust is not permitted. Adultery itself is prohibited in a manner that transcends time and nation, and the reason can be found in this betrayal of trust.

Again, it might initially seem that some periods and societies tolerate theft, prohibited by the eighth commandment, or lying, prohibited by the ninth. The essence of theft does not, however, lie in merely taking another's possessions but in the betrayal of trust in an established relationship of ownership. In a society where plundering by the strong is regarded as legitimate, taking another's possessions does not in fact enter the realm of theft as long as the weak do not trust that they will not be looted by the strong. If among the plunderers themselves, however, one seeks to appropriate the spoils for himself, he will be ostracized as a thief. In other words, it is inconceivable that theft representing a betrayal of trust would be sanctioned at any time in history. As far as lying is concerned, it is true that military commanders who defeat the enemy through deceit are frequently commended, but scheming in war is strategy and does not constitute lying. Even in societies at war, deceiving an ally is abhorred as a betrayal. It is inconceivable that lying that constitutes a betrayal of trust would be endorsed in any society. In short, regardless of time or place, both theft and lying are considered to be wrong, and this is precisely because they are tantamount to a betrayal of trust.

Here I have attempted to establish the grounds for the sixth to ninth commandments based on the fundamental perspective underlying Watsuji's ethics. So, does his reasoning as to the grounds for the Ten Commandments succeed? Exploring this question is the task of the next chapter.

Notes

1. Exod 20:1–17 = Deut 5:6–21.
2. Exod 20:22–23:33.
3. Deut 12–26.
4. Lev 17–26.
5. Lev 1–7.
6. Lev 11–15.
7. A. Alt, "Die Ursprünge des israelitischen Rechts (1934)," in *Grundfragen der Geschichte des Volkes Israel: Ein Auswahl aus den "Kleinen Schriften"* (Munich: Beck, 1970), 203–57.
8. Exod 21:12, *mot yumat* construction.
9. Deut 27:16, *'arur* construction.
10. Exod 20:13, *lo'* + imperfect form.

11. R. Killian, *Literarkritische und formgeschichtliche Untersuchung des Heiligkeitsgesetzes* (Bonn: Hanstein, 1963); G. Fohrer, "Das sogenannte apodiktisch formulierte Recht und der Dekalog," *Kerygma und Dogma* 11, no. 1 (1965), 49–74.

12. G. E. Mendenhall, *Law and Covenant in Israel and the Ancient Near East* (Pittsburgh: Presbyterian Board of Colportage of Western Pennsylvania, 1955), reprinted from *Biblical Archaeologist* 17, no. 2–3 (May–September 1954).

13. H. W. Wolff, *Bibel: Das Alte Testament: eine Einführung in seine Schriften und in die Methoden ihrer Erforschung* (Stuttgart: Kreuz-Verlag, 1970), 53–54; H. J. Boecker, *Law and the Administration of Justice in the Old Testament and Ancient East*, trans. Jeremy Moiser (Minneapolis: Augsburg, 1980), 156, 166, translation of *Recht und Gesetz im Alten Testament und im Alten Orient* (Neukirchen-Vluyn, Germany: Neukirchener Verlag, 1976).

14. Tetsurō Watsuji, *Watsuji Tetsurō's Rinrigaku*, trans. Seisaku Yamamoto and Robert E. Carter (Albany: State University of New York Press, 1996), 287ff., translation of *Rinrigaku: Jō* (Ethics, Vol. 1), *Watsuji Tetsurō zenshū*, Vol. 10 (Watsuji's Collected Works) (Tokyo: Iwanami shoten, 1962), 303ff.

15. This name is used in contrast with the "ritual Decalogue" or the "Twelve Commandments" (Exod 34:14–26). Usually the term "Decalogue" refers to the ethical Decalogue.

16. J. J. Stamm with M. E. Andrew, *The Ten Commandments in Recent Research*, 2nd ed. (London: S. C. M., 1967), 15. Views on where to segment each commandment diverge slightly among (1) the Greek Orthodox Church and Protestant Reformed Churches, (2) Roman Catholics and Protestant Lutherans, and (3) Judaism. See, for instance, the chart in O. H. Steck, *Arbeitsblätter Altes Testament für Einführungskurse* (Zürich: Theologischer Verlag Zürich, 1983), 9c. The present book follows the method adopted by group (1).

17. See the first section in chapter 1 of Tetsurō Watsuji, *Ningen no gaku toshite no rinrigaku* (Ethics as the study of man), *Watsuji Tetsurō zenshū*, Vol. 9 (Watsuji's Collected Works) (Tokyo: Iwanami shoten, 1962).

18. For a more detailed examination of the discussion of the Ten Commandments that will be presented here and in the following chapter, see Seizō Sekine, *Transcendency and Symbols in the Old Testament: A Genealogy of the Hermeneutical Experiences*, trans. Judy Wakabayashi (BZAW 275; Berlin: Walter de Gruyter, 1999), 16ff., originally published as *Kyūyaku ni okeru chōetsu to shōchō: kaishakugaku-teki keiken no keifu* (Tokyo: University of Tokyo Press, 1996).

19. A. Jepsen, "Du sollst nicht toten! Was ist das?" *Evangelisch-Lutherische Kirchenzeitung* 13 (1959) 384f.

20. See, for example, Gen 18:7–8; 43:16.

21. See, for example, Exod 12:6; Lev 1:5.

22. See, for example, Exod 21:17; 22:18; Lev 20:13.

23. See, for example, Num 21:2–3; Deut 2:34; 7:2–5.

24. "If anyone kills another, the murderer shall be put to death on the evidence of witnesses; but no one shall be put to death on the testimony of a single witness."

25. See also Tadashi Inoue, "Rinrigaku o koeru mono kara" (From something transcending ethics), in *Rinrigaku no susume* (An exhortation to ethics), ed. Toshio Satō (Tokyo: Chikuma Shobō, 1970), 295–96.
26. Gen 1:28; 9:3–6.
27. Isa 2:2–4 = Mic 4:1–3.
28. Isa 45:18–24; 55:1–5.
29. Matt 5:21–22: "You have heard that it was said to those of ancient times, 'You shall not murder. . . .' But I say to you that if you are angry with a brother or sister, you will be liable to judgment; and if you insult a brother or sister, you will be liable to the council; and if you say, 'you fool,' you will be liable to the hell of fire."
30. See, for example, Lev 20:10; Ezek 16:32; Hos 3:1.
31. Hos 1:2; 3:3.
32. Exod 34:15, 16; Lev 17:7; 20:5, 6.
33. Deut 22:21.
34. Gen 38:24.
35. Num 15:39; Lev 19:29.
36. See "Kan'in" (adultery), in *Kyūyaku Shin'yaku Seisho Daijiten* (Encyclopedia of the Old and New Testament Bible) (Tokyo: Kyōbunkan, 1989), 341.
37. Deut 22:20ff.
38. Lev 18:6–18.
39. Gen 19:5; Lev 18:22; Deut 23:18.
40. Exod 22:19; Lev 18:23; Deut 27:21.
41. Gen 38:9–10.
42. Matt 5:27–28: "You have heard that it was said, 'You shall not commit adultery.' But I say to you that everyone who looks at a woman with lust has already committed adultery with her in his heart." For an examination of the interpretation of this, see my "Sei to kekkon o seisho ni tou" (Seeking biblical answers to questions of sex and marriage), in *Sei to kekkon: Kōza gendai kirisuto-kyō rinri dainikan* (Sex and marriage: Lectures on contemporary Christian ethics, Vol. 2), ed. Seizō Sekine (Tokyo: Nihon Kirisutokyōdan Shuppankyoku, 1999), 13–49.
43. A. Alt, "Das Verbot des Diebstahls im Dekalog," in *Kleine Schriften zur Geschichte des Volkes Israel I* (Munich: Beck, 1953), 333–40.
44. See Sekine, *Transcendency and Symbols in the Old Testament*, 22–23.
45. Kanzō Uchimura, "Mōse no jikkai" (The Ten Commandments of Moses), in *Gendai nihon shisō taikei daigokan "Uchimura Kanzō"* (Modern Japanese thought systems, Vol. V: Kanzō Uchimura) (Tokyo: Chikuma Shobō, 1963), 339ff.
46. Num 35:30; Mic 6:3.
47. M. A. Klopfenstein, *Die Lüge nach dem Alten Testament: ihr Begriff, ihre Bedeutung und ihre Beurteilung* (Zürich: Gotthelf-Verlag, 1964), 19.
48. 1 Kgs 21:5–14, and the New Testament story in Acts 6:12–13 and 7:59–60.
49. See the story of Susanna in the apocryphal book of Daniel and Susanna.
50. Exod 21:1–3, 6–8; Prov 24:28.
51. Deut 19:16–21.

52. Num 35:30; Deut 19:15.

53. M. Luther, *Der Große Katechismus* (Göttingen: Vandenhoeck & Ruprecht, 1983), 73ff. Luther himself admits (p. 73) that this commandment deals primarily with perjury in court. See also, for instance, Uchimura, "Mōse no jikkai" (The Ten Commandments of Moses), 344ff., and H. J. Boecker, "Recht und Gesetz: Der Dekalog," in *Altes Testament*, ed. H. J. Boecker, H. Hermission, J. Schmidt, and L. Schmidt (Neukirchen-Vluyn, Germany: Neukirchener, 1983), 219, etc.

54. See, for example, L. Köhler, *Old Testament Theology*, trans. A. S. Todd (London: Lutterworth, 1957), 202.

55. See Takezō Kaneko, *Girishia shisō to heburai shisō* (Greek and Hebrew thought) (Tokyo: Ibunsha, 1978), 5–6.

56. I. Kant, *Grundlegung zur Metaphysik der Sitten*, Philosophische Bibliothek, Vol. 41 (Hamburg: Meiner, 1965), 43.

57. Kant, *Grundlegung zur Metaphysik der Sitten*, 44. The quote is, however, an amplification based on H. J. Paton, *Der kategorische Imperativ: Eine Untersuchung über Kants Moralphilosophie* (Berlin: Walter de Gruyter, 1962), 182f.

58. W. K. Frankena, *Ethics*, 2nd ed. (Englewood Cliffs, NJ: Prentice-Hall, 1973), 31.

59. G. W. F. Hegel, *Lectures on the History of Philosophy*, trans. E. S. Haldane, Vol. III-3 (London: K. Paul, Trench, Trübner & Co., 1896), 460–61; trans. of *Vorlesungen über die Geschichte der Philosophie* (Berlin: Duncker und Humblot, 1840).

60. Frankena, *Ethics*, 31f.

61. See, for instance, the criticism in Takeo Iwasaki, *Rinrigaku* (Ethics) (Tokyo: Yūhikaku, 1971), 72ff., to the effect that whereas the universality of the "universal laws" spoken of by Kant originally meant something with which all people should agree, Kant changed it to mean that everyone has the right to act equally in the same manner. For a rebuttal of Iwasaki's argument, see Sekine, *Transcendency and Symbols in the Old Testament*, 28.

62. The direction of this criticism traces back to Hegel (*Lectures on the History of Philosophy*, 110–11), but I would like to focus on Watsuji in particular because he does not stop at criticism of the categorical imperative but also presents an alternative viewpoint, setting forth an impressive argument.

63. The quotations in this paragraph are from Watsuji, *Watsuji Tetsurō's Rinrigaku*, 249.

64. Watsuji, *Watsuji Tetsurō's Rinrigaku*, 279.

65. Watsuji, *Watsuji Tetsurō's Rinrigaku*, 286.

66. The following is from Watsuji, *Watsuji Tetsurō's Rinrigaku*, 289–90.

67. Watsuji, *Watsuji Tetsurō's Rinrigaku*, 278.

68. Watsuji, *Watsuji Tetsurō's Rinrigaku*, 288.

69. Watsuji, *Watsuji Tetsurō's Rinrigaku*, 288ff.

CHAPTER 9

The Ten Commandments (2): Focusing on the First Commandment

1. A Reexamination of the Grounds for the Sixth to Ninth Commandments: Doubts about Watsuji's Theory

The previous chapter examined Watsuji's theory, which offers a comprehensive explanation of the grounds for the ethical imperatives that are relevant in all historical periods and societies, that is, the sixth to the ninth commandments in the Decalogue, which prohibit murder, adultery, stealing, and lying. Watsuji presents an outstanding and well-balanced argument. Yet if we reexamine the Ten Commandments from within Old Testament thought, it seems to me that there is at least one other conceivable rationale behind the Ten Commandments. This does not necessarily preclude Watsuji's interpretation based on a broad understanding of ethics as a whole. I am simply suggesting the possibility of locating the core of the Ten Commandments in a somewhat different position. Let me start by venturing to raise a few basic doubts about Watsuji's argument.

THE POSITION OF THE COMMANDMENTS ABOUT RELATIONS WITH GOD

Watsuji states, "I have already mentioned that four of the Ten Commandments, which have something in common with the Buddhist five Commandments, are concerned with the prohibition of a betrayal of trust. But there is no difference as regards the fact that even the other commandments also uphold this point."[1] Yet is this actually so? Watsuji goes on to discuss only the fifth and tenth commandments specifically. What about the first four commandments, which deal with relations with God? Is not Hebrew ethics characterized by the very fact that the commandments pertaining to God are given precedence as a unit over those concerning human relationships? Does not Watsuji's argument, which ignores the first four commandments, miss this point about Hebrew ethics?

TRANSCENDENTAL ETHICAL PRINCIPLES

In view of the structure of Watsuji's overall ethics, in fact it should not be possible to let matters rest with this concept of betrayal of trust. The reason that homicide, adultery, theft, and perjury were prohibited was that they constitute a betrayal of trust. So why must such betrayals be prohibited in the first place? Here even Watsuji cannot help but proffer a transcendental principle. It is because the phenomenon of trust—whereby "the self and the other, while opposed to each other, come to have a direction of unity"—also means that "future unity is assured in the present *in advance*" (emphasis added). This is possible because a law inherent in human existence is at work, namely, "the movement of negation through which *ningen sonzai* [human existence] comes back to authentic wholeness through disruption," because "the past we shoulder in *ningen sonzai* is, at the same time, precisely the future we are going to aim at," and because a "movement coming back to authenticity" is being made. This "movement in which absolute negativity returns back to itself through negation" is also a law of human existence. Hence in both spatial and temporal terms, trust is based on laws of human existence, while betraying trust is contrary to these laws, which is exactly why it was prohibited.[2] I believe it is also necessary to discuss the first four commandments as transcendental principles in the Decalogue so to reaffirm the existence in Watsuji's ethics of such transcendental principles as the "movement of the negation of absolute negativity" and so as to reconsider the meaning of these principles.

TOWARD ANOTHER INTERPRETATION

Given such doubts, one other possible interpretation concerning the grounds for the Ten Commandments inevitably comes to mind. This is the possibility of a different—and probably more Hebraic—answer to the question of why homicide, adultery, theft, and perjury are wrong. Doing full justice to this question would entail a consideration of the remaining six commandments as well. Since space does not permit an examination of all of these, here I will focus on the first commandment as a classic example dealing with relations with God.[3]

2. On the First Commandment

The First Commandment: I Am the LORD Your God, Who Brought You Out of the Land of Egypt, Out of the House of Slavery; You Shall Have No Other Gods in My Presence.[4] It is customary to translate 'al panay as "before me," which is typically interpreted idiomatically as meaning "other than me" or "besides me." When the noun panim (face, surface) is used in conjunction with a suffixed personal pronoun, however, there is in fact not a single other occurrence in the entire Old Testament of it being used in the sense of "besides," which is why I have translated it here as "in my presence." This commandment is far from an injunction to monotheism. Tradition has perhaps insisted on the translation "besides me" because of an unwillingness to admit this fact. As pointed out in a commentary by Uchimura,[5] who relies on the Classical Japanese Bible, this is in fact an exhortation to monolatry. This commandment is not claiming that no sole absolute god exists "besides me"; instead, it assumes the existence of "other gods" and orders that these deities not be worshipped "in my presence."

The first half of the first commandment recalls the blessed events of the exodus from Egypt, which has now come to pass for "you." The second half asks how could "you" possibly have "other gods" in front of the God who manifested himself in this blessing. (Later we will discuss how the form of the Hebrew word here originally expressed not only prohibition but also a declaration of impossibility. This also occurs in the tenth commandment.) Upon meeting your God, even those of you who had previously bemoaned your nation's hidden God and wavered toward the powerful deities of other countries, particularly Egypt, must have realized the rich blessings of your God. Surely the core of this commandment's message lies in ordering "you" to abandon other gods decisively, swear fidelity to the God who has appeared to you, and in an obedient response to the commandment among these blessings, perfect your covenant and relationship with this God who has finally been revealed.

LUTHER'S COMMENTARY

We are treading on tricky ground here. That is, when Hebrew thought speaks of ethical issues in human relationships in a correlation with a personal God, how should ethics deal with this "God"? Here I would like to move away a little from the question of ethics per se and venture off in what might seem to be a detour. My reasons for doing so are that a certain degree of care is necessary to speak of "God" in ethical terms, and this is also something that hones directly in on the core of Hebrew ethics.

First, let us look back at the famous commentary on the gods in the first commandment by Luther, the sixteenth-century religious reformer:

> What is it to have a god? What is God?
> Answer: A god is that to which we look for all good and in which we find refuge in every time of need. To have a god is nothing else than to trust and believe him with our whole heart. . . . That to which your heart clings and entrusts itself is, I say, really your God. . . . Many a person thinks he has God and everything he needs when he has money and property. . . . Surely such a man also has a god—mammon [Matt 6:24] by name, that is, money and possessions. . . . So, too, if anyone boasts of great learning, wisdom, power, prestige, family, and honor, and trusts in them, he also has a god, but not the one, true God. Notice, again . . . how despondent when they lack them or are deprived of them. . . . [T]o have a God properly means to have something in which the heart trusts completely.[6]

Here Luther's commentary on the first commandment expresses an important understanding of God. First, he argues that whatever someone believes in, no matter what it might be, is a god to that person; second, there are true and false deities, and the true God is one in whom you can believe wholeheartedly.

Some might regard Luther's first point as an excessively demythologized understanding of God that does not accord with the concept of God in the first commandment. Nevertheless, as long as the first commandment mentions "other gods"—be they Egypt's Ra or Osiris or Canaan's Baal—and these deities guarantee and symbolize some form of political power, fame, or accumulation of wealth and plenty, then Luther's claim is correct. The second point, however, needs further investigation, as it is conceivable that some people might believe wholeheartedly in money for their entire life, and there are people who, as was the case with some Jews in exilic times, were drawn to the idolatrous deities of a powerful nation and were unable to believe wholeheartedly in YHWH. This does not mean, however, that Luther is saying that the former believe in the true God and the latter in false gods. Hence, there is scope to reconsider his contention that the criterion for distinguishing between true and false gods lies in whether one can believe wholeheartedly in a particular god.

TILLICH'S ARGUMENT ABOUT TRUE AND FALSE GODS

It was the leading twentieth-century theologian Paul Tillich who, influenced both directly and indirectly by Luther, took Luther's ideas on belief in true and false gods a step further in relation to faith.[7] According to Tillich,

> This character of faith [the disappearance of the opposition between subject and object] gives . . . [a] criterion for distinguishing true and false ultimacy. The finite which claims infinity without having it (as, e.g., a nation or success) is not able to transcend the subject–object scheme. It remains an object which the believer looks at as a subject. He can approach it with ordinary knowledge and subject it to ordinary handling.[8]

By contrast, in a faith that believes in a "true," "ultimate, unconditional, infinite, absolute" entity, "that which is the source of this act is present beyond the cleavage of subject and object."[9] For instance, when Paul says "it is no longer I who live, but it is Christ who lives in me" (Gal 2:20), the unconditional entity is an object that transcends "me" and is simultaneously my own subject that fundamentally allows "me" to live. "The same experience expressed in abstract language is the disappearance of the ordinary subject–object scheme in the experience of the ultimate, the unconditional."[10] Hence the criterion for distinguishing between true and false deities should be sought in whether the deity transcends this division between subject and object.

This is the gist of Tillich's argument. In fact, he agrees with Luther that, in principle, a false god that does not transcend this division cannot be believed in wholeheartedly; but even if it is not possible in principle, this is conceivable in reality, as described above, and it is a major achievement on Tillich's part to have set his sights on this reality and delved down to clarify just why this is not possible in principle. When we adopt this perspective, we realize that not only the worldly examples cited by Luther (e.g., money and goods or skills and power) but also things that are generally regarded as sacred (e.g., the church, the altar, the Bible, or the word "God") are false "gods" that lack a vital power transcending the subject–object dichotomy, so the subject that has regained composure after some time realizes that these things must be reduced to the object of a faded despair. Yet what does failure to transcend the subject–object dichotomy actually mean? The concept of symbols, used elsewhere by Tillich,[11] is helpful in clarifying this.

TILLICH'S ARGUMENT ABOUT SYMBOLS

According to Tillich's definition, symbols are things that (1) point beyond themselves to something else, (2) participate in that something else, (3) not only reveal actual levels that would be inaccessible by other methods, but (4) also reveal elements or dimensions of our soul that correspond to these levels, (5) cannot be deliberately invented, and (6) resemble living creatures in that they are born and die.[12] All ultimate and unconditional entities with which we are involved through our beliefs must be expressed by means of symbols. This is because a truly ultimate and unconditional entity infinitely transcends the domain of finite existence and cannot be expressed directly by any finite existence. Whether we refer to entities involved with us in an ultimate manner as God or by some other name, all such names are used symbolically. "It points beyond itself while participating in that to which it points. In no other way can faith express itself adequately. The language of faith is the language of symbols." The properties that we attribute to God and the reports on divine acts in the past, present, and future are all things we have taken from our daily, finite experiences and applied symbolically to matters transcending the finite and infinite.[13] So these symbols must never be interpreted literally.

Literalism consists of interpreting symbols in their denotative meaning to the letter and construing materials taken from nature and history not as something transcending that object but as the object itself. According to this approach, "Creation is taken as a magic act which happened once upon a time. The fall of Adam is localized on a special geographical point and attributed to a human individual. The virgin birth of the Messiah is understood in biological terms, resurrection and ascension as physical events, the second coming of the Christ as a telluric, or cosmic, catastrophe."[14] This gives rise to a fundamental misunderstanding in relation to faith, namely, the misconception that whereas faith entails unconditional involvement with an unconditional entity via the medium of symbols, unconditional involvement with the symbols themselves is somehow sincere and religious. Both the Bible and descriptions of it are merely symbols, however, and we must place our faith not in the symbols themselves but in the unconditional entity that they indicate. Here we learn the reason for the earlier declaration that not only money and goods, and skills and power, but also things generally regarded as sacred, such as the Bible, the godhead, the church, and the altar, are merely false "gods" that cannot transcend the subject–object schema. The reason is that they are mere symbols. In this respect they are no different from other worldly things, and we must be on constant guard against rigid worship of these symbols themselves.

MERE SYMBOLS AND INDISPENSABLE SYMBOLS

While keeping this squarely in mind, I must also agree with Tillich that the expression "only a symbol" is not necessarily appropriate.[15] First, as Tillich says, "symbolic language . . . surpasses in quality and strength the power of any nonsymbolic language,"[16] and it must not be regarded in a disparaging light. Second, even though symbols are admittedly just a means leading to the unconditional entity, there is no other way for us who dwell in this conditional and finite world to reach this entity, so symbols are not a "mere" means but are in fact indispensable. Third, we might add that the expression "only a symbol" disregards the balance between the two elements—ultimacy (unconditionality) and concreteness—in Tillich's concept of God.[17] Indeed, "God as the ultimate in man's ultimate concern is more certain than any other certainty, even that of oneself."[18] Nevertheless, in the final analysis unconditionality is merely unconditionality, and it is only rarely that we who dwell in the everyday world can perceive this unconditional entity clearly. Our only alternative in our daily affairs is to trace this unconditional God in the concreteness of the mirror of symbols, all the while complaining of the mirror's lack of clarity (1 Cor 13:12). For these reasons, the value of symbols should in no way be underestimated.

INTERPRETATION OF THE FIRST COMMANDMENT

The same applies to myths. "Demythologization . . . must be accepted and supported if it points to the necessity of recognizing a symbol as a

symbol and a myth as a myth." However, "it must be attacked and rejected if it means the removal of symbols and myths altogether." "It is
an attempt which never can be successful, because symbol and myth are
forms of the human consciousness which are always present."[19] However, "a myth which is understood as a myth . . . can be called a 'broken
myth.' Christianity denies by its very nature any unbroken myth, because its presupposition is the first commandment."[20]

Having reached this point, we can now return to the first commandment. Tillich includes in this commandment matters that I regard as pertaining to the second commandment, and he interprets the first
commandment as "the affirmation of the ultimate as ultimate and the
rejection of any kind of idolatry."[21] However, in my opinion—and here
I must part company with Tillich to some extent—nowhere in the Decalogue is there any mention that "other gods" are "idols." Moreover, it is
mere arbitrariness on Tillich's part to claim also that only "other gods"
are associated with "unbroken myths" and that "the LORD" alone embodies a "broken myth."[22] The utterance "The LORD your God, who
brought you out of the land of Egypt, out of the house of slavery" is
itself, to borrow Tillich's term, a "myth." It will depend on our interpretation as to whether or not we shatter this myth. I believe we should
interpret this as meaning that "other gods" and "the LORD" all have
their own myths and in their own symbolic ways refer to ultimate, unconditional entities, but that the first commandment is exhorting us to
discern which myth is close to "you" and is linked to the inevitability
of "your" history and through which symbol "you" can clearly relate
ultimately and unconditionally with an ultimate and unconditional entity, and to make a clear choice of one god here and now.

In other words, if we are forever simply looking at myths and symbols from the outside and comparing and weighing them up objectively,
a subjective relationship with the unconditional entity denoted by that
symbol will never eventuate. Assuming that we who dwell in space and
time are permitted to glimpse far-off unconditional entities only by
choosing some myth or symbol that in itself is merely finite and conditional and by autonomously forming a living (i.e., unconditional) relationship with this, then what should be important is not vacillating
among several gods on each occasion, with an eye to how much can be
gained in this finite world, or ridiculing "mere symbols" or "mere
myths" and looking on objectively from the sidelines, but instead deciding here and now on one god. And the time for this choice is at hand,
because through the events in the "exodus" from Egypt "I" have chosen
and saved "you," and it is "I" who am personally appearing in the here

and now as "your God." In this way, the first commandment reveals the secret of where people can encounter the unconditional. The only way to achieve this is through some kind of symbol, but the unconditional bears down on each person in a different way, so we encounter it through a symbol to which each person can relate unconditionally in his or her own fashion, by keenly sensing, when the time is ripe, the proximity of this unconditionality and by choosing that entity and sincerely perfecting this relationship.

FURTHER REMARKS

Here we have discussed the broad outlines of the interpretation of the first commandment based on a contemporary theory of symbols, but I would also like to reconfirm briefly the original meaning of the text prior to reaching this interpretation. The literal reading of the first commandment is that here a being called YHWH, who appeared to Moses on Mount Sinai (some sources call this Horeb) during Israel's time in Egypt, is recalling his work of salvation in leading the exodus out of Egypt and is demanding allegiance from the people he saved. If, however, God is an unconditional, absolute being, then, as Tillich—not to mention the Greeks Xenophanes and Aristotle (see chapters 1 and 7 in part I)— argues, surely God is not a relative being who is constrained by such fixed spatiotemporal categories and who influences and is influenced by things in this world. This is why it is necessary to demythologize and extract the true meaning of what the Old Testament authors wrote in line with the mythical concepts of God in their day and the constraints of their times. If we assume, however, that this mythical understanding still has a richness that speaks to us today in its specific representation of symbolic language and that proper demythologization first requires an accurate grasp of the myth itself, then we also need to look back and briefly ascertain the literal meaning of the myth.

This leads us directly on to the next unresolved issue. In the previous chapter, we consciously focused on exploring not just the original meaning of the sixth to ninth commandments, but also their universal spirit, that is, the range of meaning that speaks to us today as well, after the specific circumstances pertaining to Israel have been discounted. The hermeneutical appropriateness of this approach is already apparent from the above discussion. As historical products, the texts inevitably depict experiences on the basis of the particular constraints of their times, whether or not they are concerned with religious symbols, and it is right and necessary for interpreters of these texts not only to be properly aware of the texts' particularity and to clarify their specific narrow meaning, but also to boldly read into them a broad general meaning that emerges after the particularistic meaning has been excluded. This is also the direction of the philosophical hermeneutics advocated by Gadamer and Ricœur, which took the exegete's subjective horizon into account, in contrast with the hermeneutics of historical criticism, which reconstructs the objective meaning of texts (for a typical example of this, see chapter 14). When interpreting ancient texts today we should, I believe, consciously keep *both* of these approaches in mind. In the previous chapter, I simply pointed out how the interpretation of each commandment shifted between the broad and narrow readings, and I suspended judgment on which to adopt, but in reality both interpretations are appropriate in their own way.

Here I would like to bring to a close our discussion of the subtle issues surrounding the "gods" of the first commandment and return to questions of ethics.

3. An Old Testament Basis for the Ethical Imperatives

THE STRUCTURE OF THE DECALOGUE

So far we have looked at the first commandment and the sixth to ninth commandments. For the remaining commandments, I would like to simply itemize the main points. As with the first commandment, the second to fourth commandments can be interpreted as speaking of an unconditional relationship with an unconditional being through symbols, that is, as the so-called bones of faith. The fifth commandment, which decrees love for one's father and mother as representatives of one's superiors (of whom God is the ultimate), can be positioned as a bridge between the first four commandments, which relate to God, and those from the sixth commandment onward, which relate to other people. As a special commandment concerning dealings with one's near "neighbors" (*rea'*), the tenth commandment combines with the fifth and ninth commandments to frame the sixth, seventh, and eighth commandments, which relate to one's relationships with people in general. The discussion in the previous chapter bracketed the sixth to ninth commandments together as universal commandments discussing human relationships, but in terms of the over-all structure of the Decalogue, it is actually the sixth to eighth command-ments that form a unit.

What issues, then, remain unresolved? This boils down to the basis for the prohibitions on homicide, adultery, and theft, which are universal ethical imperatives, and the question of what explanation can be pro-posed on the basis of the context of the whole Ten Commandments to replace that put forward by Watsuji. I would like to bring our discussion of the Decalogue to a close by suggesting a new approach to examining these issues.

THE GROUNDS FOR PROHIBITING HOMICIDE, ADULTERY, AND THEFT—FROM A PARTICULARISTIC PERSPECTIVE

Since each of these commandments had a particular and a general aspect and the potential for both a broad and a narrow interpretation, these remaining issues must also be addressed from both of these viewpoints. Let us commence by considering matters from the particularistic view-point.

From this perspective, homicide, adultery, and theft relate not to people in general but to members of the Israelite community in particu-lar. Hence these three commandments amount to prohibitions on violat-ing the life, home, or possessions of members of this community. The reason such actions were forbidden would have been to maintain order in the community and prosperity both for the community as a whole and for its individual members. In fact, the fifth commandment, which appears at the start of the commandments concerning interpersonal rela-tions, includes the comment "so that your days may be long in the land that the LORD your God is giving you."[23]

In response to the further suggestion that surely this is the purpose rather than the grounds for these commandments, the Decalogue as par-ticularistic commandments would probably rebut this as follows: "These commandments must be obeyed because they are divine commands. Does not the surrounding text actually state that 'God' 'spoke all these words' and so the people 'listen[ed]' of necessity?"[24] Nevertheless, this argument is open to criticism as to whether it is sufficient to obey the orders of a God who is an Other and to be content with heteronomy, brushing aside questions about the philosophical grounds of the Deca-logue by presenting a *deus ex machina* argument.

THE GROUNDS FOR PROHIBITING HOMICIDE, ADULTERY, AND THEFT—FROM A GENERAL PERSPECTIVE

Next let us turn to the Hebrew wording of the Ten Commandments and reconsider this issue from the general viewpoint. The Ten Commandments are usually translated as prohibitions, but the original Hebrew takes the form of the negative particle *lo'*, to which the imperfect form has been added, and the original meaning is simply that of a negative conjecture, along the lines of "you won't kill," "you won't commit adultery," and "you won't steal." In reality, it is still possible that homicide might be committed, but in principle this possibility is rejected outright. This expression can be interpreted in two ways. When focusing on the reality that homicide does, in fact, occur, it takes on the meaning of a prohibition—"You must not kill (commit adultery, steal)"—but when leaning more toward a rejection of the possibility of killing, it also becomes a declaration of impossibility, whereby "killing (committing adultery, theft) is inconceivable."

What principle, then, underlies the Ten Commandments? This is suggested by the historical context in which the Decalogue is situated. The Ten Commandments were given to Israel, which was brought out of slavery in Egypt through the grace of God.[25] If we extract the historical particulars and retain the general principle, we are left with the fact that people have experienced the love of God. For those who have become aware of such love, it would be inconceivable to turn their back on love and violate the lives, home, or possessions of the members of the community loved by this God, or of any creature created by the same God. So killing, adultery, and theft are prohibited as being inconceivable. This constitutes the grounds for the Ten Commandments from a general perspective that focuses on the Hebrew wording and the historical context.[26]

Nevertheless, as long as we are still trotting out a personal God yet again, the complaint that this is a *deus ex machina* argument might stand. What, then, would happen if we were to take this generalization further and demythologize this finite "God" in a slightly more infinite manner? Even in the Old Testament, Qohelet offers some suggestions regarding an understanding of an infinite god (see chapter 13), but in modern religious philosophy this is sometimes explained using a metaphor such as the following. "God is a magnetic field, which is itself invisible. Yet when nails are placed in the magnetic field created by two magnets, the nails themselves turn into small magnets and are attracted to each other, joining up to form a relationship. Without such a magnetic field, the nails would remain independent of each other, with no connection to other nails. When people fail to realize the functioning of such a magnetic field, those who are essentially egoists are likewise trapped in isolation, but when they realize its functioning and place themselves within this magnetic field, they begin to have relationships with others. People anthropomorphically represent this invisible place where love functions as God, and God is essentially an infinite place in this way."[27]

If we seek the grounds for a broad interpretation of the Ten Commandments based on such an understanding of an infinite God, we could say that becoming aware of the love of God and becoming aware of love for all creatures are one and the same thing. A contemporary interpretation of the grounds for the Ten Commandments would be as follows: "When through love we realize how precious is the existence of others, it becomes impossible to violate their lives, families, or possessions. Rather than a suppression of our egoism through prohibitions, this becomes a welcome recognition of the fact that coexistence with others is indispensable to our own fullness of life. This is equivalent to obeying an infinite function that transcends the self—a function that is often represented as a personal God, but here we are speaking in more general terms—and that orients people toward such interpersonal relationships. Even if in reality people succumb to the temptation to kill, commit adultery, or steal, if one goes back to this principle and obeys its infinite function, then killing, adultery, and theft are inconceivable and must never be committed."

Regardless of whether it precedes (if we adopt an anthropomorphic view of God) or parallels (if we adopt a view of God as a more demythologized infinite function) the acts of not killing, not committing adultery, or not stealing, it is this awakening to the love of God that constitutes the nucleus of the Old Testament's answer to the question of why we must obey the sixth, seventh, and eighth commandments.[28]

TRANSCENDENTAL PRINCIPLES OF ETHICS

Let us again revisit the subtle issues surrounding transcendency. When discussing the grounds for ethics, we need to provide answers to the anticipated questions, such as the following. Why do we still bring up some kind of transcendency in the form of "god as an absolute function," even if not the personal god criticized by Xenophanes and Aristotle? If we restrict matters to the ethical commandments governing human relationships, is not Watsuji's explanation adequate, whereby one must not kill because it constitutes a betrayal of trust? We must respond to these questions by asking just why it is wrong in the first place to betray trust. As we saw in the previous chapter, betraying trust is forbidden precisely because it violates a law of human existence; essentially, this is none other than the transcendental principle of a "movement of the negation of absolute negativity."[29] We must conclude, therefore, that beyond the point we reach when we seek the grounds of ethics, there likewise lies in Watsuji's argument a transcendental principle as an unverifiable postulate. No doubt this is the case not just with Watsuji. As we saw with Tillich's remarks in the addendum on the first commandment, if it is paradoxically possible that faith consists not just of revering the "God" of an established religion but also in the very act of unconditional involvement, and that all people, including atheists, have a belief (that is, if we can rephrase this to say that even people who advocate the transcendental principle that "there is no transcendental principle of God" believe in a god in the form of a different transcendental principle), then the study of ethics, which inquires into the grounds for ethical behavior, must also trace right back to the transcendency in which everyone believes in some sense or other.

Naturally, we must take great care not to idolize the actual symbols pointing to transcendency. We must also be wary of the rise of totalitarianism under the guise of transcendency, and we must be prepared to criticize any dogmatism on the part of individuals who believe in transcendency. Yet if, out of fear of such consequences, we were to go out of our way to avoid speaking of transcendency itself and were to remain silent on this, would we not then lose sight of the source of ethics itself? An attempt to determine the general grounds for the Ten Commandments inevitably seems to confront us with such questions.

WONDER AT TRANSCENDENCY

Let me add a further point. Transcendency is itself the object of a certain faith, albeit through symbols or myths, and it is a decidedly religious matter. It might be more appropriate and advisable for the study of ethics, which is concerned with an ethics for human relationships in this world, to focus not on transcendency itself but on the preceding stage, that is, on people's feelings in the presence of transcendency and on their feeling of "wonder" at something that transcends humankind. In fact, the "wonder" at something transcending us that we observed in the case of the Greeks is also a keyword in the Hebrew Ten Commandments. This wonder is expressed in the following way.

First, the book of Exodus has Moses make the following statement to his people after receiving the Ten Commandments:

> God has come only to test you and to put the [reverential] fear [*yir'ah*: wonder, awe, fear; from here on it will be translated as "reverential fear"] of him upon you so that you do not sin.[30]

As if in concert with this, Deuteronomy states that Moses conveyed the following words of God to his people immediately on receiving the Ten Commandments:

> If only they had such a mind as this, to [reverently] fear [*yare'*] me and to keep all my commandments always, so that it might go well with them and with their children forever![31]

The original *yir'ah* (*yare'* is the verb form) refers to a sense of reverential fear and awe whereby one is amazed and overawed on perceiving the true nature of things of which one has previously been unaware.[32] The Ten Commandments are indeed linked to such a sense of wonderment. The contemporary philosopher of Judaism A. J. Heschel has commented on this passage as follows:

> Indeed, there is no perception that may not be suspected of being a delusion. But there are perceptions which are so staggering as to render meaningless the raising of such a suspicion. A cosmic fear enveloped all those who stood at Sinai, a moment more staggering than the heart could feel. . . . At that moment the people of Israel not only were able to entertain a feeling but also to share in an awe that overtook the world. Only in moments when we are able to share in the spirit of awe that fills the world are we able to understand what happened to Israel at Sinai.[33]

Finally, however, we must ask where people can "share in the spirit of awe." Even if we accept that an interpretation of this short passage along the lines of that by Heschel is possible, the reality is that shortly afterward the people of Israel forgot this sense of wonder and awe and instead looked back with fondness on the fleshpots of Egypt and cursed the fact that they had been brought into the wilderness of Sinai.[34] Even if in normal, everyday life people avoid the sins of homicide, adultery, and theft and are accustomed to not allowing themselves to commit perjury against or feel envious of their neighbors, and even if the Ten Commandments—which provide standards for acting as if one has encountered God, even if one still has not done so—can be regarded as a signpost to prevent people from taking a wrong turn and as an indirect blessing from God, who does not permit himself to be seen directly, the core of the Decalogue lies not merely in negative prohibitions but also in positive love and in matters based on an awakening to wonder at transcendency and an awareness of that love. Observing the Ten Commandments in the true sense, then, must boil down to the questions of where we can encounter transcendence again and whether we will be filled with a sense of awe at this.[35]

In fact, it is these very questions that the subsequent history of Israel continued to raise. Returning to a sense of wonder and seeking anew the time and place of transcendent epiphany seems to be a fundamental issue when inquiring into Hebraic ethical thought, along with the other books in the Old Testament that, while lamenting Israel's sin in having lost the sense of wonder and having lost sight of God, asked when and where God would again become manifest and continued to explore these questions. Keeping the extent and range of this issue in mind, in the following chapters I would like to shift perspective a little before returning to this fundamental issue in chapters 13 and 14 of part III.

Notes

1. Tetsurō Watsuji, *Watsuji Tetsurō's Rinrigaku*, trans. Seisaku Yamamoto and Robert E. Carter (Albany: State University of New York Press, 1996), 296, trans. of *Rinrigaku: Jō* (Ethics, Vol. 1), *Watsuji Tetsurō zenshū*, vol. 10 (Watsuji's Collected Works) (Tokyo: Iwanami shoten, 1962), 313.

2. Watsuji, *Watsuji Tetsurō's Rinrigaku*, 269–72.

3. There are strong views that regard the fourth commandment, which concerns the Sabbath, as the core of the commandments concerning relations with God. Cf. N. Lohfink, "Zur Dekalogfassung von Dtn 5," in *Studien zum Deuteronomium und zur deuteronomistischen Literatur I* (Stuttgart: Verlag Katholisches Bibelwerk, 1990), 193–209; E. Otto, *Theologische Ethik des Alten Testaments* (Stuttgart: Kohlhammer, 1994), 215ff. In this connection, A. J. Heschel (*God in Search of Man: A Philosophy of Judaism* [New York: Farrar, Straus & Cudahy, 1955], 417) also emphasizes the importance of the commandment about the Sabbath within the Ten Commandments: "The whole text has been faithfully translated into English and yet it reads as if it were originally written in English. But, lo and behold! There is one Hebrew word for which no English equivalent has been found and which remained untranslated: *Sabbath*. . . . Perhaps Sabbath is the idea that expresses what is most characteristic of Judaism." Nevertheless, along with commentators such as W. H. Schmidt (*Alt-

testamentlicher Glaube in seiner Geschichte, 6th ed. [Neukirchen-Vluyn, Germany: Neukirchener Verlag, 1987], 74–81, especially 67ff.), here I will regard the first commandment as central and restrict my discussion to that commandment. Naturally, if space permitted, I would like to discuss all the commandments. For a discussion of the remaining five commandments, refer to my *Transcendency and Symbols in the Old Testament: A Genealogy of the Hermeneutical Experiences*, trans. Judy Wakabayashi (BZAW 275; Berlin: Walter de Gruyter, 1999), 47–73, originally published as *Kyūyaku ni okeru chōetsu to shōchō: kaishaku-gaku-teki keiken no keifu* (Tokyo: University of Tokyo Press, 1996).

4. Exod 20:2–3 = Deut 5:6–7; adapted from the NRSV.

5. Kanzō Uchimura, "Mōse no jikkai" (The Ten Commandments of Moses), in *Gendai nihon shisō taikei daigokan "Uchimura Kanzō"* (Modern Japanese thought systems, Vol. V: Kanzō Uchimura) (Tokyo: Chikuma Shobō, 1963), 306.

6. M. Luther, *Der Grosse Katechismus*, Part I, the first commandment, in *The Book of Concord: The Confessions of the Evangelical Lutheran Church*, trans. T. G. Tappert (Philadelphia: Fortress, 1959), 365–66.

7. P. Tillich, *Dynamics of Faith* (New York: Harper & Brothers, 1958).

8. Tillich, *Dynamics of Faith*, 11.

9. Tillich, *Dynamics of Faith*, 11.

10. Tillich, *Dynamics of Faith*, 11.

11. Tillich, *Dynamics of Faith*, 41–54.

12. Tillich, *Dynamics of Faith*, 41f.

13. Tillich, *Dynamics of Faith*, 45.

14. Tillich, *Dynamics of Faith*, 51–52.

15. Tillich, *Dynamics of Faith*, 45.

16. Tillich, *Dynamics of Faith*, 45.

17. Tillich, *Dynamics of Faith*, 46.

18. Tillich, *Dynamics of Faith*, 47.

19. Tillich, *Dynamics of Faith*, 50.

20. Tillich, *Dynamics of Faith*, 50–51.

21. Tillich, *Dynamics of Faith*, 51.

22. Tillich, *Dynamics of Faith*, 51.

23. Exod 20:12 = Deut 5:16.

24. Exod 20:1, 19.

25. Exod 20:2 = Deut 5:6.

26. In Japan this was first pointed out by Masao Sekine in *Isuraeru shūkyō bunka-shi* (A cultural history of Israelite religion) (Tokyo: Iwanami Shoten, 1952), 53–54, and in *Kyūyaku seisho josetsu* (An introduction to the Old Testament), *Sekine Masao chosakushū* (The works of Masao Sekine), vol. 4 (Tokyo: Shinchi Shobō, 1985), 97, etc. I examine this theory in detail in *Transcendency and Symbols in the Old Testament*, 75–90, based on an analysis of Hebrew usage. Masao Sekine's counterargument appears in *Seisho no shinkō to shisō—Zen seisho shisō-shi gaisetsu* (Faith and thought in the Bible—An overview of the thought of the entire Bible) (Tokyo: Kyōbunkan, 1996), 57–59. My rebuttal of his argument appears in *Kyūyaku seisho no shisō: 24 no danshō* (The thought of the Old Testament: 24 fragments) (Tokyo: Iwanami Shoten, 1998), 89–92.

27. Seiichi Yagi and Katsumi Takizawa, *Kami wa doko de miidasareru ka* (Where can God be found?) (Tokyo: San'ichi Shobō, 1977), 82.

28. In terms of the whole Old Testament, nor can we overlook an answer along the lines of the theory of creation.

29. Watsuji, *Watsuji Tetsurō's Rinrigaku*, 118.

30. Exod 20:20.

31. Deut 5:29.

32. Gen 3:10; 28:17; Exod 1:17, 21; 3:6; 9:20, 30; 14:31; 15:11; 34:10, 30; etc.

33. Heschel, *God in Search of Man*, 196.

34. Exod 16:3; 14:11; 17:1ff.; 32:1ff.; etc.

35. We could, to be sure, understand Jesus's emotional-ethical analysis of the sixth and seventh commandments in the Sermon on the Mount from a perspective of neighborly love that takes the tenth commandment into account. Yet judging from the surrounding paradoxical and revolutionary tone, perhaps the following intent could also be read into this. That is, the intention lay precisely in addressing, in particular, those people who make light of the difficulties of obeying God's commandments and entering heaven, and in overturning this commonly held view and making these people realize that obeying the commandments in the true sense is not a matter of outward form but a question of the reality of one's relationship with God, and that it is far from an easy matter. See "Sei to kekkon o seisho ni tou" (Seeking biblical answers to questions of sex and marriage), in *Sei to kekkon: Kōza gendai kirisuto-kyō rinri dainikan* (Sex and marriage: Lectures on contemporary Christian ethics, Vol. 2), ed. Seizō Sekine (Tokyo: Nihon Kirisutokyōdan Shuppankyoku, 1999).

CHAPTER 10

Legal Codes: The Book of the Covenant, the Deuteronomic Code, and the Holiness Code

Any scholarly discussion of Hebrew ethics, which is premised on the existence of a personal God, requires an appropriate methodology, and that is why it was necessary in the first two chapters of part II to delve into hermeneutics and into ethics in general. Hence we had no choice but to narrow our textual focus down immediately to several commandments from the Decalogue. This is a key text representing the principles of Hebrew ethics, but other wide-ranging ethical texts are also scattered throughout the "Law" of the Old Testament. Based on the fundamental stance of the scholarly style adopted in the previous two chapters, in the present chapter I would like to examine the legal codes that have a close connection with ethics.

As we saw in chapter 8, the "Law" (*Torah*), which represents the first part of the Old Testament, has both a broad and a narrow meaning, but in the narrow sense the Torah refers to ethical, legal, and ritual "teachings." The word *torah* is related to the verb *yarah* (a causative form meaning "to teach" or "to give instructions"), and the Torah has various settings in everyday life, such as in worship[1] and education.[2] If, however, we look only at the Pentateuch, then the fundamental setting of the Torah in its narrow sense in everyday life was in trials. We could modify Alt's argument and classify all of the laws other than the Ten Commandments as "casuistic law" (*kasuistisches Recht*) (see chapter 8) and define them all as relating to trials, whose deliberations resolve doubts raised about various cases (*Kasus*) in actual life. Fundamentally, these are written laws, but it is usual for them to be supported by historical instructions and to be developed through admonitory teachings and so forth, so that they possess such an ethical framework. This is a striking feature of the major codes of Hebrew law, namely, the Book of the Covenant, the Deuteronomic Code, and the Holiness Code.

1. The Book of the Covenant

The Book of the Covenant (Exod 20:22–23:33) is the oldest legal code in the Old Testament. Its name derives from the fact that Exod 24:7—"Then he [Moses] took the book of the covenant, and read it in the hearing of the people"—was linked to this legal code, which in current redactions is placed immediately prior to that verse. It is likely, however, that before this legal code was incorporated into the Sinai pericope[3] this name referred instead to the Decalogue. In either case, this code—which consists of a part that has a quasi-apodictic style similar to that of the Ten Commandments and a part that is pure casuistic law, by which the Ten Commandments are applied to more concrete scenarios in life—is significant as a supplement to the Decalogue. In that sense, it is not entirely inappropriate for it to be placed immediately after the Ten Commandments and to be called the Book of the Covenant. Here "Covenant" (*berith*) refers to the agreement reached by YHWH with the people of Israel on Mt. Sinai[4] whereby, in return for YHWH's rescuing them from Egypt and for his acts of grace, Israel vowed to obey his "laws" (*torah*) and to be faithful to him.[5]

STRUCTURE AND GENESIS

The Book of the Covenant consists of the following six sections:

(1) Preface (Exod 20:22)
(2) Guidelines for worship (20:23–26)
(3) Casuistic laws concerning slaves, injuries, debts, and marriage (21:1–22:16)
(4) Various quasi-apodictic regulations aimed at maintaining the community (22:17–23:13)
(5) Additional guidelines for worship (23:14–19)
(6) Warnings from God (23:20–33)

Of these, sections (2), (4), and (5) are for the most part pure Israelite, but section (3) has many parallels in the ancient Near East, and its core is thought to comprise legal material that the Israelites inherited in the land of Canaan. In fact, as Max Weber long ago perceptively pointed out, "the law of the Book of the Covenant is not that of semi-nomads. . . . The interests of village and town-dwelling peasants are almost the exclusive concern of the law."[6] Framed by sections (1) and (6), the Covenant as a whole is of course edited under the authority of the covenant God, YHWH. There is, however, no mention at all of kings. Hence the Book of the Covenant can be traced back to the period after the settling in

Canaan but prior to the united kingdom period, that is, to the time of the Judges in the twelfth to eleventh centuries BCE. (Many scholars postulate that it was the Elohist source of around the eighth century BCE, rather than the Yahwist source of around the tenth century BCE, that was the collection of narratives in which this covenant was passed down, but there is no conclusive evidence on this point.)

CONNECTION WITH ANCIENT NEAR EASTERN LAW

There is debate about the continuity or lack thereof between the law and ethics, but for our particular topic of ethical thought, it is appropriate here to focus on section (4) of the Book of the Covenant. This is because the examples for section (3) have counterparts in the ancient Near East and on the whole are laws. Sections (2), (4), and (5) are unique to the Hebrews, but even here sections (2) and (5) relate to worship. (Alt classifies many of the stipulations in section (4) as "apodictic law," but in the light of criticisms of his views—see chapter 8—I regard pure apodictic law as consisting solely of the Ten Commandments, so here I will refer to the stipulations in section (4) as "quasi-apodictic.")

I would, however, like to note a couple of classic examples from section (3) in connection with ancient Near Eastern law.

> When you buy a male Hebrew slave, he shall serve six years, but in the seventh he shall go out a free person, without debt.[7]

What is at issue here is not tramontanes who have been captured in war and put into slavery, but Hebrew people who have been sold into slavery because of poverty or crimes. It is thought that they can repay their debts through six years of labor. Compared with other regulations, such as the Code of Hammurabi in Babylonia in the eighteenth century BCE, this does not seem a particularly generous provision.

> If a man be in debt and sell his wife, son or daughter, or bind them over to service, for three years they shall work in the house of their purchaser or master; in the fourth year they shall be given their freedom.[8]

In the Code of Hammurabi, it is the debtor's family that is sold into slavery to pay the debt, but they are given their freedom after three years—half the time of the Hebrew code. Perhaps, however, in addition to this "work" in "service," there is also a condition here whereby the "debt" must be repaid separately.[9] By contrast, with the Hebrews the labor was itself applied to repayment of the debt. The following Hebrew provision is unusual in that it shows that slaves had the right to protection from injury:

> When a slaveowner strikes the eye of a male or female slave, destroying it, the owner shall let the slave go, a free person, to compensate for the eye. If the owner knocks out a tooth of a male or female slave, the slave shall be let go, a free person, to compensate for the tooth.[10]

This is a generous provision for slaves, with no parallel in the entire legal culture of the ancient Near East,[11] including of course the Code of Hammurabi. In addition, the provision in Exod 21:20 that "When a slaveowner strikes a male or female slave with a rod and the slave dies immediately, the owner shall be punished [*naqam*: undergo reprisal]" is in striking contrast to clause 116 in the Code of Hammurabi, which stipulates different punishments depending on whether the victim is freeborn or a slave. This conveys the surprising information that the lives of slaves were treated on a par with those of the freeborn. Hence we could conclude that the Book of the Covenant generally pays a level of attention to protecting the rights of slaves that was unprecedented in ancient times.

As pointed out at the end of part I, in contrast to Greek ethics, which applied to free citizens, the Hebrews speak of laws or ethics that apply to slaves as well. This ethical ethos is developed further in the purely Israelite quasi-apodictic law code in section (4) of the Book of the Covenant.

CONSIDERATION FOR PEOPLE AT THE LOWER LEVELS OF SOCIETY

> You shall not wrong or oppress a resident alien, for you were aliens in the land of Egypt. You shall not abuse any widow or orphan. If you do abuse them, when they cry out to me, I will surely heed their cry; my wrath will burn, and I will kill you with the sword.[12]

After slaves, the people on the next lowest rungs of Hebrew society were the "alien," the "widow," and the "orphan." This apodictic law prescribes that their rights too must be protected, because "you were aliens in the land of Egypt" and "you know the heart of an alien" (Exod 23:9).[13] Since the Hebrews had experienced the suffering of those from the lower ranks of society, they were exhorted to be considerate of such people. This nondiscriminating attitude is of course directed not only at people from the lower ranks, but also at one's equals and even one's adversaries.

> If you take your neighbor's cloak in pawn, you shall restore it before the sun goes down; for it may be your neighbor's only clothing to use as cover; in what else shall that person sleep? And if your neighbor cries out to me [YHWH], I will listen, for I am compassionate [*hannun*: benevolent].[14]

> When you come upon your enemy's ox or donkey going astray, you shall bring it back. When you see the donkey of one who hates you lying under its burden and you would hold back from setting it free, you must help to set it free.[15]

The prevailing belief is that *agapē*, whereby one overcomes the exclusivity of *philiā* as a love between people with common interests and deliberately tries to love even those with different interests, is a New Testament discovery,[16] but in fact *agapē* can also be found in places in the Old Testament. The last passage above is an example of this and can be construed as an exhortation to love one's enemies. Similar examples can be found in the Deuteronomic Code and the Holiness Code, so I would like to examine these and then close with an overall discussion of the *agapē*-like ethos of the Old Testament.

CORRELATION WITH THE TEN COMMANDMENTS

For now let us continue examining several characteristic statements in section (4) of the Book of the Covenant, a section that is a collation of apodictic laws. The following commands that overlap with and elaborate on the Ten Commandments are worthy of note.

> You shall not spread a false report. You shall not join hands with the wicked to act as a malicious witness. You shall not follow a majority in wrongdoing; when you bear witness in a lawsuit, you shall not side with the majority so as to pervert justice.[17]

This corresponds with the ninth commandment, which prohibits perjury. If we suppose that the expression "You shall not spread a false report" extends beyond trials to prohibit false and groundless rumors in general, then it should be noted that this commandment takes on a broad semantic range that also allows the interpretation proposed by Luther (see section 8.2), who construed the ninth commandment as a prohibition on lying and calumny.

> Six days you shall do your work, but on the seventh day you shall rest, so that your ox and your donkey may have relief, and your homeborn slave and the resident alien may be refreshed.[18]

This is consistent with the fourth commandment, which decrees observance of the Sabbath, but in fact Exodus's version of the Ten Commandments attributes the grounds for this to following God's example in his work of creation (Exod 20:11; cf. Gen 2:2–3), while the version in Deuteronomy (5:14) attributes it to giving male and female slaves a rest. The idea in the Book of the Covenant is closer to that in Deuteronomy, and this provision also covers a broader range. We could also say that the command "Do not invoke the names of other gods; do not let them be heard on your lips"[19] is related to the first commandment, and that "Whoever lies with an animal shall be put to death"[20] is related to the seventh commandment in the broad sense. In this way, the apodictic parts of the Book of the Covenant overlap with several of the Ten Commandments, but completely different statements also occur. Exod 22:18, which speaks of the execution of sorceresses, and Exod 22:29, which orders that God be given the firstborn son as a sacrifice, are examples of this. With regard to the latter practice, in slightly later times the custom of offering up the eldest child as a sacrifice was replaced with animal sacrifices[21] or rejected outright,[22] but in the famous episode of Abraham's offering of Isaac[23] this practice still seems to be alive in an ambivalent form.[24] In either case, the influence of the Canaanite ritual of human sacrifice[25] was probably still strong in the Book of the Covenant, which is the oldest legal code, dating back to the twelfth–eleventh centuries BCE.

RELATIONS WITH GOD

As we have seen, relations with God implicitly or explicitly underpinned not only sections (2) and (5), which are pure worship regulations, but also section (4), which constitutes regulations for the community. YHWH's "anger will be aroused" against people who bring suffering to the "alien," "widow," or "orphan," as well as people who do not return their "neighbor's cloak" that they had taken in pawn are assured of the revenge of a God who is "compassionate" to the weak. This divine retribution is formulated as follows in the final section (6).

> You shall worship the LORD your God, and I will bless your bread and your water; and I will take sickness away from among you. No one shall miscarry or be barren in your land; I will fulfill the number of your days.[26]

> But if you listen attentively to his voice and do all that I say, then I will be an enemy to your enemies and a foe to your foes. . . . I will send my terror in front of you, and will throw into confusion all the people against whom you shall come, and I will make all your enemies turn their backs to you.[27]

Here the emphasis of God's work does not lie in "compassion" for the weak in Israel but shifts to the happiness of Israel as a whole and to protecting it against others. Note that in the final passage the "wonder" at the transcendent, which this book has consistently focused on as the undercurrent of ancient thought, is expressed as "terror" (*'emah*) that will "make . . . your enemies turn their backs to you." In v. 28 *'emah* is replaced by *tsir'ah*, which refers to "hornets" or the panic aroused by hornets. In either case, this passage portrays how one's enemies will sense a transcendental force behind some specific object and will be awed with fear.

Assuming that we have now grasped the broad outlines of the Book of the Covenant, which is the oldest of the Hebrew legal codes and also the most important in terms of ethical thought, let us now supplement this discussion with a brief consideration of the later codes—the Deuteronomic Code and the Holiness Code.

2. The Deuteronomic Code and the Holiness Code

THE STRUCTURE AND GENESIS OF THE DEUTERONOMIC CODE

The Deuteronomic Code broadly corresponds to Deuteronomy, but in the narrow sense it refers to its core, the part about laws in chapters 12–26. Various views are possible in relation to the structure of the Deuteronomic Code in the narrow sense, but here I would like to focus on the correlation with the Ten Commandments and divide the Code into eight sections, each consisting of the laws corresponding to these commandments:

(1) First and second commandments (Deut 12)
(2) Third commandment (13:1–14:27)
(3) Fourth commandment (14:28–16:17)
(4) Fifth commandment (16:18–18:22)
(5) Sixth commandment (19:1–13; 20:1–22:8)
(6) Seventh commandment (22:9–23:19)
(7) Eighth, ninth, and tenth commandments (23:20–25:19), and finally,
(8) Regulations for worship and the promise of happiness (ch. 26).

These are guidelines laid down during the religious reforms of King Josiah in 622 BCE.[28] Deuteronomy as a whole is variously referred to as the Law (*Torah*),[29] the Book of Law,[30] the Book of the Law of Moses,[31] or the Book of the Covenant (*berith*).[32] This final term is easily confused with that in Exodus, but it expresses the fundamental motif of Deuteronomy as a whole. Deuteronomy is a "federal theology" text. According to this theology, YHWH bestowed land on the people of Israel in fulfillment of his promise to the tribal chiefs, but this gift and other blessings were tied to various demands, such as that discussed below.

THE LAW REGARDING LOVE OF A MONOTHEISTIC GOD

> Hear, O Israel: The LORD is our God, the LORD alone. You shall love the LORD your God with all your heart, and with all your soul, and with all your might.[33]

Deuteronomy 6:4–5 is the law commanding love for only one God, which Jesus describes in the New Testament as the "greatest . . . commandment"[34] of the Old Testament. From here on down, the various demands in federal theology consist of nested regulations relating to worship—from stipulation of the place of worship in section (1) through to confession to a priest in section (8)—and they encompass every conceivable situation in life from sections (2) to (7). For instance, the Israelites are told that they should always keep the law and its main commandments in their hearts[35] and that obedience will lead to happiness and disobedience to being cursed.[36]

> [A]ll these blessings shall come upon you and overtake you, if
> you obey the LORD your God. . . . But if you will not obey
> the LORD your God by diligently observing all his com-
> mandments and decrees, which I [Moses] am commanding you
> today, then all these curses shall come upon you and overtake
> you.[37]

The Deuteronomistic History that follows Deuteronomy in Joshua,
Judges, Samuel, and Kings was an attempt by the "Deuteronomistic his-
torians" to interpret the long history from gaining the promised land up
until captivity in Babylonia by linking these events to the Deuteronomic
Code. Here a theodical interpretation of history based on the federal
theology of the Deuteronomic Code is evident, whereby catastrophes in
the form of the kingdom's destruction and the Babylonian captivity were
the result not of YHWH's lack of power but of his punishment for and
curse on Israel's breaking of the covenant by not observing the ethical
laws.[38]

THE STRUCTURE AND GENESIS OF THE
HOLINESS CODE

A somewhat different concept lies behind the Holiness Code, the laws
collected together in Lev 17–26. The main contents of this Code are as
follows:

(1) Regulations about sacrifices and a prohibition on the eating of
    blood (Lev 17)
(2) Various regulations concerning sexual relations (ch. 18)
(3) The Decalogue and various legal regulations (ch. 19)
(4) Regulations concerning the death penalty (ch. 20)
(5) Regulations concerning priests (21:1–22:16)
(6) Regulations concerning offerings (22:17–33)
(7) Regulations concerning feasts (ch. 23)
(8) Regulations concerning the lamps and shewbread (24:1–9)
(9) Example of and punishment for blasphemy (24:10–23)
(10) Regulations for the Sabbatical year and the year of Jubilee (ch. 25)
(11) Exhortations via rewards and punishments (ch. 26)

It is thought that in later years—opinion is divided as to whether this
was before or after the captivity in the sixth century BCE—this code was
written in the form of YHWH speaking to Moses or to the Israelites

through Moses, and it was incorporated into the Sinai pericope. The motivation behind prescribing various regulations can be found in particular in formulas such as those below.

BEING "HOLY"

> Speak to all the congregation of the people of Israel and say to them: You shall be holy [*qadosh*], for I the LORD your God am holy.[39]

> Consecrate yourselves therefore, and be holy [*qadash*]; for I am the LORD your God.[40]

The repetition of this word "holy"[41] has led researchers to refer to this code as the "Holiness Code." As in Deuteronomy,[42] if one obeys the commandments and becomes holy, one shall live.[43] In a context resembling that in Deuteronomy (ch. 28), the end of the declaration[44] speaks of the good "fruit" of good deeds and punishment for misdeeds, and also again of "terror" (*behalah*).[45] Unlike in Deuteronomy, however, the actual words "happiness" and "curse" are not used. In any case, inasmuch as the Deuteronomic Code sets forth this retribution whereby rewards and punishment are meted out strictly and impartially, this Code stands out from the surrounding Priestly materials. Of course, the Priestly materials also relate directions for people, such as the "covenant with Noah,"[46] Abram's being called to walk before God and be blameless (*tamim*),[47] the subsequent command to be circumcised,[48] and above all, the numerous worship regulations given at Sinai. Nevertheless, the Priestly materials avoid any discussion of the possibility of losing salvation as a result of disobedience. In general, in the Sinai pericope the Priestly materials shy away from the concept of a "covenant." By contrast, in the Holiness Code, as in the Deuteronomic Code and the Deuteronomistic History, we can see a struggle with the question of how to grasp the extent of the impact of humans' good deeds and particularly their misdeeds in relation to divine retribution. This was an issue that attracted particular attention in the times of crisis leading up to the Babylonian captivity.

3. Reconsidering *Agapē*

LOVE FOR ONE'S NEIGHBORS

Here we have taken a cursory look at the Deuteronomic Code and the Holiness Code, but in bringing this chapter to a close we cannot overlook the following utterance from part (3) of the Holiness Code: "Love your neighbor as yourself."[49]

Along with Deut 6:4–5, this is a crucial commandment listed among the "greatest commandments" by Jesus, who said, "On these two commandments hang all the law and the prophets."[50] In his Sermon on the Mount, Jesus again referred to this commandment:

> You have heard that it was said, "You shall love your neighbor and hate your enemy." But I say to you, Love your enemies and pray for those who persecute you.[51]

As many commentators have pointed out, Lev 19:18 lies behind this "love your neighbor," and nowhere in the Old Testament does the expression "hate your enemy" appear.[52] Nevertheless, although as far as I am aware no commentators have mentioned this,[53] not only is there no reference to hating one's enemies, but also the following passage appears before the "love your neighbor as yourself" of Lev 19:18:

> You shall not hate in your heart anyone of your kin. . . . You shall not take vengeance or bear a grudge against any of your people.[54]

In other words, among all one's "neighbors," here the focus is on those who would naturally be the subject of "vengeance"—those who have done wrong to "you" and whom you "hate" and "bear a grudge against," that is, "enemies" in the broad sense. This means that the command to love one's enemies was already the message conveyed in Lev 19:18.[55]

Naturally, since the idea of hating one's enemies is also present in the Old Testament[56] and this passage remains an exhortation to specific action, without going as far as a general formulation such as that pronounced by Jesus or an internalization toward "prayer," it would be more appropriate to say it contains the embryonic idea of loving one's enemies. We have, however, already verified that consideration for people at the lower levels of society, such as slaves, aliens, widows, and orphans, lies at the foundation of Hebrew law. Similar expressions occur frequently in the Deuteronomic Code and the Holiness Code, though I will not cite them individually here.[57] Again, in the Book of the Covenant this concern crystallizes in the exhortation to literally "help" "your enemy" impartially when he is in distress.[58] We must be wary of stereotypically overemphasizing the innovativeness of Christian thought in the New Testament. We should candidly recognize that the idea of loving one's enemies, which corresponds to the ethos of *agapē*, is already evident in places in the Hebrew thought of the Old Testament, at least in embryonic form.

FURTHER REMARKS

Let me add a few final remarks.

First, I would like to confirm that the exhortation to *agapē*, which in this way treats people who are of no value to oneself impartially, has its grounds in divine mercy and benevolence. Since God is "merciful," he also had to return what he had taken "in pawn."[59] And the Israelites must "not wrong . . . a resident alien" because, if Israel's origins are traced back in time, "you were aliens in the land of Egypt" but were rescued through divine mercy.[60] In the final analysis, the fact that the very origin of humans' ethical action—which boils down to love—resides in God's love in this way also holds true for the Ten Commandments examined in the previous two chapters, and it forms a striking contrast with the Greeks.

Second, we could also tentatively point out that this concern for slaves and others on the lower rungs of society is rather lacking in Greek ethics, which focuses on free citizens. (There are subtle nuances surrounding this point, which will be revisited in chapter 15.)

Third, the fundamental stance in the Decalogue was that one must encounter God in order to observe ethics properly, but the legal codes examined in this chapter seem instead to adopt the view that one must observe ethics in order to encounter God. In other words, observing the law is a means of enjoying divine blessings (this concept is also in common with the faith in the law expressed in Pss 1, 19:8–15, and 115, for instance, and it represents another origin of Old Testament thought). In either case, note the logical circle: unless one observes the law one cannot encounter God, but unless one encounters God one cannot in the true sense observe the law. I will set aside for later a consideration of the question of how to construe this in overall terms (see section 14.4 in part III).

Fourth, let me add that the idea of loving one's enemies appears not only in the Law sections, but also in various other books of the Old Testament, particularly Proverbs,[61] with greater clarity than it appears in the New Testament.[62] In the following chapter, therefore, I would like to focus on this concept in Proverbs, along with a range of other issues.

Notes

1. Jer 18:18: "Then they said, 'Come, let us make plots against Jeremiah—for instruction shall not perish from the priest, nor counsel from the wise, nor the word from the prophet. Come, let us bring charges against him, and let us not heed any of his words.'"

2. Prov 6:20: "My child, keep your father's commandment, and do not forsake your mother's teaching." Prov 13:14: "The teaching of the wise is a fountain of life, so that one may avoid the snares of death."

3. Exod 19–Num 10.

4. Exod 24:8; also 19:5; 34:10, 27.

5. Exod 24:3, 7; also 19:8.

6. M. Weber, *Ancient Judaism*, trans. Hans H. Gerth and Don Martindale (New York: Free Press, 1967), 62, trans. of *Das antike Judentum*, 4th ed. (Tübingen, Germany: J. C. B. Mohr, 1966), 66f.

7. Exod 21:2.

8. *The Code of Hammurabi*, trans. R. F. Harper (Chicago: University of Chicago Press, 1904), 41, clause 117.

9. Ichirō Nakada, *Genten-yaku: Hanmurabi 'Hōten'* (Translation of the original text: The 'Code' of Hammurabi) (Tokyo: Riton-sha, 1999), 34, n. 89, adopts a free rendition along the lines of "if he himself has been given as security for a debt."

10. Exod 21:26–27.

11. H. J. Boecker, *Law and the Administration of Justice in the Old Testament and Ancient East*, trans. Jeremy Moiser (Minneapolis: Augsburg, 1980), 186, trans. of *Recht und Gesetz im Alten Testament und im Alten Orient* (Neukirchen-Vluyn, Germany: Neukirchener Verlag, 1976).

12. Exod 22:21–24a.

13. Tomonobu Imamichi (*Ekoetika* [Eco-ethica] [Tokyo: Kōdansha gakujutsu bunko, 1990], 110ff.), who advocates the creation of contemporary new ethical virtues, cites "*philoxenia*" (the love of strangers) alongside "punctuality," "cosmopolitanism," "the mastering of languages and equipment," and "*eutrapelia*" (mental diversion). Such statements by the Hebrews, who from ancient times were sandwiched between great nations and had no choice but to be outward looking, suggest the background to the virtues demanded of societies that have tended to be insular, such as Japan, and also seem to have contemporary implications.

14. Exod 22:26–27.

15. Exod 23:4–5.

16. See Seizō Sekine, "Ai" (Love), in *Rinri shisō jiten* (Dictionary of ethical thought), ed. Tsutomu Hoshino, Teruo Mishima, and Seizō Sekine (Tokyo: Yamakawa Shuppansha, 1997), 25–27.

17. Exod 23:1–2.

18. Exod 23:12.

19. Exod 23:13b.

20. Exod 22:19.

21. Exod 13:12–13 and Exod 34:19–20 by the redactor of the Yahwist [J] and Elohist [E] sources in the seventh century BCE; Num 3:44ff. in the sixth–fifth centuries BCE.

22. Micah 6:7–8, from an eighth-century BCE prophetic book.

23. Gen 22, from the hand of the Elohist in the eighth century BCE.

24. For an explanation of this story, see Seizō Sekine, *Kyūyaku seisho no shisō: 24 no danshō* (The thought of the Old Testament: 24 fragments) (Tokyo: Iwanami Shoten, 1998), chapters 5 and 6, particularly 62ff.

25. Ps 106:37–38; Ezek 23:37ff.

26. Exod 23:25–26.

27. Exod 23:22, 27.

28. 2 Kgs 22–23.

29. Deut 4:8.

30. Deut 28:61.

31. Josh 8:31.

32. 2 Kgs 23:2. Compare this with 2 Kgs 22:8, 11.

33. Deut 6:4–5.

34. Mark 12:28–34; Matt 22:34–40; Luke 10:25–28.

35. Deut 6:6–9; Josh 1:8.

36. Section (8) above and Deut 28.

37. Deut 28:2, 15.

38. This is the ground-breaking claim put forward by M. Noth in *Überlieferungsgeschichtliche Studien I* (Halle [Saale]: Niemeyer, 1943), but suggestions that include not only theodicy but also, more positively, promises of divine protection and a call for turning to YHWH have been made for modifying Noth's view. For example, see G. von Rad, *Old Testament Theology*, Vol. I (New York: Harper & Row, 1962), 334–47, trans. of *Theologie des Alten Testaments*, Vol. I (Munich: Kaiser, 1960), 346–58.

39. Lev 19:2.

40. Lev 20:7.

41. It also appears in Lev 20:26; 22:2 and elsewhere.

42. Deut 30:15–20.

43. Lev 18:5.

44. Lev 26:3ff.

45. Lev 26:16.

46. Gen 9:1–7.

47. Gen 17:1.

48. Gen 17:9–14.

49. Lev 19:18. A noteworthy new Japanese translation by Tetsuo Yamaga renders this along the lines of "Treat your neighbors in a spirit of friendship as being similar to you yourself," in *Shutsu-Ejiputo-ki; Rebi-ki* (Exodus and Leviticus), trans. Tetsuo Yamaga and Fujiko Kohata, Kyūyaku seisho ni (Old Testament II) (Tokyo: Iwanami Shoten, 2000), 331. The grounds for this rendition are explained in detail in note 13 on the same page.

50. Matt 22:40.

51. Matt 5:43–44; see also Luke 6:27–28, 35.

52. E. Schweizer, *The Good News According to Matthew*, trans. David E. Green (originally *Das Evangelium nach Matthäus*; Atlanta: Knox, 1975), 370; J. Schniewind, *Das Evangelium nach Matthäus* (Göttingen: Vandenhoeck & Ruprecht, 1968).

53. For details of the argument below, see chapters 16–18 in my *Kyūyaku seisho no shisō* (The thought of the Old Testament), particularly 218ff.

54. Lev 19:17–18.

55. See E. Otto, *Theologische Ethik des Alten Testaments* (Stuttgart: Kohlhammer, 1994), 247. Otto also recognizes this passage as being about loving one's enemies, and he infers that the redactors of the Holiness Code took it from Exod 23:1–8, particularly vv. 4–5 in the Book of the Covenant.

56. Ps 139:21–22; Isa 41:11–13; 49:25–26; etc.

57. Deut 10:18; 14:21, 29; 16:11, 14; 24:17, 19, 20, 21; 26:12, 13; 27:19; Lev 19:10, 33, 34; 23:22; etc.

58. Exod 23:4–5.

59. Exod 22:25–26.

60. Exod 22:20–23a.

61. Prov 25:21–22.

62. Rom 12:19–20.

CHAPTER 11

The Wisdom Literature (1): Proverbs

1. The Wisdom Literature and Proverbs

WISDOM LITERATURE

Of the "Writings" that comprise the third category of Hebrew scripture, the genre most closely related to ethical thought is that known as "Wisdom Literature" (*Weisheitsliteratur*). The Apocrypha and the Pseudepigrapha also contain a number of interesting books of wisdom, such as Sirach (Ecclesiasticus), which transmits the laws and wisdom of later Judaism, and the Wisdom of Solomon (the Book of Wisdom) and 4 Maccabees, both of which have Hellenistic overtones. Here, however, we will restrict our discussion to the canon, focusing on Proverbs, Job, and the Qohelet. (Psalms also contains a small number of wisdom psalms, such as Pss 37, 73, and 119, but they will not be examined here.) Over the next three chapters I would like to look at each of these books in turn.

THE WISDOM LITERATURE'S SETTING IN LIFE

Before taking up this task, let me mention briefly the lifestyle under which Israel's Wisdom Literature came into being in the first place, that is, its "setting in life" (*Sitz im Leben*).

Wisdom literature was prevalent in the ancient world. There were schools in Mesopotamia and Egypt, and many of the clay tablets and papyruses used there for reading and writing have survived today. Wisdom about social conventions and customs seems to have been taught at these schools quite systematically, suggesting that wisdom (*hokhmah*) was probably also taught at schools in Israel.[1] For instance, the existence of such teachers of wisdom is perhaps intimated by the reference to the "officials of King Hezekiah of Judah" who were involved in the copying mentioned in Prov 25:1, and by the reference to "the wise" who provided "counsel" in Jer 18:18. Nevertheless, some scholars argue that there is as yet no definitive evidence of this, and that pleasant memories of exchanging witty remarks and matching wits at the *sod*[2] were gradually compiled into a collection of adages.[3] These two theories are not, however, mutually exclusive, and we can assume that even without a formal school system Israel, too, had places where reading, writing, and the commandments and proprieties were taught in some fashion or other, with this function having been fulfilled by the *sod* prior to their establishment.

So what is the *sod*?[4] The lonely prophet Jeremiah lamented that "I did not sit in the company [*sod*] of merrymakers, nor did I rejoice."[5] The *sod* refers to evening gatherings to which the villagers looked forward with anticipation. The *sod* is a venue where, after the day's work is done and dinner at home is over, the men gather in small groups in a corner of the village at the fall of dusk and ask each other how things are going, swapping information about their days and discussing the weather and harvest prospects. After chatting about various matters for a while, the assembly falls silent. As if waiting for this moment, someone suddenly stands up and starts to speak.

> Two things I ask of you;
> do not deny them to me before I die.[6]

While everyone is wondering what this means, some quick-witted person chimes in:

> Remove far from me falsehood and lying;
> give me neither poverty nor riches.[7]

Nobody is sure what has prompted the first utterance, including the person who responded to it, but that is of no import. The enjoyment lies in how the conversation starts off in this way and how everyone plays a part in steering it in different directions, so that it develops along more meaningful lines. A third person picks up the thread:

> Three things are too wonderful for me.[8]

A fourth person breaks in, saying,

> four I do not understand.[9]

An old man known for his wisdom starts off in a grave tone:

> the way of an eagle in the sky,
>   the way of a snake on a rock.[10]

Here he becomes at a loss for words. A young man takes over and continues:

> the way of a ship on the high seas.[11]

All are filled with admiration for this nice turn of phrase. A wag continues, leading to a roar of laughter,

> and the way of a man with a girl.[12]

In this fashion, their collective wisdom works in a direction unimagined by the initial speaker, ending up with something akin to a proverb.
    Or there are simpler exchanges of wit. When one man begins with

> The legs of a disabled person hang limp,[13]

someone cynically remarks,

> so does a proverb in the mouth of a fool.[14]

When another says,

> There are sixty queens and eighty concubines,
>   and maidens without number.[15]

a young man in love replies,

> My dove, my perfect one, is the only one.[16]

The night wears on. One by one, the men turn in and the evening's *sod* draws to a close. The stillness of the night envelops the surroundings. Yet some recall the finest epigrams from that night and relate them to their family, while others lie alone in bed, enjoying repeating these sayings over and over. In this way several aphorisms stick in people's minds and might be repeated or refined at the *sod* the following day, and they are gradually passed on down. This is thought to be how several of the wisdom books originated and were handed down. Already apparent in the examples above is a perspective on ethical virtues and vices, such as integrity and love, respecting the virtue of the mean, and disdain for foolishness. What shall emerge if we examine this a little more systematically?

PROVERBS AS A CATALOGUE OF VIRTUES

Wisdom literature could provisionally be defined as literature that, through cultivating Hebrew wisdom, seeks standards for good actions and right conduct. In that sense it can be regarded as an outstanding gleaning of Hebrew ethical thought. Various genres are used, such as allegories, dialogues, disputes in court, proverbs, and lists of everything from flora and fauna to virtues and vices. The above quotations from Proverbs generally consist of proverbs, sayings, and dialogues, but it seems to me that the whole of Proverbs could be read as a "catalogue of virtues." There is no direct equivalent for the word "virtue" in Hebrew, and since the Septuagint renders the glorious acts of God (*tehillah*) as *aretē*,[17] it is usual to refer to descriptions of God's powerful actions as *Aretalogie* or to include them in a typology whereby relatively short passages—such as the Ten Commandments, Ps 15:2–5, and Job 31, as well as the New Testament passages of Rom 1:29–31 and Gal 5:19–23— are referred to as a "catalogue of virtues" (*Tugendkatalog*) or, conversely, a "catalogue of vices" (*Lasterkatalog*). In terms of ethical thought, however, it seems to me that Proverbs as a whole can be regarded as a list of virtues and vices, that is, as a "catalogue of virtues" in the broad sense. This catalogue, however, is presented in a somewhat confused and complicated fashion. When interpreting it, therefore, I would like to incorporate a comparison with the Greek catalogue of virtues. The Greek theory of virtue—particularly that expounded in books III to VI of Aristotle's *Nicomachean Ethics*—arranges its discussion of virtue in philosophical terms. A comparison with this will, I believe, allow us to systematize and restructure the complicated account in Proverbs, and certain features of the Hebrew theory of virtue will also be revealed through a comparison with that of the Greeks. Here I would like to attempt to bring order to Proverbs by reading it from this perspective of a comparison with Greek virtues.

THE STRUCTURE OF PROVERBS

First I would like to touch briefly on the structure of Proverbs. It consists of five parts that have different sources and dates of origin.

(1) Chapters 1–9: A collection of general admonitory instructions. This is thought to be of the most recent origin, but there is debate over whether it was written before the period of captivity in the sixth century BCE or in the early years after captivity.
(2) Chapters 10:1–22:16: This has the title "The proverbs of Solomon," but it is impossible to determine which parts are in fact attributable to Solomon. In any case, this is assumed to be the oldest passage in Proverbs, dating from the kingdom period in the tenth century BCE.
(3) Chapters 22:17–24:34: Two collections of "sayings of the wise."
(4) Chapters 25–29: A sequel to "The proverbs of Solomon," copied by "the officials of King Hezekiah of Judah."
(5) Chapters 30–31: Four short teachings originating mainly in Edom, to the south of the Dead Sea.

In this rather chaotic fashion, the book of Proverbs brings together sayings of different vintages and origins. My approach here consists of rearranging these and reading Proverbs as an ethical "catalogue of virtues" through a comparison with that of the Greeks. In this chapter, we will follow Proverbs, which consists of these sections, in learning about the foundations of wisdom, while chapter 12 will trace the subsequent development of wisdom in Job, which was written at a later date, and chapter 13 will examine this further in relation to the Qohelet.

2. Virtues Shared with Greece

THE MEAN AND MODERATION

Aristotle certainly has no monopoly on the virtue of the "mean." The verse cited above, "give me neither poverty nor riches" (Prov 30:8), continues as follows:

> feed me with the food that I need
> or I shall be full, and deny you,
>   and say, "Who is the LORD?"
> or I shall be poor, and steal,
>   and profane the name of my God.[18]

This states that the extremes of gluttony and starvation or of wealth and poverty both risk a turning against God, so the best course lies between these extremes, that is, the mean corresponding to "the food that I need." As is evident in the quote,

> It is not good to eat much honey,
>   or to seek honor on top of honor.[19]

this approach can be construed both as extolling moderation, which prohibits excess in physical pleasures, and as an exhortation to the mean in relation to honor. Examples of the former include,

> 1 When you sit down to eat with a ruler,
>   observe carefully what is before you,
> 2 and put a knife to your throat
>   if you have a big appetite.
> 3 Do not desire the ruler's delicacies,
>   for they are deceptive food.
> 4 Do not wear yourself out to get rich;
>   be wise enough to desist.
> 5 When your eyes light upon it, it is gone;
>   for suddenly it takes wings to itself,
>   flying like an eagle toward heaven.
> 6 Do not eat the bread of the stingy;
>   do not desire their delicacies;
> 7 for that is like a hair in the throat.
>   "Eat and drink!" they say to you;
>   but they do not mean it.
> 8 You will vomit up the little you have eaten,
>   and you will waste your pleasant words.[20]

This rather lengthy passage is divided into three sections. Verses 1–3 caution against gluttony when one is invited to dinner by a ruler, vv. 4–5 expound on the foolishness of trying to increase one's wealth, and vv. 6–8 are somewhat unclear but could be construed as meaning that if one is invited by the "stingy" and "desire[s]" too much of their food, one will incur their enmity. Verse 7a follows the Septuagint. The hair in one's throat triggers a bout of vomiting. This is similar to "Do not covet the property of the dependent. . . . The property of a dependent blocks the throat, It is vomit for the gullet," which appears in the Egyptian *The Instruction of Amenemope* (ch. 11:4), which is the parallel text for the surrounding passage, Prov 22:17–23:14, so I have adopted the Septuagint translation. Even the Hebrew Masoretic text says, "He is like one keeping accounts," which could be interpreted as meaning that the host is a stingy person who will later begrudge the things offered, and your compliments will have been in vain, so you should not eat to excess. In any case, all three passages urge restraint and moderation in eating.

Of the passages exhorting people to the mean, as stated above, Prov 30 originated in Edom, Prov 23 resembles Egypt's instructional literature, and Prov 25 is thought to be pure Israelite. Note here that the "mean" regarded by Aristotle as lying at the root of all virtues is emphasized in the "Proverbs" of various peoples. Since our concern in this book lies with Greek and Hebrew ethics, however, I would prefer not to broaden the scope too much, and instead narrow the focus down to the question of which of the virtues enumerated by Aristotle in books III to VI of the *Nicomachean Ethics* can also be found in the Hebrew Proverbs.

TRUTH AND AFFECTION

"Truth" and "affection" are included in the virtues listed in book IV of the *Nicomachean Ethics*. What Aristotle meant by "truth" was "the mean between boastfulness and self-depreciation" (*Nicomachean Ethics* IV, 7, 1127a13).[21] In the above passage it means that the stingy host who nevertheless puts on a feast is being boastful, while the guest who wants to partake of this feast and so compliments the host on it is exhibiting self-depreciation. Rather,

> The getting of treasures by a lying tongue
> is a fleeting vapor and a snare of death.[22]

and

> Righteous lips are the delight of a king,
> and he loves those who speak what is right.[23]

Indeed, "truth" is also regarded as a virtue in the Hebrew Proverbs:

> Truthful lips endure forever,
> but a lying tongue lasts only a moment.
> Deceit is in the mind of those who plan evil,
> but those who counsel peace have joy.[24]

What about affection (*stergein*)? As with "truth," in chapter 6 of book IV of the *Nicomachean Ethics* Aristotle also defines "affection" as a "mean" in "social" situations between "the complaisant," who agree to everything, and the "quarrelsome," who disagree with everything,[25] and we have already seen (section 6.3 in part I) how in books VIII and IX Aristotle further develops a multifaceted inquiry into all aspects of "love" (*philiā*). The Hebrew book of Proverbs also values such love and is intent on describing various desirable forms of love, such as the following:

> Better is open rebuke
>   than hidden love.
> Well meant are the wounds a friend inflicts,
>   but profuse are the kisses of an enemy.[26]

Particularly in relation to the education of children, passages such as

> Those who spare the rod hate their children,
>   but those who love them are diligent to discipline them.[27]

argue that mouthing nice pleasantries does not constitute love.

> Some friends play at friendship
>   but a true friend sticks closer than one's nearest kin.[28]

But

> A friend loves at all times,
>   and kinsfolk are born to share adversity.[29]

This is why such kinsfolk are said to be better than one's kin by birth.

> Do not forsake your friend or the friend of your parent;
>   do not go to the house of your kindred in the day of your calamity.
> Better is a neighbor nearby
>   than kindred who are far away.[30]

In this way love is extolled, as in the following:

> Perfume and incense make the heart glad,
>   but the sweetness of a friend is better than one's own counsel.[31]

> Better is a dinner of vegetables where love is
>   than a fatted ox and hatred with it.[32]

The object of this love extends beyond one's friends to encompass also "the poor," "the weak," and one's "enemies."

Those who despise their neighbors are sinners,
but happy are those who are kind to the *poor*.[33]

Whoever gives to the *poor* will lack nothing,
but one who turns a blind eye will get many a curse.[34]

Whoever is kind to the *poor* lends to the LORD,
and will be repaid in full.[35]

If you close your ear to the cry of the *poor*,
you will cry out and not be heard.[36]

By loyalty and faithfulness iniquity is atoned for,
and by the fear of the LORD one avoids evil.
When the ways of people please the LORD,
he causes even their *enemies* to be at peace with them.[37]

If *your enemies* are hungry, give them bread to eat;
and if they are thirsty, give them water to drink;
for you will heap coals of fire on their heads,
and the LORD will reward you.[38]

It is this final passage that, even more than the New Testament, is the main text that speaks of loving one's enemy, as was indicated in the previous chapter.[39] This passage is quoted in modified form by Paul in the New Testament.[40] He omits the final line, no doubt in an attempt to interpret this passage in the sense of "YHWH will retaliate on your behalf against your enemies," and he links the preceding passage to "Vengeance is mine [YHWH's]" from Deuteronomy,[41] highlighting this sense of revenge. By contrast, in view of the usage in Prov 19:17, it would be more natural to construe the "reward" (*shillam*) in Proverbs in the sense of good deeds being met with rewards, rather than taking revenge on one's enemies.[42] In addition, "heap coals of fire on their heads" refers to making them metaphorically burn with shame, and it involves inducing one's enemies, who are no longer able to bear the agony, to abandon their enmity. We could conclude, then, that the idea in Proverbs is that the good ordained by God consists of "you" and "your enemies" dissolving your mutual enmity and coexisting. The prevailing view that the idea of *agapē*, which entails loving one's enemies, first appeared in the New Testament is far from correct, and although the idea of hate for one's enemies is very strong in the Old Testament (e.g., Ps 139:21–22), we should follow up on the previous chapter by noting that this penetrating idea of loving one's enemies is also mentioned occasionally in the Old Testament.[43]

GOOD TEMPER AND JUSTICE

It is evident that this idea of love, whereby one loves one's enemies, emphasizes a mild-tempered disposition and the pursuit of a justice that protects also the weak in society. Next I would like to look at these two virtues, which are also included among those cited by Aristotle.

According to chapter 5 in book IV of the *Nicomachean Ethics*, "good temper" represents "a mean with respect to anger," and the midway position between "hotheads" and "the weak-spirited" (simpletons) is an even-tempered person.[44]

> Do not quarrel with anyone without cause,
>   when no harm has been done to you.[45]

This assumedly means that if "harm has been done to you" by "anyone" you should "quarrel" with that person, and if you don't, you are "weak-spirited." Yet the Greek insight that "To good temper we oppose the excess more than the deficiency; for it is more common"[46] is directly applicable to Hebrew views. Most of what is spoken of in Proverbs is an exhortation to even temperedness without excessive anger.

> Scoffers set a city aflame,
>   but the wise turn away wrath.[47]

> A fool gives full vent to anger,
>   but the wise quietly holds it back.[48]

> Whoever is slow to anger has great understanding,
>   but one who has a hasty temper exalts folly.[49]

> A soft answer turns away wrath,
>   but a harsh word stirs up anger.[50]

> Those who are hot-tempered stir up strife,
>   but those who are slow to anger calm contention.[51]

The feature of Hebrew thought, however, is that it superimposes such even-tempered people who restrain their anger in this way with those who leave justice up to God.

> Do not fret because of evildoers.
>   Do not envy the wicked;

for the evil have no future;
the lamp of the wicked will go out.⁵²

By contrast,

[The LORD] stores up sound wisdom for the upright;
he is a shield to those who walk blamelessly,
guarding the paths of justice
and preserving the way of his faithful ones.⁵³

In this way, justice derives from God.⁵⁴ Of course, it should not just be left up to God alone, but it is also something that people should strive to carry out themselves. In this respect, the Hebrew understanding of justice overlaps with that of the Greeks. Naturally, Proverbs is totally lacking in a description such as that in the *Nicomachean Ethics* (V, 1–5), where justice is subdivided into general and special justice, with the latter being further subdivided into distributive justice, corrective justice, and reciprocal justice (justice in exchange) and these then being analyzed in philosophical terms.⁵⁵ Nevertheless, the basis of Aristotle's theory of justice, which argues that "'the just' means that which is lawful or that which is fair,"⁵⁶ is shared by Proverbs. For instance, Prov 29 is a classic example that considers these two aspects.

By justice a king gives stability to the land,
but one who makes heavy exactions ruins it.⁵⁷

The righteous know the rights of the poor;
the wicked have no such understanding.⁵⁸

The poor and the oppressor have this in common:
the LORD gives light to the eyes of both.⁵⁹

Where there is no prophecy [*hazon*], the people cast off restraint,
but happy are those who keep the law [*torah*].⁶⁰

"Keep[ing] the law" corresponds to "justice," and this justice also entails protecting the rights of the oppressed "poor." This is because both the oppressed and the "oppressor" have equally been given life by "the LORD" so that they will have "light to the eyes." The regaining of such equality is commanded by prophetic "revelation,"⁶¹ laid down by "the law"⁶² and also mentioned repeatedly in Proverbs, including in a form urging charity toward the destitute.⁶³

WIT AND WISDOM

Here we have inquired into those virtues that, despite certain subtle differences, are common to both the *Nicomachean Ethics* and Proverbs. Finally, let us also take a brief look at "wit" and "wisdom."

Again, the philosophical analysis of "wit" set out in chapter 8 of book IV of the *Nicomachean Ethics* is naturally absent in Proverbs, but surely all would agree that actual examples of wit, including black humor, are scattered here and there throughout Proverbs. The previously cited passage,

> The legs of a disabled person hang limp;
>   so does a proverb in the mouth of a fool.[64]

and

> Like a dog that returns to its vomit
>   is a fool who reverts to his folly.[65]

are examples of black humor and might be frowned upon in some quarters. However, passages such as

> It is better to live in a corner of the housetop
>   than in a house shared with a contentious wife.[66]

appear in various permutations,[67] and though they could be construed as being spoken in bitterness, they are contrasted with positive expressions such as "a prudent wife is from the LORD"[68] and "A capable wife . . . is far more precious than jewels."[69] Considered in conjunction with the fact that Proverbs as a whole concludes with a tribute to good wives,[70] then these excerpts can probably be interpreted as instances of endearing humor.[71] Furthermore, other passages seem vaguely amusing, such as:

> A stone is heavy, and sand is weighty,
>   but a fool's provocation is heavier than both.[72]

> Whoever blesses a neighbor with a loud voice,
>   rising early in the morning,
>   will be counted as cursing.[73]

> For as pressing milk produces curds,
>   and pressing the nose produces blood,
>   so pressing anger produces strife.[74]

Commenting on any more witty aphorisms would be "boorish,"[75] how-ever, so here I will content myself with simply citing the examples above. After having analyzed "ethical excellence" from the latter half of book III through to book V of the *Nicomachean Ethics*, Aristotle went on in book VI to discuss "intellectual excellence." "Virtue" in the nar-row sense would fall under the former category, but since "wisdom" also represents "excellence" (*aretē*), it could be included in "virtue" (*aretē*) in the broad sense. Obviously, there are abundant references to "wisdom" in the Wisdom Literature, so again I will confine myself to noting two or three classic examples.

> Doing wrong is like sport to a fool,
>   but wise conduct [*ḥokhmah*] is pleasure
>   to a person of understanding.[76]
>
> Do not withhold discipline from your children;
>   if you beat them with a rod, they will not die.
> If you beat them with the rod,
>   you will save their lives from Sheol.
> My child, if your heart is wise,
>   my heart too will be glad.
> My soul will rejoice
>   when your lips speak what is right.[77]

It should be added that wisdom is also considered in relation to God, as in

> The fear of the LORD [fearing the LORD] is the beginning of
>   knowledge;
>   fools despise wisdom and instruction.[78]

or

> The LORD by wisdom founded the earth;
>   by understanding he established the heavens;
> by his knowledge the deeps broke open,
>   and the clouds drop down the dew.[79]

Wisdom is also positioned as the opposite of arrogance, as in the fol-lowing:

> The talk of fools is a rod for their backs,
>   but the lips of the wise preserve them.[80]
>
> The wise are cautious and turn away from evil,
>   but the fool throws off restraint and is careless.[81]

3. Virtues Particular to Greece

This last point is important. Books III to VI of the *Nicomachean Ethics* list a total of twelve virtues, including wisdom, and we have already seen how eight of these—the mean, moderation, truth, affection, good temper, justice, wit, and wisdom—appear in Proverbs as well. Yet if the wisdom spoken of in Proverbs is incompatible with arrogance, does it not mean that Hebrew ethics is at odds here with the Greek theory of virtues, which emphasizes how inclusive it is, even encompassing arrogance? In other words, it is anticipated that the Hebrews might not include among their virtues the remaining four virtues of bravery, liberality, magnificence, and high-mindedness.

BRAVERY AND LIBERALITY

Of these, the situation is unclear with regard to "bravery" and "liberality." Passages such as

> One wise person went up against a city of warriors
> and brought down the stronghold in which they trusted.[82]

and

> Wise warriors are mightier than strong ones,
> and those who have knowledge than those
> who have strength.[83]

seem to regard "bravery," which is "a mean with regard to fear and courage,"[84] as a virtue in connection with "wisdom," while

> A generous person will be enriched,
> and one who gives water will get water.
> The people curse those who hold back grain,
> but a blessing is on the head of those who sell it.[85]

can be described as an example that regards "liberality," which is "a mean with regard to property" between "wastefulness" and "stinginess,"[86] in a positive light. It should be noted, however, that Proverbs contains very few such instances. Whereas for the other eight virtues there are numerous examples in addition to those listed above,[87] the several examples cited here more or less exhaust those relating to "bravery" and "liberality."

MAGNIFICENCE AND HIGH-MINDEDNESS

There are virtually no examples at all for "magnificence" and "high-mindedness."

"Magnificence" refers to lavish consumption, such as equipping a fleet for the sake of the nation.[88] In view of their general standard of living, this would have been unlikely for the Hebrews, who, as mentioned earlier, offered up prayers such as "give me neither poverty nor riches, feed me with the food that I need."[89]

"High-mindedness" entails believing in one's own worth and actually living up to that,[90] but for the down-to-earth ("Better to be despised and be a servant, than to be self-important and lack food")[91] and religious Hebrews ("Toward the scorners he is scornful, but to the humble he shows favor"),[92] perhaps this is a matter of no consequence.

As the saying goes,

> When pride comes, then comes disgrace;
> but wisdom is with the humble.[93]

It seems that for the Hebrews it was *shefal ruah* (humble-heartedness, humility) that was a virtue, rather than the *megalopsychiā* (greatness of soul, high-mindedness) of the Greeks.

Based on these preliminary conclusions from an examination of the virtues shared by the Greeks and Hebrews, as well as those particular to Greece, we will now move on to a consideration of the virtues specific to the Hebrew people.

4. Virtues Particular to the Hebrews

HUMILITY

There are three instances in the Old Testament of the expression *shefal ruah*, meaning "humility," with two of these appearing in Proverbs (the other occurrence is Isa 57:15). One is:

> It is better to be of a *lowly spirit* among the poor
> than to divide the spoil with the proud.[94]

Humility is sometimes linked with poverty, but associating it with peace and one's conscience[95] and hence regarding it as intrinsically nobler than wealth is a Hebraic value concept. By contrast, arrogance leads to abuse and conflict[96] and involves paying no heed to correction[97] and ignoring God,[98] so it leads people to ruin.[99] One other example referring to "the humble" is,

> A person's pride will bring humiliation,
> but one who is *lowly in spirit* will
> obtain honor.[100]

Haughtiness entails an inflated opinion of oneself, so one will eventually be cut down to size and brought "humiliation" (the causative form of *shafel*, which has the same root as *shefal*). By contrast, since one knows one's station in life, humility is more closely matched to reality than is haughtiness, and it will eventually bring "honor." The verse above, "When pride [*zadon*] comes, then comes disgrace; but wisdom is with the humble [*tsanua*]," [101] likewise portrays this situation. Indeed, in certain respects this calls to mind Socrates' "knowledge of ignorance." [102] This is also apparent in such variations as

> Do you see persons wise in their own eyes?
> There is more hope for fools than for them.[103]

or

> Answer fools according to their folly,
> or they will be wise in their own eyes.[104]

People should be aware of their own ignorance, and since "proud" people lack the "wisdom" of their "ignorance," they will witness "disgrace."

In the final analysis, this ignorance is in comparison with God. Whereas in Socrates' case the emphasis was on the fact that ignorance entails not "know[ing] anything . . . noble and good [*kalon kagathon*]," [105] Proverbs seems to be characterized by the fact that human beings' ignorance and impuissance are contrasted with God's omniscience and omnipotence.[106]

All our steps are ordered by the LORD;
how then can we understand our own ways?[107]

Do not be wise in your own eyes;
fear the LORD, and turn away from evil.[108]

In the case of the Hebrew "knowledge of ignorance," the reason that a "person's pride will bring humiliation"[109] is not only because it is based on an erroneous understanding, but also because this is abhorred by God.[110] Conversely, we can also take the view that the reason "one who is lowly in spirit will obtain honor"[111] is that God esteems such humility.[112] In other words,

Toward the scorners he is scornful,
but to the humble he shows favor.[113]

The Hebrew word translated here as "humble" is 'ani in the Received Text and 'anaw in the Masoretic emendation; in either case, it is the adjectival form of 'anawah (humility). Although the adjectival form is used more frequently,[114] the fundamental meaning of this root is expressed clearly in the following two nominal usages:

The reward for humility ['anawah] and fear of the LORD
is riches and honor and life.[115]

The fear of the LORD is instruction in wisdom,
and humility ['anawah] goes before honor.[116]

So it turns out that "humility" consists of "lowering oneself" before God and "fearing the LORD." Although duly noted in relation to the other virtues as well, the fact that an ethical virtue is conceived of in relation to God in this way seems to be a general feature of the Hebraic theory of virtue, in contrast with that of Greece. Let us next review this point in several passages from Proverbs.

DIVINE FAITH

It is written that

The eyes of the LORD are in every place,
keeping watch on the evil and the good.[117]

The fundamental understanding in Proverbs is that the existence of God lies at the basis of ethical good and evil:

> The fear of the LORD is hatred of evil.
> Pride and arrogance and the way of evil
>   and perverted speech I hate.[118]

Based on an awareness of such a divine being,

> The *fear* [*yir'ah*; wonder and dread] of the LORD
> is instruction in wisdom.[119]

That is, to "wonder" at something that transcends us is also the basis and point of departure for Proverbs. The following famous utterance is a formulation of this:[120]

> The *fear* [*yir'ah*] of the LORD
> is the beginning of knowledge.[121]

As we saw also in section 9.3 in relation to the Ten Commandments, the word *yir'ah* refers to the emotion felt when one's eyes open to something one had previously been unaware of and one feels a sense of wonder and dread. Here it is provisionally translated as "fear." Similar expressions occur not only on these two occasions in Proverbs but also in Ps 111:10, forming the fundamental tenet of Hebrew wisdom.[122] It is written that through this "fear" people can avoid the temptation to sin,[123] and they can live long[124] and achieve good understanding.[125]

Without such a "fear,"

> Haughty eyes and a proud heart—
> the lamp of the wicked—are sin.[126]

By contrast,

> In [a humble] fear of the LORD one has strong confidence,
>   and one's children will have a refuge.
> The fear of the LORD is a fountain of life,
>   so that one may avoid the snares of death.[127]

This God is concerned not with the good or evil of people's outward behavior, but with whether they have a faith that rests in God.

> All one's ways may be pure in one's own eyes,
>   but the LORD weighs the spirit.

> Commit your work to the LORD,
> and your plans will be established.[128]

Likewise we must also refrain from judging people and retaliating on the basis of outward rights and wrongs.

> Do not say, "I will repay evil";
> wait for the LORD, and he will help you.[129]

YHWH is a God of retribution who rewards goodness based on faith with happiness, and evil based on a lack of faith with woe.

> The righteous are delivered from trouble,
> and the wicked get into it instead.[130]

> The righteous have enough to satisfy their appetite,
> but the belly of the wicked is empty.[131]

The essence of wisdom lies in perceiving in the phenomena of this world the workings of this retributive God who presides over the world.

> For whoever finds me finds life
> and obtains favor from the LORD;
> but those who miss me injure themselves;
> all who hate me love death.[132]

As was the case throughout the admonitory instructions in Prov 1–9, the first-person reference to "me" here signifies personified "wisdom." Those who "find" wisdom will understand the workings of the God of retribution, and for trusting in this they will be rewarded with "life," while those who do not will attain "death."

5. On Retribution Ethics

WISDOM ABOUT RETRIBUTION

In addition to those cited above, there are innumerable other sayings about retribution ethics:

> The good obtain favor from the LORD,
> but those who devise evil he condemns.[133]

> [I]f you hold back from rescuing those taken away to death,
> those who go staggering to the slaughter;
> if you say, "Look, we did not know this"—
> does not he who weighs the heart perceive it?
> Does not he who keeps watch over your soul know it?
> And will he not repay all according to their deeds?[134]

> Whoever is kind to the poor lends to the LORD,
> and will be repaid in full.[135]

This is just a tiny sample of these sayings. Faith in such retribution urges people also to entrust to God's hands the penalty for evil and revenge on one's enemies.

> [F]or though [the righteous] fall seven times, they will rise again;
> but the wicked are overthrown by calamity.
> Do not rejoice when your enemies fall,
> and do not let your heart be glad when they stumble,
> or else the LORD will see it and be displeased,
> and turn away his anger from them.[136]

More plainly,

> Do not say, "I will do to others as they have done to me;
> I will pay them back for what they have done."[137]

There are also cases where God does not himself preside over such retribution, which is instead already inherent in the matter itself under the so-called law of cause and effect.

> Misfortune pursues sinners,
> but prosperity rewards the righteous.[138]

> Those who mislead the upright into evil ways
> will fall into pits of their own making,
> but the blameless will have a goodly inheritance.[139]

THE BREAKDOWN OF RETRIBUTION

To begin with, the fact that the Hebrew word *ra'*, which means ethical "evil,"[140] also signifies the resultant "suffering,"[141] and *tsedaqah*, which refers to "righteousness,"[142] implies the ensuing "happiness"[143] can also be taken as an indication that the law of good cause–good effect/bad cause–bad effect was simply too self-evident to the Hebrews.[144] Conversely, since there are cases where retribution does not work, it might also be construed as a hidden theodicy exonerating God. Though few in number, in fact there are also cases in Proverbs where there is a recognition of the reality that evil flourishes and righteousness is not rewarded.

> [T]he wicked will not go unpunished
>   no matter how many generations pass,[145]
>   but the descendants of the righteous will escape.[146]

The "proverbs of Solomon" in chapters 10–22, within which section this verse is located, fall under category (2) according to the classification in section 11.1. In other words, this constitutes the oldest part of Proverbs, and on the face of it this passage, too, espouses the traditional law of cause and effect. It is also possible, though, that there is already a latent awareness of the injustice whereby even if subsequent descendants are "punished" for "generations," there are "wicked" people who escape punishment in a single generation. The following two passages, which are thought to be the product of a later period, do not make the far-fetched claim that the law of cause and effect is in operation because these people will be punished eventually; instead, these passages demonstrate a franker awareness of the breakdown of retribution and a clear unease at this:

> Like a muddied spring or a polluted fountain
>   are the righteous who give way before the wicked.[147]

> Under three things the earth trembles;
>   under four it cannot bear up:
> a slave when he becomes king,
>   and a fool when glutted with food;
> an unloved woman when she gets a husband,
>   and a maid when she succeeds her mistress.[148]

In this way the wisdom of the book of Proverbs consists of an awareness that the law of retribution underpins the phenomena of this world, but if we take a comprehensive look at the real world, where wrongdoers prosper and the just perish, in the end we are also impelled to a frank recognition of the breakdown of retribution. It seems that wisdom must also evolve toward somehow formulating a theodicy that demonstrates the justness of a God who overlooks evil and fails to reward good. This theme is explored in the books of Job and the Qohelet. Hence our task in the next two chapters consists of reading further in the later Wisdom Literature from this perspective of the breakdown of retribution.

6. Conclusion

The aim of this chapter lay in reading Proverbs, a work of early Wisdom Literature, as a catalogue of virtues. Since the discussion has ranged widely, in closing I would like to summarize the thrust of my argument and link it to the next chapter.

First, the *Nicomachean Ethics* listed a total of twelve virtues, and we have verified that eight of these—the mean, moderation, truth, affection, good temper, justice, wit, and wisdom—are regarded as important virtues in Proverbs as well. There were numerous examples of these virtues in Proverbs, but very few instances of the virtues of "bravery" and "liberality" that are also cited in the *Nicomachean Ethics*, while examples of "magnificence" and "high-mindedness" are nonexistent in Proverbs. Rather than such Hellenic *megalopsychiā* (greatness of soul), Proverbs emphasized *shefal ruah* (humble-heartedness). Compared with the Greeks, "humble-heartedness," or "humility," is a virtue particular to the Hebrews, and it is linked to their fundamental stance of stressing "faith in God," who is omniscient and omnipotent. On the ethical horizon, this God needs to be a God of "retribution" who commends humility and abhors arrogance, and who rewards good with happiness and evil with misfortune. The main topic of early Wisdom Literature, then, lay precisely in discerning divine retribution behind worldly phenomena. A schism was already vaguely apparent even in early retribution ethics. How was this issue interpreted in later Wisdom Literature, which criticized the fact that causal retribution does not operate more directly? In closing, we ascertained this point as an issue that remains to be resolved.

Notes

1. G. von Rad, *Weisheit in Israel* (Neukirchen-Vluyn, Germany: Neukirchener Verlag, 1970), part I, ch. 2.

2. Jer 15:17; Ezek 13:9.

3. L. Köhler, *Der Hebräische Mensch* (Tübingen, Germany: Mohr, 1953), ch. 5.

4. On this question, see also my *Kyūyaku seisho no shisō: 24 no danshō* (Thought of the Old Testament: 24 fragments) (Tokyo: Iwanami Shoten, 1998), 95–97.

5. Jer 15:17.
6. Prov 30:7.
7. Prov 30:8.
8. Prov 30:18.
9. Prov 30:18.
10. Prov 30:19.
11. Prov 30:19.
12. Prov 30:19.
13. Prov 26:7.
14. Prov 26:7.
15. Song 6:8.
16. Song 6:9.
17. Isa 42:8, 12; 63:7; Hab 3:3.
18. Prov 30:8–9.
19. Prov 25:27.
20. Prov 23:1–8.
21. Aristotle, *The Nicomachean Ethics*, trans. H. G. Apostle (Dordrecht, Netherlands: Reidel, 1975), 74, hereafter *NE*.
22. Prov 21:6.
23. Prov 16:13.
24. Prov 12:19–20.
25. *NE* IV, 6, 1126b11ff.
26. Prov 27:5–6.
27. Prov 13:24.
28. Prov 18:24.
29. Prov 17:17.
30. Prov 27:10.
31. Prov 27:9.
32. Prov 15:17.
33. Prov 14:21; emphasis added.
34. Prov 28:27; emphasis added.
35. Prov 19:17; emphasis added.
36. Prov 21:13; emphasis added.
37. Prov 16:6–7; emphasis added.
38. Prov 25:21–22; emphasis added.
39. In relation to the following discussion, see Sekine, *Kyūyaku seisho no shisō* (Thought of the Old Testament), 217.
40. Rom 12:19–20.
41. Deut 32:35.
42. Also see, however, Prov 20:22.
43. Other examples include, for instance, Lev 19:17–19. For an interpretation of this, see Sekine, *Kyūyaku seisho no shisō* (Thought of the Old Testament), 215–19.
44. *NE* IV, 5, 1125b26ff.
45. Prov 3:30.
46. *NE* IV, 5, 1126a29–30.

47. Prov 29:8.
48. Prov 29:11.
49. Prov 14:29.
50. Prov 15:1.
51. Prov 15:18.
52. Prov 24:19–20.
53. Prov 2:7–8.
54. Prov 2:9; 6:33.
55. We might recall how Boman once argued that ethics (which deals with thinking) and psychology (which deals with understanding) are two different modes of knowing, and that the Greeks excelled at the former while the Hebrews were good at the latter. See Thorleif Boman, *Hebrew Thought Compared with Greek*, trans. Jules L. Moreau (New York: Norton, 1960), 193ff., trans. of *Das hebräische Denken im Vergleich mit dem griechischen*, 2nd ed. (Göttingen: Vandenhoeck & Ruprecht, 1954).
56. *NE* V, 1, 1129a34.
57. Prov 29:4.
58. Prov 29:7.
59. Prov 29:13.
60. Prov 29:18.
61. Isa 1:17, 23; 10:2; Jer 22:3; 7:5–6; etc.
62. Deut 10:17–19; 27:19; Lev 19:34; etc.
63. Prov 8:18, 20; 10:2; 11:4–5, 18–19; 12:28; 13:6; 14:34; 28:8, 27; etc.
64. Prov 26:7.
65. Prov 26:11.
66. Prov 21:9.
67. Prov 21:19; 25:24. Also Prov 19:13; 27:15.
68. Prov 19:14.
69. Prov 31:10.
70. Prov 31:10–31.
71. We might recall that, as Tomonobu Imamichi points out in *Ekoetika* (Eco-ethica) ([Tokyo: Kōdansha Gakujutsu bunko, 1990], 120), the Greek word *eutrapelia*, which is translated as "wit," originally meant a "clever shift," and it was an approach that used humor and wit to shift one's mood to happiness.
72. Prov 27:3.
73. Prov 27:14.
74. Prov 30:33.
75. According to the *NE* IV, 8, 1128a9, "boorishness" is the opposite pole of "buffoonery" (where humor is taken to excess), and it refers to something that is simply awkward.
76. Prov 10:23.
77. Prov 23:13–16.
78. Prov 1:7; see also Prov 9:10, which is discussed below.
79. Prov 3:19–20.
80. Prov 14:3.
81. Prov 14:16.

82. Prov 21:22.
83. Prov 24:5.
84. *NE* III, 6, 1115a6–7.
85. Prov 11:25–26.
86. *NE* IV, 1, 1119b23ff.
87. In addition to those cited above, there are literally too many examples in Proverbs to list here, such as Prov 12:12; 16:32; 23:29–35; 25:16–17; 27:7; 28:22 in relation to the mean and moderation; 2:14–15, 21; 4:24; 6:16–19; 8:6–8; 11:3; 12:17; 14:5 in relation to truth; 11:17–19; 12:28; 17:9; 21:13; 31:26 in relation to affection; 12:16; 14:17, 30; 16:32; 22:24; 25:15; 29:9, 22 in relation to good temper; 1:3; 2:9, 21; 8:6–8; 11:3; 12:5; 13:23; 16:8; 21:3 in relation to justice; 14:4; 17:10–12, 14–16, 28; 26:17–25; 30:15–16, 24–28 in relation to wit; and 1:2–6; 12:1; 13:15–16; 14:1, 18; 15:14, 20–21; 16:16, 21–23; 17:27–28; 19:2–3; 18:15; 20:15; 21:11, 20; 23:12; 24:3–5, 14; 28:26; 29:8–9; 31:26 in relation to wisdom.
88. *NE* IV, 2.
89. Prov 30:8.
90. *NE* IV, 3.
91. Prov 12:9, adapted from the NRSV.
92. Prov 3:34.
93. Prov 11:2.
94. Prov 16:19; emphasis added.
95. Prov 15:16–17; 17:1.
96. Prov 7:19; 13:10; 16:28–30.
97. Prov 15:32.
98. Prov 8:13.
99. Prov 16:18.
100. Prov 29:23; emphasis added.
101. Prov 11:2.
102. Plato, *Apology of Socrates* 21Aff.; see also chapter 3 of this book.
103. Prov 26:12.
104. Prov 26:5.
105. *Apology of Socrates* 21D, trans. T. G. West (Ithaca, NY: Cornell University Press, 1979), 26.
106. Naturally, such a viewpoint was not totally lacking in Greece. For instance, refer to section 3.1 in relation to Socrates and back to section 1.3 in relation to Heraclitus to see the implications of a comparison with God's knowledge. Admittedly, however, in Greece the emphasis was not explicitly placed on this aspect.
107. Prov 20:24.
108. Prov 3:7.
109. Prov 29:23.
110. Prov 3:34; 6:16–19; 15:25; 16:5; 21:4.
111. Prov 29:23.
112. Prov 3:34; 15:25, 33; 18:10; 22:4.
113. Prov 3:34.
114. In Proverbs, *'anaw* appears in 3:34 (*Qere*); 14:21; 16:19 (*Qere*); *'ani* appears in 3:34 (*Kethiv*); 15:15; 22:22; 30:14; 31:9, 20.

115. Prov 22:4.
116. Prov 15:33; the other example of 'anawah in Proverbs is in 18:12.
117. Prov 15:3.
118. Prov 8:13. "I" refers to personified "wisdom."
119. Prov 15:33a.
120. E. Otto (*Theologische Ethik des Alten Testaments* [Stuttgart: Kohlhammer, 1994], 162ff.) emphasizes the contrast whereby old wisdom is spoken of through an "inductive" method based on empirical observations, whereas the wisdom in the new era portrayed in Prov 1–9 is described "deductively" based on the principle of a fear of God. After the captivity "wisdom sets out not from experience, but from trust in YHWH, the God of Israel and the creator of the world" (trans. from Japanese by Judy Wakabayashi).
121. Prov 1:7 = Prov 9:10.
122. See also Qoh 12:13.
123. Prov 1:10ff.
124. Prov 9:11.
125. Ps 111:10.
126. Prov 21:4.
127. Prov 14:26–27.
128. Prov 16:2–3; a similar statement occurs in 21:2.
129. Prov 20:22.
130. Prov 11:8.
131. Prov 13:25; a similar expression occurs in 15:6.
132. Prov 8:35–36.
133. Prov 12:2.
134. Prov 24:11–12.
135. Prov 19:17.
136. Prov 24:16–18.
137. Prov 24:29.
138. Prov 13:21.
139. Prov 28:10.
140. Gen 2:9, 17; 3:5, 22; 6:5; 8:21; Deut 15:21; 17:1; etc.
141. Gen 44:34; 48:16; Jer 7:6; 25:7; 48:16; etc.
142. Gen 30:33; Deut 9:4, 5, 6; Isa 45:23; etc.
143. Isa 46:12, 13; 51:6; 54:14; Ps 24:5; 98:2; etc.
144. K. Koch, *Um das Prinzip der Vergeltung in Religion und Recht des Alten Testaments* (Darmstadt: Wissenschaftliche Buchgesellschaft, 1972), 160ff.
145. *Yad* and *leyad* can also be construed in the emphatic sense of "be assured," but along with the Japanese New Common Bible Translation, I understand this as "descendants for generations."
146. Prov 11:21; trans. from Japanese by Judy Wakabayashi.
147. Prov 25:26.
148. Prov 30:21–23.

CHAPTER 12

The Wisdom Literature (2): The Book of Job

1. The Theme and Structure of Job

THEME

"The book of Job is a work that takes readers through a state of 'resignation' and leads them to a site of rebellion against the 'God of the theologians.'"[1] In other words, its theme lies in going beyond "resignation" at the irrational reality that the just sometimes suffer to air frank doubts about what on earth the "God of the theologians" is up to, since by rights he should praise the just and punish the sinner. In terms of the Wisdom Literature's key words that we ascertained in the previous chapter, the theme of the book of Job lies in confronting the reality that "retribution ethics" is not operating and in questioning God's responsibility for this.

STRUCTURE

The book of Job consists of forty-two chapters, framed at the beginning (chs. 1–2) and end (42:7–17) by a folk narrative in old prose. Between this, Job's lament (three chapters) is placed in dramatic prose, and a dispute with his friends Eliphaz, Bildad, and Zophar is described in three places (chs. 4–14, 15–21, and 22–27). Finally, a hymn to wisdom (ch. 28) and Job's last long speech (chs. 29–31) are related, but the poetic section can be regarded as climaxing with Elihu's speech (chs. 32–37), God's answer from out of a whirlwind on two occasions (38:1–40:2 and 40:7–41:26), and Job's brief replies (40:4–5 and 42:2–6).

JOB IN THE FRAME NARRATIVE

The frame narrative first speaks of how, with God's permission, Satan completely destroys the just man Job's wealth, health, and children in order to test whether he *"fear[s] [yare']* God for nothing."[2] Yet even when told that all his children have suddenly died, Job simply says,

> Naked I came from my mother's womb, and naked shall I return there; the LORD gave, and the LORD has taken away; blessed be the name of the LORD.[3]

And even when his wife sees his whole body covered in sores and tells him to curse God and die, the Job of the frame narrative remains composed and obedient to God to the end, saying:

> Shall we receive the good at the hand of God, and not receive the bad?[4]

HIS FRIENDS' CRITICISMS

In the dispute discourses, however, a completely different and defiant Job appears, becoming angry, beating his chest, and challenging God. What triggers this defiance is the criticism levied at him by his three friends on the basis of a steadfast and deep-rooted "retribution ethics." They believe that Job must be undergoing such great suffering because he has committed sins that deserve this, so they urge him to repent. For instance, Eliphaz says,

> Think now, who that was innocent ever perished?
>   Or where were the upright cut off?
> As I have seen, those who plow iniquity
>   and sow trouble reap the same.[5]

Bildad also admonishes Job:

> Does God pervert justice?
>   Or does the Almighty pervert the right?
> If your children sinned against him,
>   he delivered them into the power of their transgression.
> If you will seek God
>   and make supplication to the Almighty,

if you are pure and upright,
    surely then he will rouse himself for you
    and restore to you your rightful place.⁶

JOB'S REBUTTAL

Job replies that although he would not claim to be entirely free of sin,⁷ he
cannot believe he deserves such great suffering. To his friends he pleads:

O that my vexation were weighed,
    and all my calamity laid in the balances!
For then it would be heavier than the sand of the sea;
    therefore my words have been rash. . . .
Teach me, and I will be silent;
    make me understand how I have gone wrong. . . .
Turn now, my vindication is at stake.⁸

And to God, Job appeals:

If I sin, what do I do to you, you watcher of humanity?
    Why have you made me your target?
    Why have I become a burden to you?
Why do you not pardon my transgression
    and take away my iniquity?
For now I shall lie in the earth;
    you will seek me, but I shall not be.⁹

Gradually Job's appeals to God become increasingly censorious:

I will say to God, Do not condemn me;
    let me know why you contend against me.
Does it seem good to you to oppress,
    to despise the work of your hands
    and favor the schemes of the wicked?¹⁰

Or

How many are my iniquities and my sins?
    Make me know my transgression and my sin.
Why do you hide your face,
    And count me as your enemy?¹¹

Finally he challenges God defiantly, saying:

> O that I had one to hear me!
> (Here is my signature! Let the Almighty answer me!)
> O, that I had the indictment written by my adversary!
> Surely I would carry it on my shoulder;
>   I would bind it on me like a crown;
> I would give him an account of all my steps;
>   like a prince I would approach him.[12]

If we construe the "adversary" in the final passage and the two occurrences of "him" as referring to Job's friends who started the debate, it would mean that Job is maintaining his innocence here in the face of his friends' ethical condemnations. Since, however, these words are in the singular and are unlikely to refer to several friends, and since it would be more natural for this to refer to "the Almighty" himself (in view of the fact that Job 40:2 contains a similar expression, "Anyone who argues with God"), this passage could be read as Job provoking the arrogant God who is "Almighty"—an exceptional provocation for the Hebrews. In that case, wearing the "indictment . . . on my shoulder" can be construed as conforming with the custom whereby innocence is proven if one's body remains unharmed despite ordeals. This seems to highlight how Job argues with God, believing he is right even if denounced by God. Job persists in the hope[13] that when "the Almighty answer[s] me" his unjust suffering will be redeemed, but he becomes impatient with the "Almighty" who never "answer[s]," and in this final plea Job reaches the point of irreverently challenging the hidden Almighty.[14]

2. Kierkegaard's Interpretation

PRAISE FOR JOB

One thinker who shows infinite sympathy for Job's attitude is Søren Kierkegaard. In his enigmatic work *Gjentagelsen* (*Repetition*), into which Kierkegaard poured his hopes for winning back his fiancée, Regina, after he had broken off their engagement, he excitedly states that "here he thinks he has found what he sought, and in this little circle of Job and the wife along with three friends the truth . . . seems more glorious and joyful and true than in a Greek symposium."[15] Kierkegaard says, "Every word of his is food and clothing and medicine for my ailing soul"; "In the whole Old Testament there is no figure one approaches with so much confidence and frank-heartedness and trustfulness as Job."[16] The reason is that "everything about him is so human."[17] Why is it "human"? Is it because Job humbly and calmly says "the LORD gave, and the LORD has taken away; blessed be the name of the LORD"?[18] In fact, the opposite is true, writes Kierkegaard. Job utters these words "at the beginning and did not repeat [them] later. But Job's significance is that the border conflicts incident to faith are fought out in him, and that the prodigious insurrection of the wild and bellicose powers of passion are here set forth."[19]

THEOPHANY

"Job represents as it were the whole weighty pleas presented on man's behalf in the great suit between God and man, the prolix and dreadful process of justice which had its ground in the fact that Satan raised a suspicion against Job, and which ends with the explanation that the whole thing is a trial of probation."[20] Kierkegaard observes, "This category, 'trial of probation,' is neither aesthetic, nor ethical, nor dogmatic, it is entirely transcendent."[21] Kierkegaard is of the view that this "transcendent" category "places man in a purely personal relationship of contradiction to God," and it is expressed effectively and symbolically by the "whirlwind" in Job 38 onward. Rather than the appearance of God out of the "whirlwind" and rather than the actual "repetition" whereby Job's possessions are subsequently restored twofold over what they had been before,[22] Kierkegaard fervently desires the coming of this "transcendental" "whirlwind."[23]

"How much good a thunderstorm does after all! . . . Ordinarily a man is so likely to harden himself against reproof; when God passes judgment a man loses himself and forgets the pain in the love which is intent upon educating."[24] The whirlwind will "make me capable of being a husband. That will crush my whole personality—I am ready for it. It will make me unrecognizable in my own eyes."[25] Kierkegaard, who could thus hardly wait for the "whirlwind," subsequently abandoned the later part on learning that Regina had become engaged to someone else, thereby ending these manuscripts rather abruptly.

In either case, this presents a classic reading of the book of Job—along lines that find the solution to everything in God's appearance from amid the whirlwind in chapter 38 onward. According to this view, Job's

sufferings are ultimately not an ethical punishment, but a religious "ordeal" for the purpose of reaching this point.

Yet is it really acceptable to suspend ethical judgments in religion?
(This is also the theme of another work written by Kierkegaard around
the same time, *Frygt og Boeven* [*Fear and Trembling*].) Does God's appearance out of the whirlwind described in Job 38 and following truly
contain a reality that will resolve everything? Perhaps the straight question posed below by C. G. Jung,[26] who instead emphasizes ethicality, has
a more persuasive ring for those with these lingering doubts.

3. Jung's Interpretation

JOB'S CRITICISM OF GOD

Jung takes the view that the "amoral" "darkness"[27] of God is portrayed
in the book of Job. "He 'multiplies my wounds without cause.'"[28] This
God of "savagery"[29] "does not care a rap for any moral opinion and does
not recognize any form of ethics as binding."[30] "[H]e, who watched so
jealously over the fulfillment of laws and contracts," had little trouble in
breaking his own vow to "not violate my covenant."[31] "Modern man,
with his sensitive conscience, would have felt the black abyss opening
and the ground giving way under his feet, for the least he expects of his
God is that he should be superior to mortal man in the sense of being
better, higher, nobler—but not his superior in . . . moral flexibility."[32]
By contrast, "the greatest thing about Job" is probably that he "clearly
sees" the following fact: he clearly recognizes that YHWH is both "evil"
and "good," "both a persecutor and a helper in one," and "Yahweh is
not split, but is an *antimony*—a totality of inner opposites—and this is
the indispensable condition for his tremendous dynamism, his omniscience and omnipotence."[33] Accordingly, Job's response to the appearance of YHWH from out of the whirlwind is as follows:

> See, I am of small account; what shall I answer you?
> I lay my hand on my mouth.
> I have spoken once, and I will not answer;
> twice, but will proceed no further.[34]

Interpreting this utterance by Job, Jung states: "In spite of his pitiable
littleness and feebleness, this man knows that he is confronted with a

superhuman being who is personally most easily provoked. He also knows that it is far better to withhold all moral reflections, to say nothing of certain moral requirements which might be expected to apply to a god."[35]

YHWH'S VIOLENT NATURE

So why does YHWH visit such "savagery" on Job and cause him such "wounds" in the first place? Jung conjectures that YHWH is hurt extremely easily and is highly suspicious, so when egged on by Satan he doubts "Job's faithfulness" "amazing[ly] . . . easily."[36] For no reason, YHWH puts Job through a meaningless moral ordeal that involves acts of "robbery, murder, bodily injury with premeditation, and denial of a fair trial," with the result that God "flagrantly violates at least three"[37] of the prohibitions that he laid down in the Ten Commandments.

In any case, Jung's view is that at the end of this ordeal, from out of the whirlwind YHWH "thunders reproaches at the half-crushed human worm (Job 38:2): 'Who is this that darkens counsel by words without insight?' In view of the subsequent words of Yahweh, one must really ask oneself: *Who* is darkening *what* counsel?"[38] "The answer to Yahweh's conundrum is therefore: it is Yahweh himself who darkens his own counsel and who has no insight. He turns the tables on Job and blames him for what he himself does." This is despite the fact that "for seventy-one verses he proclaims his world-creating power to his miserable victim . . . [and] Job has absolutely no need of being impressed by further exhibitions of this power."[39] And despite the fact that "he pays . . . little attention to Job's real situation, . . . one cannot help but see how much he is occupied with himself. The tremendous emphasis he lays on his omnipotence and greatness makes no sense in relation to Job, who certainly needs no more convincing."[40] Jung continues on in this vein, soundly berating YHWH.

EVALUATION OF JUNG'S ANALYSIS

In this analysis, Jung's awareness of the difference between the being called God and the God who is a complete mental fabrication on the part of the writer of the book of Job seems somewhat confused.[41] Insofar as Jung fails to question this writer's intentions, instead hurling abuse at God himself, it is understandable why Christian circles have criticized

Jung's book as blasphemous or ignored it as nonscholarly. Nevertheless, we cannot overlook Jung's achievement in having candidly suggested that God's response in Job 38 presents no answer at all in ethical terms.

4. Retribution Ethics in the Book of Job

THE DOGMA OF RETRIBUTION

In fact, we might suggest that the question of retribution ethics remains unresolved in the book of Job. Job's friends are constrained throughout by the dogma of retribution, whereby good people should receive good rewards and bad people bad rewards, and they denounced this without examining Job's reality. Yet as far as remaining constrained by the dogma of retribution is concerned, Job himself, who continues to rebuke God without making any attempt to realize that God transcends this dogma, has not moved a step beyond this. This is because Job argues to God, who has not rewarded him appropriately for his goodness, that "You have done wrong."[42] As long as people remain bound by this concept of God from a human perspective, they will be unable to accept the reality of a God who transcends this concept. Instead, protesting one's righteousness merely results in a vicious circle whereby one becomes more and more distant from God in his true light. It seems that what brought greater suffering on Job than the disasters that befell him was the chaotic darkness in which he had lost sight of God in this fashion (particularly ch. 26 onward). In that case, God's appearance from amid what Kierkegaard describes as a "transcendental" "whirlwind" has to be something that would interrupt this vicious circle—something not at the level of self-justification of God in relation to retribution, but something that would force a focus on the essence of matters completely transcending this. That is why God starts to speak about the beginning of time when the earth was created:

> Where were you when I laid the foundation of the earth?
> Tell me, if you have understanding.
> Who determined its measurements—surely you know!
> Or who stretched the line upon it?[43]

Human beings cannot, on the basis of a human-centered eudaemonism, force on God laws that are ideal in the world of humans. The writer of the book of Job does not view God as an ideal fabrication that suits humans. Instead, he believes that the disclosure, that is, self-revelation, of God as being beyond such human ideas and as the transcendental source that gives humans life should consist of a remembering of creation.

THE CONCLUSION TO THE BOOK OF JOB

At this point the answer to Satan's question "Does Job fear God for nothing?"[44] also becomes apparent. People usually feel that they encounter the God of love and justice in the reward of happiness. Yet on experiencing calamities to a degree they feel unjustified, they either encounter a God contrary to the usual concept of God or they fall into a state whereby they lose sight of the God of love and justice. Passing by God represents the greatest suffering for a religious person, so this is even more difficult to endure than actual calamities. Satan's petty suspicion that the reason people "fear God" lies in the "reward"[45] of being able to keep their "house and all that" they have[46] and their "bone and . . . flesh"[47] is by no means accurate, but even for such a highly religious person as Job, there is after all a certain reason for "fear[ing] God." This refers to the self-serving circumstances of his persistent desire to encounter God. The conclusion of the book of Job as a whole is that beyond the despair and agony of having his happiness destroyed, having his commonsensical concept of a God of retribution shattered, and losing sight of God, instead Job truly experiences an encounter with the real God (ch. 38 onward). Hence he confesses that

> Therefore I have uttered what I did not understand,
> > things too wonderful for me, which I did not know. . . .
> I had heard of you by the hearing of the ear,
> > but now my eye sees you;
> therefore I despise myself,
> > and repent in dust and ashes.[48]

This passage too speaks of the "wonder" (*pele'*) at something transcendental that lies at the basis of Greek and Hebrew ethics. The word translated as "things too wonderful" (*nifla'ot*; Niphal participle) is a denominative verbal form of *pele'* and refers to the wondrous workings of God that transcend human understanding.[49] The earlier interpretation by Jung—which regards even this as a self-protective pose on the part of Job, who has realized that "entertaining critical thoughts" toward this irrational God is taboo—reads too much into this. For a start, there are no direct textual grounds for Jung's overinterpretation that YHWH allows these calamities to befall Job because of YHWH's suspicious mind. Instead, the straightforward interpretation would be that God allows these calamities as an "ordeal"[50] aimed at upsetting the idealistic view of God into which even Job has fallen. Elihu's argument from chapter 32 to chapter 37, which sets forth the edifying significance of suffering, does in that sense correctly suggest the direction of a solution to the matter and is appropriately placed here as an introduction to God's appearance in chapter 38 and following. (The fact that God's rebuke starting in 42:7 is restricted to Job's three friends can be viewed as testimony to the fact that the final redactor of the entire book of Job also approved of Elihu's speech, rather than as a result of the fact that the frame narrative is unaware of Elihu's existence.)

BEYOND RETRIBUTION ETHICS

Looked at in this light, to the author of the book of Job, God was the basis of an existence that goes beyond retribution ethics—a mysterious creator who, in a state beyond good and evil, barely manages to encounter people. In closing, however, it must be noted that in the long run this, too, is merely an understanding of God on the part of the author of the book of Job. The Old Testament explores various other concepts of God and other explanations of this mystery. In terms of ethical thought, further questions arise as to whether the ethical justice of such a God is really proven and whether the Old Testament bears witness to a God who appears not only beyond retribution ethics but also very much in this world. Our task in the final section, part III, lies in advancing our discussion by going back to square one in relation to this point and other issues.

Notes

1. H. W. Wolff, *Bibel: Das Alte Testament: eine Einführung in seine Schriften und in die Methoden ihrer Erforschung* (Stuttgart: Kreuz-Verlag, 1970), 151, trans. from Japanese by Judy Wakabayashi.
2. Job 1:9. In view of its relationship with the verb *hanan*, which means "to

bestow favor on" or "take pity on," the word *hinnam* can be restricted to meanings such as "without reward" or "without compensation" (e.g., Gen 29:15; Isa 52:3, 5), but interpreting it in the broader sense of "without reason" or "to no purpose" fits both the context here (see below) and general usage (e.g., Job 2:3; 9:17; 22:6; I Sam 19:5; 25:31; I Kgs 2:31; Ezek 6:10; 14:23).

3. Job 1:21.
4. Job 2:10.
5. Job 4:7–8.
6. Job 8:3–6.
7. See, for example, Job 7:20–21; 10:14; 19:4.
8. Job 6:2–3, 24, 29b.
9. Job 7:20–21.
10. Job 10:2–3.
11. Job 13:23–24.
12. Job 31:35–37.
13. Job 9:34–35; 13:3, 15, 21–22; 16:20–21.
14. For an interpretation of this passage, see my *Kyūyaku seisho no shisō: 24 no danshō* (The thought of the Old Testament: 24 fragments) (Tokyo: Iwanami Shoten, 1998), 180–81.
15. S. Kierkegaard (under the pseudonym Constantin Constantius), *Repetition: An Essay in Experimental Psychology* (*Gjentagelsen*), trans. Walter Lowrie (New York: Harper & Row, 1964), 90.
16. Kierkegaard, *Repetition*, 109.
17. Kierkegaard, *Repetition*, 109–10.
18. Job 1:21.
19. Kierkegaard, *Repetition*, 115.
20. Kierkegaard, *Repetition*, 115.
21. Kierkegaard, *Repetition*, 115.
22. Job 42:10.
23. Kierkegaard, *Repetition*, 117, 119.
24. Kierkegaard, *Repetition*, 117.
25. Kierkegaard, *Repetition*, 119.
26. C. G. Jung, *Answer to Job*, trans. R. F. C. Hull (New York: Meridian, 1960), trans. of *Antwort auf Hiob* (Zürich: Rascher, 1952).
27. Jung, *Answer to Job*, 22.
28. Jung, *Answer to Job*, 26.
29. Jung, *Answer to Job*, 22.
30. Jung, *Answer to Job*, 28.
31. Jung, *Answer to Job*, 30.
32. Jung, *Answer to Job*, 30–31.
33. Jung, *Answer to Job*, 28.
34. Job 40:4–5.
35. Jung, *Answer to Job*, 25–26.
36. Jung, *Answer to Job*, 37–38.
37. Jung, *Answer to Job*, 40. The last two of the four commandments listed by Jung are not part of the Ten Commandments, so this "three" should be "two."

38. Jung, *Answer to Job*, 42.
39. Jung, *Answer to Job*, 43.
40. Jung, *Answer to Job*, 43–44.
41. In his preface (particularly Jung, *Answer to Job*, 18–19), Jung himself distinguishes between the "image" of God and the "transcendental x to which it points," but he does not consistently maintain this distinction in his text. While mentioning both "the author of the Book of Job" (37) and "the poet of this drama" (54), Jung directly portrays throughout his whole book not just the YHWH of Job's day but also the transformations in YHWH himself, such as the YHWH of the Ps 89 period (31ff.) and the YHWH of Proverbs times (60ff.).
42. Job 36:23; Elihu's summary of Job's statement.
43. Job 38:4–5.
44. Job 1:9.
45. See n. 2 above.
46. Job 1:10.
47. Job 2:5.
48. Job 42:3, 5–6.
49. Exod 15:11; Ps 77:15; 119:129; etc.
50. The word *bahan* in Job 34:36 is the key word. See also Job 7:18; 12:11; 23:10; 34:3.

Part III

THE CONSEQUENCES OF HELLENIC AND HEBREW ETHICS

CHAPTER 13

Retribution Ethics in Hebrew Religion: Focusing on the Qohelet

1. Wonder and Retribution

WONDER

As pointed out in the introduction and in various places throughout this book, a major feature of ancient ethical thought was the richness of this idea of "wonder." Our final task in the closing three chapters and the conclusion will be to revisit "wonder" and reconsider its meaning. In chapters 13 and 14, I will follow up on the consequences of the ultimate destination of the "wonder" in Hebrew religious ethics.[1] Then, in chapter 15, I will use the Greek discourse on philosophical and universal reason as a means of reflecting on and gaining a fresh grasp of the matters to which these symbols of religious faith point. Bringing these two approaches together in the conclusion, I will turn to what these "origins of ethical thought" can teach us today.

QUESTIONS ABOUT THE GOD OF RETRIBUTION

For the Hebrews, the main object of "wonder" was God's work in history. In terms of the correlation with ethical issues, it was the work of the God of retribution, who rewarded ethical goodness with happiness and evil with calamities, that was the object of the "awe" displayed by the writer of Proverbs and that was sincerely acclaimed by the psalmist. Yet where in fact are God's works seen, and where can we verify the existence of such a God of retributive ethics? As if to put a damper on this enthusiasm for "wonder," such questions continued to be hinted at in the book of Job, for instance. These were questions on which the Hebrew people, who had experienced a history of hardship where the just suffered and sinners prospered, had continued to carp in the midst of their suffering. As we saw in chapters 3 and 4, Plato also pointedly asked whether justness receives its due reward, although here the element of divine retribution retreats into the background. In general, this possibility of retribution has been widely questioned whenever ethical matters are considered, regardless of the place and time.

In contemporary Japan, which is not only atheistic but also economically affluent, this question might, however, seem remote. Yet is that really the case? In this chapter, I would like to keep the link to contemporary issues in mind and start out by noting that such questions and answers about retribution can be found here and there, in the pages of our newspapers, for instance. The following two examples are typical yet contrasting instances that testify to how such questions are by no means unconnected to our lives.

EXAMPLES FROM CONTEMPORARY JAPAN

In January 2001, an incident occurred at Shin-Ōkubo Station in Tokyo in which two men who tried to help a drunken man who had fallen down onto the railway tracks themselves ended up as victims, with all three being run over by a train and killed. In the ensuing media reports, some weekly magazines lauded the courage of the two men who acted on the spur of the moment in an attempt to save a total stranger. The media also criticized the unethical behavior of a fourth man who had been drinking with the first man on the platform and who had him go and buy alcohol several times, yet made no attempt to help when he fell onto the tracks. I am unaware of the exact details of what happened, but this was reported in terms of the irony of fate, whereby just men seemingly died in vain, and it was discussed in connection with the question of whether any God or Buddha exists. We frequently see such ironies in our lives.[2] The majority of Japanese today seem to share a vague feeling that a God who rewards ethical behavior obviously does not exist.

There are, however, some who disagree, as illustrated by an article by Hidekazu Yoshida, a leading music critic, written after the first anniversary of the sarin poisoning on the Tokyo subway.

> The other day I saw a repeat on TV of the first-anniversary memorial for those employees who died in the course of their duties during the sarin gas incident. This was a true tragedy. These people lost their own lives saving many others. . . . They are remarkable people.

Easily moved to tears as I get older, I found it difficult to keep watching, so I switched the TV off. Afterward I wondered if these people's souls go to paradise. I hope they do, but I also heard a voice inside me saying, "Do you really believe that?"

If all that were a fabrication, how would the loss of these lives be compensated for? Uncertain how to answer this question, I reiterate my respect for these people whose actions prevented an even greater tragedy.[3]

In the midst of such "uncertain[ty]," one sometimes hears this idea that if one is not rewarded in this world one must surely be rewarded by God in heaven. I believe that quite a few Japanese think along these lines, not just this critic above.

These two typical examples suffice to show that the question of whether an ethical God of retribution exists is by no means completely remote from us today. When confronted with this question, are we not often torn between an affirmative and a negative reply?

KANT'S ANTIMONY AND ITS VALIDITY

In the history of Western ethical thought, it was Kant who discussed this aporia between positive and negative responses as an antimony of practical reason relating to the correspondence between virtue and happiness. In his "Dialectic of Pure Practical Reason" in *Kritik der praktischen Vernunft* (*The Critique of Practical Reason*), Kant argues with equal authority both the thesis that morality and happiness are interrelated (i.e., ethical behavior will be rewarded) and the thesis that there is no such connection (i.e., ethical behavior is not rewarded). Kant finds the reason for this in the distinction between the material world and the world of the intellect, and on that basis he proposes the immortality of the soul and the existence of God as practical requirements.[4] This is a classic argument in the history of ethical thought questioning retribution ethics, but we will not explore this further here. It should be noted, however, that in view of the point of departure of Kantian ethics—which, for the sake of moral autonomy, did away with material motives dependent on eudaemonism and argued that the grounds for determination of the will should be questioned solely from a formal perspective—Kant is being inconsistent here by smuggling in the concept of happiness. Even setting aside the validity of Tetsurō Watsuji's criticism to the effect that demanding such a God of retribution is "Kant's concession to the times" and that he should instead have "detected God in the depths of . . . his essential self" as the spontaneity of reason,[5] we must regard Kant as guilty of inconsistency. In any case, the fact that this aporia must relate to the question of the soul's immortality and the existence of God is already naturally foreshadowed here.

THIS APORIA AMONG THE HEBREWS

In the history of ethical thought, Hebrew thought was the first and probably the greatest (albeit a diachronic) example that explored this aporia to its lengths. Partly as a review of our discussion up to chapter 12, let us examine several related passages.

For example, the psalmist believed the proposition that ethical behavior is rewarded, as expressed in the following:

> For the LORD loves justice;
>   he will not forsake his faithful ones.
> The righteous shall be kept safe forever,
>   but the children of the wicked shall be cut off forever.[6]

The writer of Proverbs also regarded as self-evident the premise that

> The LORD does not let the righteous go hungry,
>   but he thwarts the craving of the wicked.[7]

With regard to the law of retribution, whereby a good cause has a good result and a bad cause a bad result, traditional wisdom argued that God is just, so he must be ruling this world.

In later times, however, doubts were cast on this belief, arising from an awareness of the cold reality that this law does not work in practice. In the Hellenistic period, the nihilist Qohelet formulated this doubt as follows:

> There is a vanity that takes place on earth, that there are righteous people who are treated according to the conduct of the wicked, and there are wicked people who are treated according to the conduct of the righteous. I said that this also is vanity.[8]

In this way, the Hebrew people were likewise torn between a positive and negative response when faced with this same question of whether an ethical God of retribution does in fact exist. So on what grounds did the Hebrews argue for these antithetical propositions? Next I would like to touch on the arguments on which these two propositions are based.

THE HEBREWS' THESIS

First, various actual examples demonstrate the grounds for the thesis that ethical behavior is rewarded, both in the case of individuals and communities. The people of Sodom, who gave themselves over to homosexuality (hence the origin of the term *sodomy*) and dissipation, were destroyed by burning sulfur, along with their town. By contrast, Lot, who sought to sacrifice his own daughters to protect the messengers of God from the men of Sodom, escaped this disaster together with his family.[9] Abimelech, who became king by murdering seventy of his brothers, paid the penalty by being killed when a woman dropped a millstone on his head and cracked his skull.[10] By contrast, Hezekiah was known as a particularly pious king even among the long line of kings,[11] and it is said that he "had very great riches and honor."[12] As we saw also in chapter 11, this principle of retribution was regarded as all too self-evident. Thus, in Hebrew the word *ra'*, meaning ethical "evil," also signifies the "calamities" resulting from this; *tsedaqah*, which refers to "justice," also indicates the resulting "happiness"; and *'awon*, which expresses "sin," also implies the "calamities" that are its price. Moreover, divine retributive will was embodied in the law, and compensation and punishment were demanded for wrongful acts. "[Y]ou shall give life for life, eye for eye, tooth for tooth."[13] In this way, retributive justice for moral behavior was also guaranteed by law.

Naturally, it is also possible for the just to perish, but this is explained in terms of the principle of collective responsibility, whereby these people are stained by the sins of their fellow creatures[14] and must bear the sins of their ancestors.[15] Since they are stained by the wrongs of others and are themselves not perfectly righteous, it is conceivable for them to perish. This is the main thrust of this thesis.

THE HEBREWS' ANTITHESIS

What, then, are the grounds for the antithesis? Psalms and Proverbs, which were quoted earlier, belong to what is known as Wisdom Literature, but they originate in the happy days before captivity, when the Hebrews had not yet experienced a crisis of wisdom. In those days Israel consisted of multiple groups that were on an equal footing. In ethnosociological terms, it was a segmented (*segmentär*) society. Furthermore, the principle of collective responsibility was still in operation. After the period of captivity, however, when huge empires such as Babylonia centralized the economy, this segmented social structure collapsed, and a situation arose where unjust people who turned their backs on YHWH and adopted the religious ethics of the heathen nations slipped through the meshes of the law and prospered economically, while those who did not do so were brought to ruin. This cannot be explained by the principle of collective responsibility. In fact, it runs counter to simple laws of retribution based on this principle. This jeopardized the ancient wisdom that spoke of retributive lessons of life. The person who faced up to this reality and proclaimed that the law of retribution was a pack of lies was the above-mentioned hero of later Wisdom Literature, Qohelet. Going against tradition, he argued that ethical behavior is not in fact rewarded. And when pointing out the "vanity" resulting from the breakdown of retributive justice, Qohelet took the view that the original source of this "vanity" was the God who carries out such "retribution." It is vain because "God will judge the righteous and the wicked,"[16] and "they cannot find out what God has done"[17]—in other words, God is unreasonable.

Some might still cavil at this, arguing that if there is no retribution in this world, then in the next world the just will ascend to heaven and sinners will plunge to hell, so that retribution will make sense. Yet Qohelet's cool-headed view is that such arguments premised on the soul's immortality are in the final analysis mere wishful thinking.

> For the fate of humans and the fate of animals is the same. . . .
> For all is vanity, . . . all are from the dust, and all turn to dust
> again.[18]

In this way, Qohelet also resignedly rejects how people imagine a hereafter and gloss over the vanity of the breakdown of retribution in this world. He maintains that ethical behavior is rewarded neither here nor elsewhere.

2. Qohelet and Nietzsche

CONTRAST WITH NIETZSCHE'S NIHILISM

Qohelet's attitude brings to mind Nietzsche's essentialist argument, and a focus on their similarities is inevitable. Nietzsche's understanding of nihilism chopped and changed, but a passage thought to have been written in his mature years (from the fall of 1887 to the spring of 1888), immediately before he became mentally deranged, reads as follows:

> *Nihilism as a psychological state* will have to enter on the scene, *first*, when we have sought a "meaning" in all events that is not in them: so that the seeker eventually becomes discouraged. . . . Nihilism as a psychological state arises, *secondly*, when one has posited a *totality* . . . in all occurrences . . . so that a soul that craves to adore and revere wallows in the general notion of some supreme form of domination and governance. . . . Nihilism as a psychological state has yet a *third* . . . form . . . to invent a world that would lie beyond it, as the *true* world. But, as soon as man finds out how that world is fabricated, solely out of psychological needs . . . the final form of nihilism emerges.[19]

This passage is given much weight by people such as Heidegger,[20] who regard it as the *terminus ad quem* of Nietzsche's understanding of nihilism. Let us take a look at this, referring back to Heidegger's commentary. The first form of nihilism, "meaning," is also rephrased by Nietzsche himself as "purpose," and as examples of this Heidegger cites overarching goals such as "eternal peace" and the "greatest good of the greatest number." Heidegger explains the second form, "totality," as "unification . . . of all things into one." It was Nietzsche's insight that even if there is no purpose that gives meaning to life in this world and no unity that imparts order to the world, what is left in the end as an "escape" is the "fabrication" of the concept of "a world that would lie beyond it, as the *true* world," that is, "eternal bliss beyond" (Heidegger). Yet when people recognize that in the long run this, too, is no more than an "illusion," they become immersed in the feeling that everything is without value, and in this way nihilism finally emerges.

Qohelet obviously meets the second condition with his declaration that divine retribution does not function anywhere. His denial of the existence of a hereafter meets the third condition. And when he reaches the conclusion "vanity of vanities! All is vanity,"[21] he also fulfills the first condition, because "vanity" means that "there was nothing to be gained,"[22] which is tantamount to a perception[23] that, broadly speaking, there exists no "purpose" to be achieved. In my view, this leads to the conclusion that Qohelet was thus a nihilist in the full sense of the word.

WAS QOHELET A NIHILIST?

This question might seem problematical to some, on the grounds that nihilism is a diachronic artifact of modern European anthropocentrism and it is wrong to generalize this concept synchronically. This seems to be the main reason that Old Testament scholars have not, to the best of my knowledge, regarded Qohelet as a nihilist in the past, even if they described him as a pessimist or a skeptic.

Diachronically speaking, no doubt, nihilism was first discovered in the consciousness of Nietzsche.[24] We should, however, note the following observation by Heidegger: "by nihilism we do not mean something merely present or, indeed, 'contemporary' to Nietzsche's time. The name *nihilism* points to a historical movement that extends far behind us and reaches forward far beyond us."[25] In other words, "Since it is deeply rooted synchronically in history . . . it has been brilliantly disclosed diachronically in these modern times that have endorsed anthropocentrism."[26] In that case, boldly defining Qohelet's thought in ancient times as nihilism and using an analogy with the nihilism that modern-day philosophy has consciously reflected on and come to terms with, so as to understand how Qohelet speaks in the midst of confused trial and error, is a privilege available to contemporary commentators precisely because they have experienced nihilism so keenly. If failure to do that means that we would wander into the same maze of unawareness as the ancient text, then this could in fact be regarded as an obligation on the part of contemporary commentators.[27]

In any case, the issue that I would like to take up here is the underlying perception among nihilists that "God is dead." As readers are no doubt aware, it was Nietzsche who declared that "God is dead. . . . We have killed him,"[28] and it was Heidegger who interpreted Nietzsche's words as meaning that the subjectivist metaphysics ever since Descartes had led to the demise of the whole of European metaphysics, including Christianity.[29] If we follow this line of thought, it seems we could also say that Qohelet likewise announced the death of the traditional God and was of the opinion that what killed him was the idea of retribution ethics. So did Qohelet generally deny the existence of God? No. He did deny the existence of the traditional God of retribution, but I believe we can say that Qohelet himself was searching for a new God to replace this. So what kind of new God did he discover?

3. Qohelet's Overcoming of Nihilism

ENCOUNTER WITH THE HIDDEN GOD

The following passage is worthy of note:

> I know that there is nothing better for them than to be happy
> and enjoy themselves as long as they live; moreover, it is God's

gift that all should eat and drink and take pleasure in all their toil. . . . God has done this.[30]

Qohelet managed to encounter the hidden God in these small pleasures in life. It seems that the conclusion reached in the whole of the Qohelet—repeated in variations in 3:22, 5:18, 8:15, and 9:7—is that it is only in such pleasures that the emptiness of life is clearly filled, albeit only slightly.

THE REDUCTION OF SUBSUMING PURPOSES TO NOTHING

But what is happening here? Qohelet rejected both meaning in life and order in the world, and in the end he also rejected the idea of salvation in the next world. He also denied the existence of the traditional God of retribution who guaranteed these. This was Qohelet's nihilistic perception that there are no all-subsuming values. Yet he became aware that even though there is no such subsuming value, this sense of emptiness is overcome whenever we love a relative value such as food, drink, or work. Naturally, if we return to the question of ultimate purpose, saying, "What use is it?"[31] then life is still meaningless, because in the ultimate analysis it entails no "gain" whatsoever. Yet was it not this very way of thinking—whereby everything was viewed in the light of such an ultimate purpose and subsumed into a series of teleological means to that end—that was the culprit that gave rise to nihilism? As long as we remain shackled by such thinking we cannot encounter what juts out from this series of teleological means, and since that purpose is in the long run something that the person has himself established, he will be unable to transcend egoism and encounter others. As Seiichi Yagi points out in his perceptive analysis in relation to Jesus, in the case of the New Testament it was perhaps this very feeling of emptiness from having reached an impasse—the feeling of a drying up of life, whereby one is alienated from the relationships one should by rights have with others—that constituted meaninglessness itself.[32] In fact, Qohelet never did experience an encounter with others.

EGOISM

Again I saw all the oppressions that are practiced under the sun. Look, the tears of the oppressed—with no one to comfort

> them! . . . And I thought the dead, who have already died,
> more fortunate than the living, who are still alive. . . . This also
> is vanity and a chasing after wind.[33]

This passage unintentionally reveals an intellectual who is merely toying with the paradox that one is better off dead, sheltering behind the nihilistic understanding that everything is meaningless when viewed in the light of an ultimate purpose. He ends up merely standing idly by without raising a hand to help the oppressed. Crüsemann,[34] who takes the view that here Qohelet was speaking cynically of the impossibility of changing the present state of affairs and that he was trying to preserve the privileges of the upper classes to which he himself belonged, also points out Qohelet's jealousy of later generations:

> I hated all my toil in which I had toiled under the sun, seeing
> that I must leave it to those who come after me. . . . This also
> is vanity.[35]

As Yagi has indicated, such jealousy is nothing but the "distress" of an egoist for whom it is no longer possible to "be conceited" about the "fulfillment and perfection of the ego."[36] Apart from this jealousy, Qohelet evinces no interest in later generations, including his own children.[37] Parents and neighbors do not even rate a mention, and on the whole, women are merely an object of scorn.[38] It seems that even when Qohelet did express an interest in others, in the long run he was unable to see beyond the egotistical viewpoint of whether or not something was to his own personal gain. For instance, he says, "Two are better than one,"[39] but the reason is that this is more beneficial, "For if they fall, one will lift up the other. . . . Again, if two lie together, they keep warm."[40] Hence we are perhaps forced to conclude that the God discovered by Qohelet after having rejected the God of retribution was merely a God whom Qohelet barely managed to sense in his own egotistical pleasures, a God who excluded others.

EVALUATION OF QOHELET

It does indeed seem that Qohelet cool-headedly faces up to the reality that the law of retribution had broken down and that he discovers a way of overcoming the nihilism originating in egoism, through a change in thinking whereby he negates the egotistical ultimate purpose. Here lies his momentous significance in the history of Hebrew thought. Nevertheless, such a change in thinking should involve ceasing to defend his own egoism whereby, sheltering behind the view that everything is meaningless in terms of subsuming values, he arrogantly declares that it is therefore also meaningless to work on behalf of others. Qohelet should also rise above turning everything into a series of teleological means under the subsuming value of his own self and protecting himself behind the barriers of egoism. Instead, he should encounter others as they are, unable to be controlled through his values, and he should be filled with a desire to coexist dynamically with others. On this point, however, we must note Qohelet's inconsistency. Right up to the end he is unable to escape his egoism, and the only way he knows to deal with other people is to exclude them or reduce everything to a question of his own gain. In this respect, unfortunately, we must recognize that Qohelet has decisive limits.

FEAR

The Qohelet concludes with the following passage, which, as various commentators have recognized,[41] is thought to be the words of the redactor, who has returned to the traditional view of God:

> Fear [*yare'*] God, and keep his commandments [*mitswot*]; for that is the whole duty of everyone. For God will bring every deed into judgment, including every secret thing, whether good or evil.[42]

Unfortunately, this redactor has failed to grasp Qohelet's true intent. Or perhaps the radical issues raised by Qohelet were too much for him, so he is trying to return to the traditional dogma and smooth things over. Yet Qohelet himself continues clinging to the sole fact that "God" is an irrational being who supposedly "bring[s] every deed into judgment," "whether good or evil," so he is not worthy of true "fear," which leads to "vanity." When claiming that the work of divine retribution in history is an object of "wonder," how are we to explain realities that escape such retribution? Rather than severing reality from the dogma of retribution, as did Job's three friends, we need to persist in honestly keeping reality in view and from there assess the validity of this dogma. Instead of simply accepting traditional faith, I have deliberately adopted a perspective that encompasses contemporary nihilism and, along with Qohelet, have questioned this faith. Nevertheless, in view of Qohelet's response and limitations as described above, we must now move on from Qohelet and direct our questions toward other Hebrew texts. These questions boil down to the issue of where can a new God be found, one who candidly admits the breakdown of retribution in reality and who can elucidate the meaning of this and also include relations with others in his perspective. Following up on this point is our task in the next chapter, which brings to a close the chapters discussing Hebraism.

Notes

1. For a more detailed discussion, see my article "Ōhō no kami wa sonzai suru ka—Shokuzai shisō no keifu to sōten" (Does a God of retribution exist? The genealogy and points of dispute in redemption thought), *Seishogaku ronshū* (Annual of the Japanese Biblical Institute) 31 (1998): 5–39. See also my *Kyūyaku seisho no shisō: 24 no danshō* (The thought of the Old Testament: 24 fragments) (Tokyo: Iwanami Shoten, 1998), 33–41.

2. For a discussion of a similar tone in media reports about the tragic collapse of Toyohama Tunnel in Hokkaidō in February 1996, see, for example, Sekine, *Kyūyaku seisho no shisō* (Thought of the Old Testament), 33.

3. Hidekazu Yoshida, "Ongaku tenbō" (Musical perspective), *Asahi Shimbun*, April 18, 1996, evening edition.

4. I. Kant, *Kritik der praktischen Vernunft* (Riga: Hartknoch, 1788), part I, book 2.

5. Tetsurō Watsuji, *Kant: Jissen risei hihan* (Kant: Critique of practical reason), *Watsuji Tetsurō zenshū* (Watsuji's Collected Works), vol. 9 (Tokyo: Iwanami shoten, 1962), 293.

6. Ps 37:28.
7. Prov 10:3.
8. Qoh 8:14.
9. Gen 19.
10. Judg 9.
11. 2 Kgs 18:3–6.
12. 2 Chr 32:27.
13. Exod 21:23–24.
14. Isa 6:5.
15. Exod 20:5; Deut 5:9. However, see also Jer 31:29 and Ezek 18:2.
16. Qoh 3:17.
17. Qoh 3:11.
18. Qoh 3:19–20.
19. F. W. Nietzsche, *The Will to Power*, trans. Walter Kaufmann and R. J. Hollingdale (New York: Random House, 1967), originally published as *Der Wille zur Macht: Versuch einer Umwertung aller Werte*, Kröners Taschenausgabe, vol. 78 (Leipzig: Kröner, 1959), 12; also in F. W. Nietzsche, *Nietzsche-Werke: Kritische Gesamtausgabe* VIII, vol. 2, 11, ed. Von G. Colli and M. Montinari (Berlin: Walter de Gruyter, 1967).

20. M. Heidegger, *Nietzsche*, trans. Frank A. Capuzzi, 3rd ed. (San Francisco: Harper & Row, 1982), 24ff.; original German edition published as *Nietzsche* (Pfullingen: Neske, 1961).

21. Qoh 1:2.

22. Qoh 2:11.

23. Qoh 4:1–3.

24. Nietzsche, *Will to Power*, preface.

25. Heidegger, *Nietzsche* (1982), 57.

26. Keiichi Kashiwabara, "Gendai to nihirizumu" (Modern times and nihilism), in *Shin Iwanami Tetsugaku Kōza* (Shin Iwanami lectures on philosophy), vol. 13, ed. Shōzō Ōmori (Tokyo: Iwanami Shoten, 1986), 61.

27. For an attempt at understanding the whole of the Qohelet from such a perspective, refer to my book, *Transcendency and Symbols in the Old Testament: A Genealogy of the Hermeneutical Experiences,* trans. Judy Wakabayashi (BZAW 275; Berlin: Walter de Gruyter, 1999), 99ff., originally published as *Kyūyaku ni okeru chōetsu to shōchō: kaishakugaku-teki keiken no keifu* (Tokyo: University of Tokyo Press, 1996). Here I will restrict my discussion to the question of the death of God.

28. F. W. Nietzsche, *Die fröhliche Wissenschaft* (Chemnitz, Germany: Verlag von Ernst Schmeitzner; New York: E. Steige, 1882), fragment 125.

29. M. Heidegger, "Nietzsches Wort: Gott ist tot," in *Holzwege* (Frankfurt: Klostermann, 1950).

30. Qoh 3:12–14.

31. Qoh 2:2.

32. Seiichi Yagi, *Iesu to nihirizumu* (Jesus and nihilism) (Tokyo: Seidosha, 1979), particularly 9ff.

33. Qoh 4:1–4.

34. F. Crüsemann, "Die unveränderbare Welt," in *Der Gott der kleinen Leute: sozialgeschichtliche Bibelauslegungen,* Vol. 1, ed. W. Schottroff and W. Stegemann (Munich: Kaiser; Gelnhausen, Germany: Burckhardthaus, 1979).

35. Qoh 2:18–19.

36. Seiichi Yagi, *Iesu Kirisuto no tankyū* (Seeking Jesus Christ) (Tokyo: Sanpō, 1976), 22, 43.

37. Qoh 6:3.

38. Qoh 7:26ff.

39. Qoh 4:9.

40. Qoh 4:10–11.

41. A. Lauha, *Kohelet*, Biblischer Kommentar 19 (Neukirchen-Vluyn, Germany: Neukirchener Verlag, 1978) 221ff.; H. Ringgren and W. Zimmerli, *Sprüche/Prediger*, 3rd ed., Das Alte Testament Deutsch 16 (Göttingen: Vandenhoeck & Ruprecht, 1980), 244ff., etc.

42. Qoh 12:13–14.

CHAPTER 14

Hebrew Religious Ethics and Atonement Ideology: Focusing on the Prophets

In the previous chapter, we verified the innovative nature of Qohelet's thinking, which holds that the God who is the object of the "wonder" underpinning Hebrew ethical thought can be perceived beyond the reality of the breakdown of retribution, and we also ascertained the limitations of Qohelet's thought, which fails to move beyond egoism. The aim of the present chapter is to seek in other Hebrew texts a God of retribution who transcends even these limitations.

1. Isaiah's Heart-Hardening Prophecies

The precaptivity prophets spring to mind first. As a typical example of these prophets, here I would like to look at Isaiah, who was active in the eighth century BCE. When Isaiah received his call from God as a prophet, he was given a puzzling mission—to prophesy so that the people "may not . . . turn and be healed."[1] Usually one thinks of prophecies as aiming to turn people and heal them, but Isaiah's prophesying was charged with the opposite task. There have been various debates over how this paradox can be explained.

According to one theory, on learning that his prophecies had merely hardened the people's hearts, Isaiah retrospectively added this to the account of his calling, as if that had been his aim from the outset.[2] This would, however, mean that he had engaged in rather makeshift falsification, and this is simply too removed from Isaiah's stance of faithfully conveying the word of God without fear of what people might think, which is the premise on which his prophecies were based. Other scholars argue that in fact Isaiah intended all along to make the people hard-hearted through his judgment prophesies,[3] but the question then remains of whether all the salvation prophecies scattered throughout the book of Isaiah can be regarded as later additions. To state only my conclusion, I would interpret this as follows: in subjective terms, Isaiah prophesied in order to have the people repent and be saved by God, but in objective terms his prophecies resulted, in the long run, in hardening people's hearts and in judgment from God.[4] Why then did such a discrepancy arise between the subjective intention of Isaiah's prophecies and their objective outcome? There are various aspects involved here, and I believe this can be explained in different ways,[5] but here I would like to take up just one of these, namely, an explanation from the perspective of depth psychology.

A DEPTH-PSYCHOLOGICAL EXPLANATION

First, we need to ascertain the specific nature of Isaiah's prophesying. This could be summed up as censuring the people. As if resisting his mission of heart-hardening prophecies, Isaiah hoped that the people would "turn and be healed." To this end, he continued to condemn their sins so that they would become aware of them. He defined sin as, for example, social injustices such as ignoring the rights of the weak,[6] behaving violently,[7] a lack of faith whereby one tries to survive in foreign relations by appealing to the mercy of a mighty nation instead of relying on God,[8] or arrogance that ultimately ignores God.[9] Here exactly the opposite qualities to the humility and consideration for the weak that were regarded as ethical virtues in the Law and the Wisdom Literature, which we have already examined, are censured as vices or sins in relations with God. Isaiah wanted to expose these sins and make people aware of them. Yet the more he denounced the people's sins, the more they resisted the prophet and hardened their hearts. In this way, contrary to his intentions, the heart-hardening prophecies were fulfilled, and in the end it did not come about that the people turned and were healed. The findings of depth psychology seem to suggest an explanation for this.

According to C. G. Jung's *Antwort auf Hiob* (1952)[10] and Yasuo Yuasa,[11] who developed this thesis on the basis of his extensive knowledge of the entire history of Christianity, the prophet insisted throughout that the people were morally unjust. Yet their sins and most crimes in general occur as a result of the impotence of their consciousness, which is powerless to control the force of demands from the unconscious. But if, relying solely on the moral judgments of the consciousness, one attempts to suppress these impulses, as did the prophet, it is not unusual for this to actually amplify the forces of natural evil and to create even greater moral evil in the form of an explosion of the evil forces that had been suppressed and pent up. Moral admonitions have no effect on people in the grip of major forces of evil. The reasoning "This is a sin. Recognize that fact!" will not lead to the demise of these evil forces. The only way to tame and reform evil is not through such verdicts but through the power of patient love. This is the understanding of sin and its healing that was achieved through depth psychology.

Jung and Yuasa do not mention Isaiah explicitly, but I believe their views offer a convincing explanation of how his heart-hardening prophecies came about. In other words, if we suppose that sin consists of a surrender to forces from the unconscious, then it is difficult for the ego-consciousness to recognize that as sin on its part. Instead, the consciousness tends only to feel a victim of unconscious forces or a casualty of the social system or of a disadvantaged home or education, shifting the blame onto such causes. That is why the people did nothing but rebel against the prophet who condemned them as if they were wrongdoers, not victims, and who made the unreasonable demand that they repent, with the upshot that they became even more obdurate. This is how depth psychology would explain how Isaiah's heart-hardening prophecies came about.

GOD OF RIGHTEOUSNESS

With this righteous God of the prophet, people do not realize their sins in interpersonal relations, so it is also impossible to mend these relations. Hence in the long run there is no "turn[ing]" to such a God and "be[ing] healed." It is probably no exaggeration to say that except in special circumstances it is generally difficult for people to encounter the God of righteousness, and they lack the necessary strength. If in Hebrew thought it was not in the God of righteousness that people found a God who could truly act as an object of "wonder," then what about the God of love? What springs to mind here as an important example extolling encounters with such a God is David's psalm at the time of the Bathsheba incident.

2. Forgiveness of Sin in David

THE BATHSHEBA INCIDENT

Two extant texts depict David's involvement with Bathsheba: 2 Sam 11–12, the historical account of the incident, and Ps 51, which portrays David's feelings at the time.[12] These passages attest to one of the most abhorrent incidents in the Old Testament. This is the adultery and murder committed by King David, where he commits adultery with Bathsheba, the beautiful wife of his faithful commander, Uriah, and then, on realizing that his scheming to conceal this has been in vain, has Uriah killed in battle. The prophet Nathan subsequently conveys God's words of forgiveness to David, who has repented of his deeds. It is then that David's anguish begins in earnest. Psalm 51 is an unparalleled song in which he frankly confesses this shuddering anguish. There is no space here to examine each verse in detail, but it is essential to grasp the following three points.

THE ORIGINS OF THE CONFESSION OF SIN

First, we should note that this psalm belongs to the literary genre of confessions of sin. Paul Ricœur, whose discussion in *La symbolique du mal* includes this psalm as an example of such confessional texts (he adopts the same perspective as that seen above in depth psychology), regards crime as something that by its nature cannot be legitimized and cannot be confessed through reason.[13] The sense of guilt for having committed a wrong is merely a vague, blind feeling that is difficult to recognize rationally, and the whole experience is veiled in emotions of fear and unease. Yet once these emotions have been expressed overtly through the language of confession and this blocked state has been overcome, these emotions manage to be objectified in discourse, albeit in halting, symbolic language.

Just how, though, does confession occur in the first place? Ricœur's discussion needs to be supplemented by a consideration of this question. Psalm 51 seems to provide a clear answer: it is only when forgiveness for sin has been declared that confession is also possible. Even when Nathan related an allegory making insinuations about David,[14] David thought it had nothing to do with him.[15] This is how difficult it is for reason to recognize sin and how easy it is to tend to hide sin both from oneself and others. When Nathan conveyed God's forgiveness for his sins,[16] however, David realized that what he had been forgiven for was indeed a sin, and this realization gave him the courage to admit this and confess. In this way, David acquired for the first time the awareness that "my sin is ever before me."[17] Sin is quite difficult to recognize on its own, and if people are simply censured, they merely make countless excuses. As we saw with Isaiah's heart-hardening prophecies, this is the way of normal, weak humans. Yet when absolution, not censure, is spoken of, people realize that sin was not an isolated concept but was linked to forgiveness. In other words, it is not until sin has been forgiven that one becomes aware of it. This seems to be one point raised by this psalm.

INTERPRETATION AS A FUSION OF HORIZONS

It was H. G. Gadamer[18] who made the insightful observation that the traditional view on the part of historical-critical hermeneutics—a view that regarded textual hermeneutics as a task that allows the text to speak through a transparent and colorless exegete and whose mission lies in accurately reproducing the writer's original intentions—was a kind of delusion. Readers inevitably bring to a text their own unique preconceptions from their own horizon. Gadamer argued that it is impossible for real exegetes to be transparent and colorless in that sense. Therefore, rather than suppressing our doubts and biases, we should not be afraid to bring them into a bold encounter with the text. If this results in a collapse of the text's horizon, it was not much of a text in the first place; trust in texts should not be something that can barely be sustained by dismissing inconvenient doubts and forcing oneself to accept questionable aspects. It must be a belief such that if part of the text collapses this also disturbs the exegete's horizon, with the potential of together reaching a higher fusion of horizons. Gadamer's philosophical hermeneutics argued that exegesis consists of such dialogues that result in a fusion with the horizon of the text. This is indeed a vital observation. Viewed in that light, conventional biblical hermeneutics had a strong tendency to muddy the waters with philological arguments that entailed nit-picking by what is known as the historical-critical method. By suppressing such doubts on the part of the exegete, this method somehow managed to still regard as Scripture dangerous texts that threatened to run counter to faith. Instead of such an approach, it is essential for hermeneutics to engage in dialogues where one boldly challenges texts with apparent anomalies and then listens to how the texts respond.

There are many problematic points in Ps 51,[19] but if we are to focus on just the most problematic, it would be the expression in v. 4, "Against you, you alone, have I sinned" (*lekha lebadekha hata'ti*). Here, "you" refers to God, but even if in a certain sense sins are committed against God by bringing disgrace on him or, particularly in the case of murder, by putting one of his creatures to death, surely these sins are not something that can be brushed aside simply by saying, "Against you, you alone, have I sinned." Above all, it was against Uriah that David had sinned. This utterance in v. 4 is not enough to dispel the suspicion that he is surreptitiously shifting the focus through a pretense of piety, thereby obscuring his responsibility for Uriah's murder.

Commentators have failed to point this out, instead putting forward misplaced defenses such as the claim that sin is a theological concept and is ultimately committed against God, and that David is remarkable for speaking of his awareness of this.[20] Yet surely this is a lie. I would suggest that such commentators are merely toying with evasive answers that pretend to piety, as did David, so that they become his unwitting accomplices.

How then should we interpret this? It is fallacious to argue that David is saying "Against you, you alone" on the grounds that sin is a matter of one's relations with God. Nevertheless, interpreting this statement as an equivocation aimed at evading the consequences of his sin against another human being would contradict the accompanying brave confession of sin that takes David's relations with others into account. This leaves us with only two options. One is to interpret this differently or exclude it when critiquing this text, and the other is the possibility of seeking a different meaning for the Hebrew word *lebadekha*, which is usually translated as "you alone." The former approach is ruled out because there is no support for this in either the Hebrew manuscripts or in ancient translations into Greek or Latin, for instance. So our sole remaining option is to come up with a different translation.

Lebadekha is a form in which a preposition (*le*) and a personal suffix (*kha*) have been added to the noun *bad*, meaning "separation." There are as many as 150 examples of *lebad* in the entire Old Testament, an examination of which reveals that the original meaning of this word was "separate from others, in particular."[21] In other words, it would be closer to the original meaning to render *lebadekha* along the lines of "Against you in particular." Translating it in this way resolves the aporia resulting from rendering it as "Against you, you alone." This is not a prevarication aimed at exonerating David from his sins against another human being. Instead, the utterance, "Against you in particular have I sinned," implies concern for Uriah, the murdered person who is the subject of David's sin. This is because "particularly" means "above all compared with others," and the "other" apart from God refers precisely to Uriah. That is, this passage is a confession meaning that "I have sinned against Uriah, and by sinning against Uriah, whom you gave me as a faithful commander, I have also committed a sin against you in particular."

In fact, in v. 14 David suddenly recalls his horrific past and speaks of the "bloodshed" of Uriah's slaying, and in v. 18 he mentions the rebuilding of the "walls of Jerusalem," an act that is thought to be an implementation of Uriah's wishes.[22] Uriah's name is too weighty to pronounce, so he is not mentioned by name. Yet David's burning desire to make amends to Uriah somehow is evident between the lines. Through forgiveness, David learns of his sin, and by doing so his concern for judgment and atonement deepens. On recognizing one's sins one can say "you are justified in your sentence"[23] and can hope to accept judgment on these sins with grace. Moreover, through these experiences David encounters the person of Uriah for the first time. Until then he has simply regarded Uriah as a means for concealing his own misconduct that was the result of his desires, and as a means for holding on to his position as king. After having gotten rid of Uriah, however, David does manage to think about him and, although too late, he has an encounter with Uriah. This is the second point made by this psalm. If we smooth matters over by saying that the expression "Against you, you alone, have I sinned" is theological and all very wonderful, David's true unspoken intent will remain forever hidden. This true intent is the response that the text offers precisely because we raise frank doubts about whether David is prevaricating here. This is an instance of what Gadamer referred to as a fusion of the reader's horizon with that of the text.

DISCOVERY OF THE GOD OF LOVE, AND THE REMAINING UNRESOLVED ISSUES

There is one other point relating to this psalm, namely, the fact that here David not only encounters Uriah, but also meets God for the first time.

Up until then David has striven to encounter God somehow. For instance, he tries to curry divine favor through acts of worship[24] and impressive works,[25] but all in vain. Even through his sermons as king and through the ideas of which he speaks so grandiosely in public[26] he is unable to encounter God. Instead, what David discovers here is that he could just barely stumble on God in the secret and wicked desires inside himself,[27] in his wretched desire for self-justification,[28] in shame such that it cannot be spoken of in public,[29] and above all, impelled by these feelings, in a sense of fault[30] and remorse[31] for having committed an irrevocable act—that is, it is only in the "inward being"[32] of the heart, which can only be called the "sin"[33] with which one is stained, that David can come upon God.[34] This can be regarded as an encounter not with the righteous God of the prophet Isaiah but with the God of love, a God of forgiveness.

Here we have explored the question of where the Hebrews came across not the God of retribution in the sense rejected by Qohelet, but a newer God in a dimension open to interpersonal relations, a God whom Qohelet failed to glimpse. It seems we have discovered a new God of love, one where there is also the potential for David to encounter the other person, Uriah.

Is it enough, however, to regard this as the *terminus ad quem* of the Old Testament view of God? In particular, if we look at this from the perspective of ethical thought, surely we cannot knowingly overlook the fact that several problems remain. We cannot forcibly suppress various doubts. For instance, what of the resentment on the part of Uriah, whose beloved wife is taken by the king and who is killed through the scheming of a king who exploits his status? How will the wrongs Uriah suffers be atoned for? Is not this psalm by the perpetrator David based on a presumption whereby he is abusing God's authority, taking too much for granted? And how in the first place can we rationalize the justice of a God who fails to punish such crimes and blindly forgives sin? We cannot feign ignorance of these doubts.

3. Atonement Thought in Isa 53 (Deutero-Isaiah)

THE PROPHET DEUTERO-ISAIAH

Burdened with such weighty questions, rather than leaning toward either righteousness or love, we must seek further for a God who integrates these two qualities. Such a God can be found in what is known as the

Fourth Song of the Servant[35] in the prophetic book of Deutero-Isaiah[36] dating from after the period of Babylonian captivity.

At the end of part I, I pointed out that whereas the Greeks spoke of ethics for the nobility and free citizens, Hebrew ethics also extended to oppressed slaves and captives. In the first three chapters of part II, we verified that in the Ten Commandments and other laws the Hebrews did in fact demonstrate a remarkably warm attitude to slaves and others in a vulnerable position, based on their own experience in having been liberated from slavery in Egypt. In the eleventh to tenth centuries BCE, the Hebrews built a kingdom in the days of Saul, David, and Solomon, and at one point they flourished. Subsequent Hebrew history, however, consisted of the north–south separation of the kingdom in 926 BCE; the downfall of the northern kingdom, Israel, in 722 BCE; and eventually the ruin of the southern kingdom, Judah, in 587 BCE. Having lost their nation, the Hebrews were carted off to Babylonia as captives and put to work (see the chronological table on page 119). With the Hebrew people facing slavery once again, it was the prophet Deutero-Isaiah who continued to probe the intentions of the God YHWH, who had driven his people to this life-or-death crisis. Deutero-Isaiah also sought an ethics that would act as a guide for living in the midst of such suffering.

THE SUFFERING SERVANT AND WONDER

In Deutero-Isaiah's song of the Suffering Servant, we again encounter "wonder." This song speaks of one apotheosis of this ancient "wonder."

> [S]o he shall startle [nazah] many nations;
>   kings shall shut their mouths because of him;
> for that which had not been told them they shall see,
>   and that which they had not heard they shall contemplate.
> Who has believed what we have heard?
> And to whom has the arm of the LORD been revealed?[37]

There are many different theories as to whom "he" (that is, God's Servant) refers. I will not go into the details here, but my conclusion is that as an individual it refers to the coming Messiah and to Deutero-Isaiah himself, and collectively it implies the whole of Israel. I interpret this passage as being written in a symbolic manner that permits these multiple readings.[38]

In any case, in the final analysis the object of the Hebrews' "wonder" was the works of God, which are said to be "revealed" in their ultimate form in this Servant of God. It was these works that astonished everyone, from the surrounding "many nations" to the "we" close to the Servant. What, then, was the specific nature of these "startl[ing]" works? This is summarized in the following sections.

ATONEMENT

> Surely he has borne our infirmities
>   and carried our diseases; . . .
> But he was wounded for our transgressions,
>   crushed for our iniquities;
> upon him was the punishment that made us whole,
>   and by his bruises we are healed.[39]

This speaks of an atonement ideology that is without parallel anywhere else in the Old Testament. That is, suffering is not meted out to "him," the just person known as the "Suffering Servant," for no reason but with the intention of atonement.

WEBER'S "THEODICY OF SUFFERING"

If we reexamine this from God's perspective, God does not mete out suffering for no reason, which means that his righteousness is demonstrated. This raises the question of what is known as theodicy. It was M. Weber who proclaimed that Deutero-Isaiah's theodicy constituted the "one truly serious theodicy of ancient Jewry" and who christened this the "theodicy of suffering" (*Theodizee des Leidens*).[40] Weber argued that what made this theodicy of suffering a serious theodicy was not its idea of atonement but the awareness that this suffering was unfair. Yet as Weber himself admits and as we saw in chapter 12, Job too suffered unfairly, and surely this cannot be regarded as the factor behind the one serious theodicy represented by Deutero-Isaiah. Moreover, I believe that Weber's positive conclusion about the glorification of the misery of being a pariah nation cannot be derived solely from the negative fact that this Servant had to undergo unreasonable suffering. Instead, I would suggest that it is precisely because of facing up to the positive issue of atonement that this Servant is glorified in such affirmative terms. In other words, Deutero-Isaiah's theodicy does constitute the one serious theodicy of ancient Jewry, but surely its claim to seriousness derives from the very atonement ideology belittled by Weber.

THE GENEALOGY OF THE IDEA OF ATONEMENT IN THE OLD TESTAMENT

No doubt Weber would object to this claim on the grounds that the idea of atonement also appears elsewhere in the Old Testament and cannot be regarded as the factor that gives Deutero-Isaiah the status of the one serious theodicy. In fact, Weber does appear to be thinking along these lines.[41] Nevertheless, he seems to lack an awareness of the clear differences in levels in the genealogy of the idea of atonement.

To be sure, Leviticus and other passages in the Old Testament do mention animal sacrifices carried out to bear the sins of human beings, and in their prayers of intercession people such as Moses[42] and Jeremiah[43] prayed to take the place of sinners. Perhaps these could likewise be regarded as belonging to a kind of atonement ideology. Yet in Isa 53 the sacrifices are neither animals nor mere prayers, as was the case with Moses, for instance. Here for the first time a human being actually "poured out himself to death."[44] This was a momentous event in the genealogy of Old Testament atonement ideology in the broad sense, and atonement ideology in the narrow sense can be regarded as having originated here. No other such instances occur anywhere else in the Old Testament. Thus, Second Isaiah embodies an unparalleled atonement ideology. In that sense we can rest assured that it was indeed the "one truly serious" idea of atonement that constituted the "one truly serious" theodicy.

THE IDEA OF ATONEMENT IN THE NEW TESTAMENT

Atonement is thought to have started with such animal sacrifices and moved on through the potential for human sacrifice in the form of prayers of intercession to the reality of human sacrifice in Isa 53. Atonement in the New Testament took the ultimate form not of animal or human sacrifices but of God himself giving his only son as a sacrifice. I quote Paul and John:

> [Our LORD] was handed over to death for our trespasses and was raised for our justification.[45]

God put forward [Christ Jesus] as a sacrifice of atonement by his blood, effective through faith. He did this to show his righteousness, because in his divine forbearance he had passed over the sins previously committed.[46]

But God proves his love for us in that while we still were sinners Christ died for us.[47]

Or

In this is love, not that we loved God but that he loved us and sent his Son to be the atoning sacrifice for our sins.[48]

INTEGRATION OF LOVE AND RIGHTEOUSNESS

Here we may conclude that an ultimate answer has been presented to the question that was posed in the previous chapter and that has disturbed the foundations of Hebrew thought, that is, whether there truly does exist a God of retribution who rewards ethical actions and who was the true object of the "wonder" expressed by the Hebrews. Traditional retributive ideology could not explain the reality that sinners prosper and the righteous suffer. It is not that this reality is glossed over to no purpose through the dogma of retribution; nor is it that the idea of retribution is completely rejected and the reality of injustice in interpersonal relations is simply derided and God is encountered in egotistical individual pleasures, as with Qohelet; nor is it that, like Isaiah, we merely proclaim the God of judgment through righteousness or that, like David, we simply throw ourselves on the God of forgiveness through love. Instead, this answer squarely confronts the realities of this world, where the principle of retribution does not function, and turns this around to speak of the discovery of a God who truly appears in that very place. In other words, this represents the discovery of a God whose righteousness would not be demonstrated if he merely forgave blindly; instead, he had one person atone for the sins of the many, thereby evincing both his righteousness and his forgiving love for the many. This is the conclusion that the genealogy from the Old Testament into the New Testament reached through numerous twists and turns in response to the ultimate question in Hebrew ethical thought as to whether there exists a God who is truly worthy of wonder and who is not at odds with our empirical reality. The conclusion is that a God of direct ethical retribution does not exist, but a God who carries out retribution in the indirect form of vicarious atonement does indeed exist.

4. Points of Contention: Three Criticisms of the Idea of Atonement, and a Rebuttal

POST-ENLIGHTENMENT CRITICISMS OF THE IDEA OF ATONEMENT

Nevertheless, this very conclusion has again become the main point of contention. Starting with Qohelet's criticism of the idea of retribution, we have seen how issues in the Bible, such as the direction of various broad and narrow interpretations of the Ten Commandments, are mutually conflicting. The idea of vicarious atonement certainly became a point of controversy in the history of secular thought, particularly after the Enlightenment. I would like to close by reviewing three leading criticisms and exploring how these criticisms might be answered.

CRITICISMS BY KANT AND THE YOUNG HEGEL

First, there is the repeated criticism of the cross by Immanuel Kant in *Religion Within the Limits of Reason Alone* (1793), particularly in books III and IV.[49] This was followed up by the young G. W. F. Hegel in fragments 44 and 46 from his Berne period (ca. 1795).[50] Their criticisms were to the effect that through having someone else atone for one's sins, the idea of atonement by the cross ignores the ethical responsibility of the individual.

NIETZSCHE'S CRITICISM

The criticism by Friedrich Nietzsche was even more trenchant. Particularly in his first essay in *The Genealogy of Morals* (1887), Nietzsche stated that the horrifying paradox of the God of the cross was fabricated to justify the *ressentiment* of the weak, and that it is an ominous temptation that regards sinners and the sick as the happiest, thereby overturning all values.[51]

LEVINAS'S CRITICISM

Third, in more recent times Emmanuel Levinas has criticized the Christian cross from the perspective of Judaism. Based on his own experience with the Nazis, in his commentary on the Talmud in *Difficile Liberté* (1963) Levinas repeatedly points out that far from being without sin, the survivors are unforgivable sinners who stayed alive by shoving aside those who ended up being killed, and that these survivors are charged with the task of continuing to testify on behalf of the victims. Levinas argues that the idea of atonement aims to set the perpetrators' minds at rest by forgiving them their sins, so this ideology should be rejected.[52]

ANSWERS FROM ATONEMENT IDEOLOGY

These are all severe criticisms, striking right at the heart of the weaknesses underlying the idea of atonement. Atonement ideology needs to humbly pay attention to such criticisms and respond as to how to avoid these pitfalls.

IN RESPONSE TO KANT AND THE YOUNG HEGEL

Here I will present only my conclusions, omitting a detailed discussion of the individual arguments. First, in response to Kant and Hegel, we must admit that the idea of atonement can indeed end up like this if not handled properly. In other words, we need to recognize the risk of this idea being used as a means of smug self-vindication, with sinners resting easy in the thought that they have been saved merely by having the Servant of atonement take on their ethical responsibilities. Yet it would be rash to abandon the whole concept simply because of this fear. There are in fact exhortations to action, such as, "We know love by this, that he laid down his life for us—and we ought to lay down our lives for one another."[53] The idea of atonement can and should be not only something where we passively accept forgiveness for our sins, but also an active idea whereby in response to forgiveness we come to a realization of our individual ethical responsibilities.

IN RESPONSE TO NIETZSCHE

There seems to be a misunderstanding on Nietzsche's part here. Sinners and the sick do not in themselves have value. The idea in the Bible is that, having had their sins forgiven or their sicknesses healed, value is bestowed on them and they should themselves then create value. By contrast, I would suggest that Nietzsche's master morality considers only sinless people of distinction and healthy people with no ailments, thereby abandoning sinners and the sick from the outset. The idea of atonement shows its true worth in its declaration of forgiveness and healing for such people. Nietzsche describes the noble and healthy as those loved by God, but is not God essentially redundant in master morality? By contrast, the idea of atonement told of where people could experience an encounter with God. It pointed out that this encounter takes place not in noble philosophy that can be pontificated on in public, but in none other than the corners of the heart that can only be described as sin, that is, in the unmentionable desires that lurk in the depths of everyone's heart, in our miserable and sick thoughts, and in our guilt and regret for past misdeeds. In this sense it seems that David's realization in the Psalms remains alive and has been passed down intact in many Hebrew texts. Arimasa Mori has produced a brilliant analysis of this in the case of Abraham in Genesis, for instance.[54]

IN RESPONSE TO LEVINAS

The third criticism, by Levinas, is to the effect that the idea of atonement is an ideology aimed at remitting the sins of wrongdoers or sinners and setting their minds at rest, so it should be rejected. This is based on Levinas's own harsh wartime experiences of being imprisoned by the Nazis and losing his family in a concentration camp. Moreover, his interpretation of Isa 53 is restricted to the Leper Scholar, so this is a particularly serious criticism that does not permit of a light rebuttal. It is also true, however, that this epitomizes the differences between Judaism and Christianity. Christianity would probably rephrase Levinas's Judaic manner of speaking as follows: survivors must be sensitive and proactive as sinners who have been forgiven and who continue to testify on behalf of the victims, and the idea of atonement should not be rejected, but accepted as a trigger that makes offenders truly aware of their own sins through forgiveness for these sins. Surely this is the Christian way of thinking. As long as we adopt this view, there is no reason to reject the idea of atonement. Instead, while fully acknowledging the issue raised by Levinas's line of thought, I believe we can explicate a position that transcends this.

This also relates to the logical circle of ethics and religion in the Old Testament that we noted at the end of chapter 10; that is to say, unless one observes the law one cannot encounter God, but unless one encounters God the law cannot be observed in the true sense. Judaism regards survivors as sinners who have not been forgiven by God, and it urges them on to further ethical acts, but Christianity takes the view that what enables ethical action in the first place is the belief that one has encountered God and his forgiveness. The Old Testament, which is Scripture for both Judaism and Christianity, contains elements of both views, and if these are examined synchronically it might seem to constitute a logical circle. Or perhaps we should say that opposing logics emerge depending on the religious horizon from which the text is interpreted.[55]

ANSWER AND CHALLENGE

Whatever the case may be, everyone who accepts this idea of atonement must continually face the question of whether one forgets one's sins and attains peace of mind through the idea of atonement, or whether the realization of one's sins moves one to atone for these sins. This represents a challenge for which each individual must be responsible. As long as we add this proviso, it seems to me that these three different criticisms can be refuted and that the idea of atonement retains in its own way its significance as the final response to fundamental issues in Jewish and Christian ethics.

5. Looking Back and Ahead

Let us bring all this together. In the question of whether a God of retribution ethics who rewards ethical behavior does actually exist, I found a problem that disturbs the foundations of Hebrew ethical thought, which espouses "wonder." This question was answered in the negative by Qohelet's nihilism, but the God he suggested instead was a substitute who could be sensed only in egotistical pleasures that ignored interpersonal relations. Therefore, while retaining nihilism's hardheaded awareness of the reality that the "unified order" consisting of direct retribution has broken down, we were forced to seek out a new view of God that incorporated the fundamental human mode of existence, that is, interpersonal relations. After examining such different figures as Isaiah and David, and eventually reaching Isa 53 and New Testament writers such as Paul, we finally discovered a God in whom, although based on the premise of the breakdown of retribution in interpersonal relations, we can find in this very breakdown the redemptive meaning of bearing the sins of others. As Paul said, it was here that people encountered a God who "show[s] his righteousness"[56] and simultaneously "proves his love."[57]

Nevertheless, in the subsequent history of thought it was this very God of atonement who became the point of contention. Here I have examined three influential criticisms and attempted to respond to them, but in doing so I naturally have no intention of adopting an apologetic approach. These criticisms point out pitfalls of atonement ideology, and my response has simply suggested ways of evading these pitfalls. No ideology is a safe vehicle that will automatically transport us across to the shores of truth if we simply place our trust in it. Instead of relaxing as if proceeding to the truth is a self-evident convention, we should constantly question whether we can escape from the truth. In that sense, these three questions should remain open to the future without reaching a conclusion.

Such a questioning stance will press on—not toward peace of mind based on a literalistic belief in atonement by the Servant of God, but toward matters that point to this symbolically—and will lead to an attitude that carefully examines the meaning of this. I would suggest that this attitude then compels us to take another step and tackle the next issue, namely, reflecting on the matters in Hebrew thought that were spoken of throughout in line with faith in God, but now using philosophical and universal language that moves away from a specific faith.[58] I would like to devote the final chapter to an attempt to review this Hebrew faith in the light of Greek philosophy. This should allow us further insights into the nature of Hellenic "wonder" and also allow us to discern what ultimately underpins both Hebrew and Hellenic thought.

Notes

1. Isa 6:10.
2. H. W. Hoffmann, *Die Intention der Verkündigung Jesajas* (BZAW 136; Berlin: Walter de Gruyter, 1974), 38–59.

3. R. Kilian, *Jesaja 1–39* (Darmstadt: Wissenschaftliche Buchgesellschaft, 1983), 128ff.

4. This is the conclusion of my article, "Yogensha ni okeru zetsubō to kibō— Izaya no tsumi rikai o megutte" (Despair and hope in the prophets: On Isaiah's understanding of sin), *Jitsuzonshugi* (Existentialism) 81 (1977). Hardmeier makes a similar claim in a different context. C. Hardmeier, "Jesajas Verkündigungsabsicht und Jahwes Verstockungsauftrag in Jes 6," in *Die Botschaft und die Boten: Festschrift für Hans Walter Wolff zum 70. Geburtstag* (Neukirchen-Vluyn, Germany: Neukirchener Verlag, 1981).

5. For a discussion of the various explanations, see "Translator's Commentary" in my *Izaya-sho* (The book of Isaiah) (Tokyo: Iwanami Shoten, 1997), particularly 338ff.

6. Isa 1:17, 23; 3:12–14.

7. Isa 1:15–16, 21.

8. Isa 30:1–5.

9. Isa 9:8.

10. C. G. Jung, *Antwort auf Hiob* (Zürich: Rascher, 1952).

11. Yasuo Yuasa, *Yungu to kirisuto-kyō* (Jung and Christianity) (1978; reprint, Tokyo: Kōdansha Gakujutsu Bunko-ban, 1996).

12. The established view in Old Testament studies in the past has been that, despite the heading of Ps 51, it is not actually related to the Bathsheba incident. However, after a detailed examination of a recent study by M. Goulder (*The Prayers of David [Psalms 51–72]: Studies in the Psalter, II* [Sheffield, Eng.: Sheffield Academic Press, 1990]), I believe that both of these texts relate to David's involvement with Bathsheba. See Seizō Sekine, *Transcendency and Symbols in the Old Testament: A Genealogy of the Hermeneutical Experiences*, trans. Judy Wakabayashi (BZAW 275; Berlin: Walter de Gruyter, 1999), section 3.3, originally published as *Kyūyaku ni okeru chōetsu to shōchō: kaishakugaku-teki keiken no keifu* (Tokyo: University of Tokyo Press, 1996). Here, however, I will omit a detailed philological discussion of this point.

13. P. Ricœur, *Finitude et culpabilité. II. La symbolique du mal* (Paris: Aubier, 1960), 11–17.

14. 2 Sam 12:1–4.

15. 2 Sam 12:5–6.

16. 2 Sam 12:13.

17. Ps 51:3.

18. H. G. Gadamer, *Wahrheit und Methode: Grundzüge einer philosophischen Hermeneutik* (Tübingen, Germany: Mohr 1960), 263ff.

19. See Sekine, *Transcendency and Symbols in the Old Testament*, 160–61.

20. This argument has been made by various scholars since the classic work of F. Delitzsch, *Biblischer Kommentar über die Psalmen*, 4th ed. (Leipzig: Dörffling und Franke, 1883), 400; cf. Sekine, *Transcendency and Symbols in the Old Testament*, 180–81.

21. Gen 21:28; Judg 6:37; etc.

22. See 1 Sam 10:6; 11:24; 5:6ff. For further details, see Sekine, *Transcendency and Symbols in the Old Testament*, 207–8.

23. Ps 51:4.
24. Ps 51:16.
25. Ps 51:18.
26. Ps 51:12–13.
27. 2 Sam 11:4ff.
28. 2 Sam 11:14ff.
29. 2 Sam 12:12.
30. Ps 51:14.
31. Ps 51:17.
32. Ps 51:6.
33. Ps 51:1–5.
34. Ps 51:5.
35. Isa 52:13–53:12.
36. Of the sixty-six chapters in the book of Isaiah, those up to chapter 39 are attributed to the eighth-century BCE prophet Isaiah, while chapters 40–55 and chapters 56–66 are regarded as the work of anonymous prophets from the exilic period in the sixth century BCE and from the postexilic period of the end of that century into the fifth century BCE, respectively. Since the late nineteenth century it has been the custom in biblical studies to refer to these prophets by the provisional names Deutero-Isaiah and Trito-Isaiah. The reason I have not used the expression "the prophet, Deutero-Isaiah" is that there are complex redactional issues involved in Second Isaiah and Third Isaiah, and it is not possible to declare Deutero-Isaiah as the sole author. For details of the redactional problems in Second Isaiah, see chapter 5 in my *Transcendency and Symbols in the Old Testament*. For a discussion of the structure and redaction of the whole of the book of Isaiah, see the commentary in *Izaya-sho*, my translation of the book of Isaiah.
37. Isa 52:15–53:1.
38. For details of the history of scholarship on this question and also for a critique of this scholarship and the grounds for my own conclusion, see Sekine, *Transcendency and Symbols in the Old Testament*, 341ff. (section 5.2.1).
39. Isa 53:4–5.
40. M. Weber, *Ancient Judaism*, trans. Hans H. Gerth and Don Martindale (New York: Free Press, 1952), 5, 369, originally published as *Das Antike Judentum*, vol. 3 of *Gesammelte Aufsätze zur Religionssoziologie* (Tübingen, Germany: Mohr, 1921).
41. Weber, *Ancient Judaism*, 376–77.
42. Exod 32:32.
43. Jer 11:14; 7:16.
44. Isa 53:12.
45. Rom 4:25.
46. Rom 3:25.
47. Rom 5:8.
48. 1 John 4:10.
49. I. Kant, *Die Religion innerhalb der Grenzen der bloßen Vernunft* (Frankfurt und Leipzig, 1793), book III, "The Victory of the Good over the Evil Prin-

ciple, and the Founding of a Kingdom of God on Earth"; book IV, "Concerning Service and Pseudo-Service under the Sovereignty of the Good Principle"; see also *Religion within the Limits of Reason Alone*, trans. T. M. Greene and H. H. Hudson (New York: Harper & Row, 1960).

50. G. W. F. Hegel, *Theologische Jugendschriften: nach den Handschriften der Kgl. Bibliothek in Berlin*, ed. von Herman Nohl (Tübingen, Germany: Mohr, 1907), 50ff.

51. F. W. Nietzsche, "Good and Evil, Good and Bad," *Zur Genealogie der Moral* (Leipzig: Naumann, 1887).

52. E. Lévinas, *Difficile Liberté: essais sur le judaïsme* (Paris: Michel, 1963).

53. 1 John 3:16.

54. Arimasa Mori, "Aburahamu no shinkō" (The faith of Abraham), in *Tsuchi no utsuwa ni* (In an earthenware vessel) (Tokyo: Nihon Kirisutokyōdan Shuppankyoku, 1976).

55. As well as their sensitivity to wonder, religions such as Christianity also focus on peace. If we assume that wonder is a state of tension and that it is also necessary to release this tension, then elements that supplement this are likewise important, such as the peace of having been forgiven for one's sins. Yet it is only natural that the task in A. J. Heschel's *God in Search of Man: A Philosophy of Judaism* (New York: Farrar, Straus & Cudahy, 1955), for instance, and the task of ethical philosophy, which has consistently maintained its questioning stance, lies in stating the position of wonder. The present book on the "origins of ethical thought" is also based on this approach, but the existence of factors that implicitly and explicitly complement this seems quite appropriate. See Seizō Sekine, Yoshihide Suzuki, and Kōichi Namiki, *Kyūyaku Seisho to gendai* (The Old Testament and the present) (Tokyo: Kyōbunkan, 2000), 38–39.

56. Rom 3:25.

57. Rom 5:8.

58. Based on post-Hegelian criticism, Jirō Watanabe (*Jinsei no tetsugaku* [Philosophy of life] [Tokyo: Hōsō Daigaku Kyōiku Shinkōkai, 1998], 61–62) has made the astute observation that he regards Kant's "rational faith" as the "best possible religious attitude for us who live in enlightened modern or contemporary times." In this way, those who discuss "religious ethics" today must constantly avoid taking on "two conflicting agonies—i.e., a leap of faith toward the absolute, and the subsequent sceptical fall."

CHAPTER 15

A Reflection on the Greek Philosophy of Love and Righteousness, Based on Aristotle

In the previous chapter, we ascertained that the ethics of Hebraism can be summed up in terms of a belief in atonement. This belief, however, carried heavy nuances of symbolic faith. What if we were to reconsider this on the plane of philosophical reason, transcending the specificity of symbols and elucidating this in general language? Our task in the present chapter is to take up the point reached by the *terminus ad quem* of Judaism and Christianity and clarify this from the perspective of Hellenic reason.

If how the Servant of God took on undue suffering and died constitutes a death of atonement, then perhaps we could say that Socrates—who, despite the unfounded charges laid against him by the public, obeyed the *daimonion*'s voice and met his death calmly—was also a servant of God whose death was a kind of death of atonement. What possesses the scope to clarify the meaning of this death of atonement in philosophical terms is the views on love of Aristotle, on whose shoulders fell Socrates' scholastic mantle. With books VIII and IX of the *Nicomachean Ethics* as our starting point, here I would like to attempt a structural clarification of why love must lead to atonement. This should also result in a reexamination of matters that lie at the foundation of ethical thought, such as the nature of love and its relationship to righteousness.

1. Aristotle's Thinking on Love

SUMMARY OF HIS VIEWS IN BOOKS VIII AND IX OF THE *NICOMACHEAN ETHICS*

Aristotle's ideas on love have already been introduced in section 6.3, so here we will set out by simply recapping these views.

Aristotle regarded love (*philiā*) as something that transcends justice: "when men are friends they have no need of justice at all, but when they are just, they still need friendship [love]; and a thing which is most just is thought to be done in a friendly way."[1]

There are three objects of love, namely, "the good or the pleasant or the useful."[2] Love of the latter two cannot be described as proper love, as it is merely self-love whereby one loves what is pleasant or useful to oneself. "Perfect friendship exists between men who are good and are alike with respect to virtue; for, insofar as they are good, it is in a similar manner that they wish each other's goods."[3]

So should all self-love be condemned? No. If, in accordance with "passions" and "the nonrational element [*alogos*] of their soul," one covets "property or . . . honors or . . . bodily pleasures," this self-love will lead to ugly competition, and it should be censured. By contrast, when one lives "according to reason [*logos*]" and the "intellect [*nūs*] rules" and is "always earnest to do, above all things, what is just or temperate," then such self-love merits praise, not reproach.[4]

In that case, a person who "wishes" well for others may also wish well for himself, and as long as he acts in accordance with *logos*, then in fact he "should love himself most of all."[5] Conversely, this implies that the meaning of "wish each other's goods" entails being careful to enhance others' virtue in line with *logos*, not pandering to a friend's egoism and allowing him the pleasures desired by bad people who are swayed by their emotions. In this way, desiring good for a friend and desiring good for oneself are not contradictory, since both desires enhance each other's virtue.

THE REMAINING ISSUES

The above is a summary of Aristotle's views on love, which we surveyed in section 6.3. Obviously, this does not exhaust the scope of his fertile thought. For instance, would it not also be possible to have a love that overcomes self-love and loves "the good or the pleasant or the useful"? What would Aristotle think of the validity of this? In particular, is his division into the rule of the "intellect" (*nūs*) and "bodily pleasures" based on a dualistic separation of mind and body? What does *nūs* refer to in the first place? Although Aristotle certainly does not discuss these questions overtly as his main focus, this does not mean he was unaware of them. Below, I would like to attempt to reformulate what can be glimpsed about these further lines of inquiry from odd fragments in Aristotle's writing, sometimes drawing out his implicit meaning.[6] This might also offer glimpses of a direction that will throw philosophical light on the doctrine of atonement.

WHAT IT MEANS TO LOVE SOMEONE'S CHARACTER

First, let us look at the claim that loving "the pleasant or the useful" is a variant of self-love and does not constitute love proper. Does this mean that moving away from what is pleasurable and useful to oneself, that is, overcoming self-love, and devoting oneself to praising the other person's beauty and the superiority of their mind constitutes love proper? Surely the answer is again in the negative, because this would entail reducing that person to certain qualities and reifying them. This does not constitute loving that person's character (*ēthos*).[7] Since a contrast is being made whereby "men who are good" love in the proper form "for the sake of their friends,"[8] we can take the view that Aristotle's argument encompasses a rejection of such reification of people.[9]

NŪS

Aristotle referred to this supra-objecthood of human beings as *nūs*.[10] *Nūs* does not merely refer to "reason"; according to *De Anima*, it is a spontaneity that transcends objects,[11] and according to the *Nicomachean Ethics*, it also consists of freedom as the basis of action[12] and is described as something divine (*theion*).[13] Thus humans are spiritual beings that transcend the mere flesh, but the spirit cannot exist separately from the flesh.[14] In this sense, Aristotle's position is not a mere mind–body dualism that simply makes a sharp distinction between spirit and flesh.[15] In other words, true human nature consists of *nūs*, and *nūs* "is reason, freedom, the spirit, the individual in the superior sense, and an existence completely different from matter, yet it cannot exist unless embodied in flesh."[16]

According to Aristotle's ontology, however, the goodness of a particular being lies in the functioning (*energeia*) of its true character.[17] True character means nature (*physis*), so this being is good when acting in accordance with nature.[18] Therefore good people are those who embody our true nature as human beings, that is, *nūs*. So "men who are good" are none other than those who live rationally in accordance with nature and who are always free and autonomous.

At this point the meaning of the earlier statements that "perfect friendship" consists of love between "men who are good" and that "they wish each other's goods" becomes clearer.[19] Instead of using the other person as a body divorced from the spirit and as a means of pleasure and usefulness, this involves—while not excluding such a perspective on the body—respecting that person as an individual and as a free agent who assumes control through reason and as an autonomous purpose, and it also involves ensuring that this person can live according to reason.

THE MEANING OF WISHING ANOTHER WELL

So just why do "men who are good" ensure this and wish "each other's goods"?[20] Aristotle makes little comment on this, but if we collate what he does say, the following ontological structure of human beings as postulated by Aristotle should become apparent.

Love Through Blood Ties

As a fundamental form of love, Aristotle first cites blood ties between parent and child and those among siblings.[21] He states that "Parents, then, love their children as they love themselves (for what comes from them is like other selves [*heteros autos*], being different by having been separated)."[22] Aristotle also observes that "brothers love each other by having been born of the same parents, for sameness [*tautotēs*] in relation to the same parents produces sameness [*tauto*] in relation to each other."[23] Aristotle broadens this latter love to encompass mental sameness, saying that "born of the same parents, they are alike in character [*ēthos*] and upbringing and have been educated alike."[24] As stated above, his understanding of humans is not a mind–body dualism that merely separates spirit and body, so in the original model of love through blood ties an analogy can likewise be made between this sameness of physical, biological being and sameness of spirit. In fact, Aristotle also states that "The friendship between brothers has the good attributes present in that between comrades; and it is a friendship to a higher degree for brothers who are *good*."[25]

Love for Friends and Neighbors

Here Aristotle moves beyond love in blood ties, which is the primal form of love, thereby opening up more broadly the field of love in relations with one's friends and neighbors. In chapter 11 of book VIII of the *Nicomachean Ethics*, Aristotle states that in despotic tyrannies "there is nothing common [*koinon*]" between the ruler and the ruled, so it is virtually impossible for love to exist.[26] The same goes for relations between master and slave. Aristotle adds, however, that "there may be friendship towards him [a slave] as a man."[27] A slave "as a slave" is merely "a living tool,"[28] but a slave "as a man"—while having the above meaning of a human who is an end, not a means—also seems to have a meaning beyond that. What leads me to this assumption is chapter 9 in book IX, which discusses the question of whether happy people need friends.

COMMUNAL EXISTENCE

In response to this question, Aristotle observes that even though happy people are self-sufficient, they are not isolated and do need friends, and he cites various reasons for this. Particularly important is the fact that "for no man with all the other goods would choose to live alone, seeing that man is a political being [*politikon*] and is disposed by nature to live with others [*syzēn pephykon*]."[29]

Yet, "liv[ing] with others" does not imply "as in the case of cattle, feeding in the same place";[30] it is something that "comes about by . . . sharing [*koinōnein*] in conversation [*logos*] and thoughts [*dianoia*]."[31] It is not difficult to imagine that this sharing refers to the situation wherein "people thinking" does not generally mean me thinking alone, but collective thinking.[32] Even my poor ideas are not something I thought of all by myself but were nurtured and shaped in encounters with the ideas of various other people—from Aristotle through to those around me today, including my family and colleagues. Understanding the person I am today is also possible by inquiring into the wide-ranging experiences of these other people beyond me.

The egoist's delusion that he has understood himself in isolation, in solitude, is merely a fictitious illusion resulting from having drawn a veil over humans' inherently communal nature, and since he fails to understand the others who are the foundation of his own existence, there is no way the egoist can properly understand himself, much less others. For people to understand themselves and others it is essential to observe the primary precept of "communal existence" and to cultivate the virtue of love in this sense. In general, opening up to other people "as a man" accords with humans' true nature. Bringing out our inherent nature is good, and this constituted happiness.[33] So for human beings to be happy, it is essential to have friends in this sense of the term. This is precisely why Aristotle states that, transcending blood ties, even slaves can be the object of love "as a man."[34]

2. Philanthropic Equity and Atonement

PHILANTHROPIC EQUITY

Here we have sketched the broad outline of the doctrine of love in books VIII and IX of the *Nicomachean Ethics*. In closing, I would like to supplement this with a discussion of the relationship between the theory of love and the theory of justice. This should also develop into a question of the interpretation of the key words *epieikeia* and *epieikēs* used by Aristotle throughout the *Nicomachean Ethics*.

(1) [B]y "a more equitable [*epieikēs*] thing" we mean a thing which is better [*dikaios*]. . . . [T]he equitable [*epieikēs*] man . . . is not overly just in insisting that his neighbour get less but is content to take less, although he has the law on his side . . . and the corresponding disposition [*hexis*] is equity [*epieikeia*].[35]

(2) [A] *good* [*epieikēs*] man is thought to *act* . . . for the sake of his friend, disregarding his own good.[36]

(3) [W]hat a *good* [*epieikēs*] man should do is just what he does, for intellect [*nūs*] in every case chooses what is best for itself, and a *good* [*epieikēs*] man obeys his intellect.[37]

(4) [T]he mean [between the obsequious and the quarrelsome] is praiseworthy. . . . No name has been given to this habit but it resembles friendship [*philiā*] most of all; for if we add affection to a man with such an intermediate habit, we shall have what we mean by "a *good* [*epieikeia*] friend."[38]

In other words, *epieikeia* is variously rendered as "goodness" or "equitableness" (Saburō Takada), "equitable tendency" or "noble character" (Shinrō Katō), and "steadfast love" or "benevolence,"[39] while *epieikēs* is its adjectival form. In a nutshell, the word seems to encompass the meanings of both impartiality and consideration. Although it is a little wordy, here I would like to translate this as "philanthropic equity" so as to encapsulate these ambiguous connotations.

INEQUITY TOWARD ONESELF

The first quotation above appears in a supplement to the discussion of distributive justice, corrective justice, and reciprocal justice (justice in exchange) that we examined in chapter 6. Aristotle argues that if we regard those who stick to legal justice in this way as formalists and that "a thing which is most just [should be] thought to be done in a friendly way,"[40] then deliberately "tak[ing] less" as a result of "philanthropic equity" is closer to the essence of justice. Naturally, Aristotle does not overlook the doubts presented,[41] for example, in the *Republic* by Plato, who questioned whether this might not in the final analysis mean distorting justice and suffering injustice, and whether it might perhaps also make unjust people arrogant.[42] "Philanthropic equity" entails not according oneself one's proper value, so Aristotle also rephrases this as "act[ing] unjustly towards [oneself]."[43] Why would one deliberately commit such an injustice?

As we saw earlier, Aristotle's theory of love encompasses a viewpoint that rejects the reification of human beings, so an interpretation along the following lines would be possible,[44] that is, "in desire I tend to subordinate the beloved to my own ends, to convert the beloved into an object. Thus it is perhaps only disinterested love that is susceptible of affecting the *thou*."[45] It is this state at which Aristotle was aiming.[46]

At the same time, the direct reason cited by Aristotle as to why one would commit an injustice against oneself would be because "a *good* [*epieikēs*] man gets more than his share of some other good, e.g., more reputation or, simply stated, more of what is noble."[47] In other words, such a person tries to live "according to reason [*logos*]" and to possess true beauty.[48] That is why Aristotle makes such statements as in quote 3 above. Such people do not act in accordance with "the nonrational element [*alogos*] of their soul" or covet "property or . . . honors or . . . bodily pleasures," being above these things. And they do not regard taking less than their share of these as real injustice toward themselves.

LOVE BASED ON RATIONAL SAMENESS

It is obvious, however, that tamely submitting to someone else's "nonrational" ego and becoming a victim does not constitute "philanthropy." In particular, in friendship between "good men" who "wish the good of their friends for the sake of their friends,"[49] such an attitude is "obsequious," as stated in quote 4 above, and as with quarrelsomeness it should be avoided. "Philanthropic equity" will at times also encompass a severity that denies the other person's nonrational desires and that attacks and destroys these desires, as did the Hebrew prophets. Aristotle can be regarded as taking the view that at such times a true love arises that is neither a slave to the other person's desires nor uses that person as a means for one's own desires but is based on rational sameness in accordance with reason.

THE POSITION OF ATONEMENT

Like Plato, Socrates' immediate disciple, no doubt Aristotle, an indirect disciple of Socrates, consciously and unconsciously thought about the meaning of Socrates' death sentence, which would be regarded as unjust from the perspective of justice. This exactly parallels and corresponds to how the Hebrew disciples of Deutero-Isaiah and also of Christ pondered the significance of their master's unjust suffering and death. The latter are religious in reading into this a personal God's intentions of vicarious atonement, as well as practical in exhorting the disciples to follow the example of their master's unjust suffering. By contrast, Aristotle is eminently philosophical in tracing back to the ontological structure of human beings to analyze where injustice intersects with love, and—no doubt out of concern that uncritical imitation of suffering might turn into a futile submission to authority in the broad sense—he is theoretical and reflective in restraining this.

PHILIĀ AND *AGAPĒ*

Naturally, such a theoretical and reflective attitude lacks practicability, and it can also be regarded as revealing the limits of *philiā* in relation to *agapē*, namely, the fact that *philiā* is not an *agapē* that encompasses people different from oneself and is in principle open to one and all but specifically remains a *philiā* among "good men" who are superior in their sameness of reason. This interpretation reads into Aristotle's *nūs* various meanings that go beyond mere "reason," and perhaps it reads too much into the scope of his theory of love. The doubts about Aristotle that were presented at the end of part I lay precisely in the fact that he disdained and abandoned the "general public" with their inferior "reason." *Nūs* primarily refers to "reason," and most of the examples in the *Nicomachean Ethics* also exemplify this sense.[50]

To start with, is love confined among "good men" who excel in reason, and do "bad men" have no choice but to be excluded and abandoned? As long as reason is stressed, must we not discard from the outset any possibility of "bad men" becoming good? Conversely, does this not mean that "good men" receive "idle" happiness on the basis of the labors of people inferior to them in reason, and that they enjoy a carefree friendship among good people? Unless we introduce the criterion of reason, is it possible to make any clear distinction between "good men" and "bad men" in the first place? Is it not the case that both qualities vie with each other in each individual?

There are plenty of reasons for criticizing Aristotle on such grounds. Nevertheless, it is not my purpose here to question the validity of this as an issue in Aristotelian interpretation. Based on the above-mentioned perspective on the diversity of *nūs* and on the contemporary discourse of otherness, all we need is to be able to extract the fact that Aristotle's theory of love has this scope, at least potentially. This is because our goal here was simply to refer to the language of Hellenic philosophy while reexamining the Hebrew tendency to believe in the doctrine of atonement.

3. Symbols and Literalness

THE DANGERS OF LITERALISM

Here I would like to shift gears and recall the three criticisms of a belief in atonement that were presented from the perspective of different philosophers at the end of the previous chapter. I would like to reconsider whether these criticisms perhaps share an ideological drawback. This should provide an object lesson even for those who believe in atonement. I would suggest that even Kant and Hegel, not to mention Nietzsche and Levinas, all interpreted the cross of Jesus overly literally. In other words, I would suggest that they interpreted this as meaning that Jesus of Nazareth took on the sins of all humankind on the cross, and they focused excessively on the validity of this claim. Was this not their ideological drawback? Based on findings from contemporary biblical studies that interpret the Bible using historical-critical methods, the awareness presented by biblical exegesis and Christian theology should have been that, as with all matters in this world, what is written in the Bible is merely referring in symbolic language to transcendental matters that cannot be spoken of. In the same way, atonement by the cross should purely and simply be no more than a symbol that sets forth the integration of the love and righteousness of the transcendental being who gives us life. We should constantly bear in mind that both believers and critics are often apt to succumb to the pitfall of confusing this symbol with a fixed reality.

In these current times of change, with such great diversity of values ever since the Cold War, conversely there is a trend toward blindly believing in religious teachings and simply clinging to that ethic, that is, a tendency to construe the holy Scriptures literally in their extremely narrow sense and to adopt a parochial fundamentalism toward oneself and others. Such fundamentalism is rampant around the world. In recent years the number of terrorist incidents around the world with a fundamentalist religion behind them reportedly totals several hundred per annum. In such times it seems vital that both religious people and philosophers not entrench the very symbols and interpret them literally, but that they always return to the fact that what is important is the transcendental matters indicated by these symbols, thereby fostering mutual tolerance and freedom of self-relativization. In that sense, too, attempts at philosophical interpretations of symbols must always be carried out in tandem with cases relating to religious ethics. This is my main reason for using this chapter to supplement the discussions in chapters 13 and 14.

SYMBOLIC LANGUAGE'S POWER TO EVOKE IMAGES

If, however, I were to add one final comment for the sake of balance, it would be that, as already pointed out in chapter 9, we must take into account not only the awareness that the matters dealt with by faith are no more than *mere symbols*, but also the fact that they are *indispensable symbols*. As Tillich observes,[51] it is only through relative symbols that those of us who dwell in this world can glimpse absolute transcendency. This means that symbols, although imperfect, are also the sole indispensable means by which we can reach this transcendency. There are times when the concrete symbol of one righteous man dying for us has a greater impact on our minds than the multifarious abstract ideological systems constructed around love and righteousness. By decoding such symbols, philosophical hermeneutics takes a critical scalpel to them and excises the superstitious elements and fossilized teachings that have become mixed in with the symbols, thereby liberating human nature from oppression and constraints and deconstructing and analyzing symbols into abstract philosophical logic. Nevertheless, as pointed out by scholars such as Ricœur,[52] we must be careful to proceed with this task in a way that ensures that we retain symbols' original power to evoke images and that recaptures this power in a simpler form.

In that sense, too, it is desirable that Hebrew religious ethics' perspective on symbols through faith and Hellenic practical philosophy's analysis of universal phenomena through reason compensate for each other's defects and form a complementary relationship of tension. This book has traced the "origins of ethical thought" in the case of the Hebrews and Greeks not merely because they form the two major streams that underpin subsequent Western ethical thought, but also because both approaches are crucial as long as human beings are understood in connection with matters that transcend humans—religion and philosophy, faith and reason—and because they are classic presentations of the ideal complementary form of both moments.

It was through "wonder" that the ancients repeatedly discovered how human beings have a relationship with something transcending themselves. This consideration should lead us to rethink the meaning of this "wonder," which highlights the "origins of ethical thought," as pointed out again and again since the introduction. I would like to close by pressing this point home.

Notes

1. Aristotle, *Nicomachean Ethics* VIII, 1, 1155a26–28. English translations here and below are from *Nicomachean Ethics*, trans. H. G. Apostle (Dordrecht, Netherlands: Reidel, 1975), hereafter *NE*.
2. *NE* VIII, 2, 1155b19.
3. *NE* VIII, 3, 1156b7–9.
4. *NE* IX, 8, 1168b15–36.
5. *NE* IX, 8, 1168b10.
6. I have benefited greatly from the invaluable discussions in *Le mystére de l'être*, 2 vols. (Paris: Aubier, 1951) and *Journal métaphysique* (Paris: Gallimard, 1935), by Gabriel Marcel, who engaged in a profound contemplation of the mystery of love for our modern times, and I have also benefited from chapter 8 of Yasuo Iwata, *Arisutoteresu no rinri shisō* (The ethical thought of Aristotle) (Tokyo: Iwanami Shoten, 1985), which contrasts these ideas with those of Aristotle. I would like to take this opportunity to express my appreciation to Marcel and Iwata.
7. *NE* VIII, 3, 1156a10–24.
8. *NE* VIII, 3, 1156b10–11.
9. See Marcel, *Journal métaphysique*, 64–65, and Iwata, *Arisutoteresu no rinri shisō* (Ethical thought of Aristotle), 294–96.

10. Iwata, *Arisutoteresu no rinri shisō* (Ethical thought of Aristotle), 298–99, points out that *nūs* has the aspect of a "persona" as a "symbol intimating supra-objecthood."

11. Aristotle, *De Anima* I, 3, 407a9–10; III, 4, 429b9; III, 5, 430a15.

12. *NE* VI, 2, 1139a31–b5; VII, 6, 1150a1–5.

13. *NE* X, 7, 1177a15, 16, 1177b28, 30; X, 8, 1178a22, 1179a22–32.

14. *De Anima* II, 1, 412b3–4; I, 1, 403a5–7.

15. Iwata, *Arisutoteresu no rinri shisō* (Ethical thought of Aristotle), 299.

16. Iwata, *Arisutoteresu no rinri shisō* (Ethical thought of Aristotle), 300.

17. *NE* I, 7, 1097b26–27; Aristotle, *Politics* I, 2, 1253a23.

18. *Politics* VII, 3, 1325b7–10.

19. *NE* VIII, 3, 1156b8–9.

20. Iwata, *Arisutoteresu no rinri shisō* (Ethical thought of Aristotle), 304.

21. *NE* VIII, 12, 1161b16ff.

22. *NE* VIII, 12, 1161b27–29.

23. *NE* VIII, 12, 1161b30–33.

24. *NE* VIII, 12, 1162a12–13.

25. *NE* VIII, 12, 1162a9–10. Iwata formulates this as follows: "Love consists of congruence (the materialization of sameness) between human beings, but since a human being is neither a mere lump of flesh nor a completely disembodied spirit, but a spirit in bodily form (a spirit that is manifest in the flesh), love too derives neither from mere physical sameness nor sameness of abstract conscious-ness separate from the flesh, but from sameness of the spirit manifested within the very sameness of the flesh." *Arisutoteresu no rinri shisō* (Ethical thought of Aristotle), 309.

26. *NE* VIII, 11, 1161a32–34.

27. *NE* VIII, 11, 1161b.

28. *NE* VIII, 11, 1161b3–4.

29. *NE* IX, 9, 1169b16–19.

30. *NE* IX, 9, 1170b13–14.

31. *NE* IX, 9, 1169b10–12.

32. Marcel calls this sharing *intersubjectivité*, and Buber views it as an "I–thou relationship," while Tetsurō Watsuji developed this as "relational betweenness." Aristotle particularly emphasizes the rational aspect of "conversation and thoughts," and here I will explore his intentions, following G. Marcel (*Le myst-ère de l'être*, vol. 1, 13). See also the cogent speculations by Iwata, *Arisutoteresu no rinri shisō* (Ethical thought of Aristotle), 313ff.

33. *NE* I, 5, 1097b24–33.

34. Iwata (*Arisutoteresu no rinri shisō* [Ethical thought of Aristotle], 319) brings this together as the "ontological structure of love": "Love consists of a union between humans as embodied spirits (persona). Originally this love arises on the basis of the factual sameness of blood ties, but more properly it derives from the fact that human beings are a 'subjective–collective existence' as logos-like beings. In other words, although human beings are individual entities, fun-damentally they are individuals within a collective, and so it is only through the materialization of true accord between I and thou as individuals that our self-

existence as individuals is enriched. To put it another way, as long as we are individuals in the narrow sense of the term, human beings are in a defective (wrongful) state; it is only by achieving sameness (*tautotēs*) with others who possess unique personas—while at the same time maintaining our own unique personas—that human beings are able to provide themselves with grounds for their existence. This sameness or commonality pertains to our true nature in the sense that human beings are the possessors of a 'logos whose essence lies in relationships' and also in the sense that humans are universally a physical being, but we cannot state that this is a fact, in that humans are not an objective existence in the sense of things. Hence love is a virtue, and we could even go further and describe it as the supreme virtue."

35. *NE* V, 10, 1137b3–1138a2.
36. *NE* IX, 8, 1168a33–35.
37. *NE* IX, 8, 1169a16–18.
38. *NE* IV, 6, 1126b17–21.
39. Iwata, *Arisutoteresu no rinri shisō* (Ethical thought of Aristotle), 332–33, n. 44.
40. *NE* VIII, 1, 1155a28.
41. See chapter 4 for a discussion of such statements as "And you must look at the matter, my simple-minded Socrates, in this way: that the just man always comes out at a disadvantage in his relation with the unjust." Plato, *Republic*, I, 343D.
42. *Republic*, I, 343C; II, 367C.
43. *NE* V, 9, 1136b19–20.
44. Iwata, *Arisutoteresu no rinri shisō* (Ethical thought of Aristotle), 323.
45. Marcel, *Journal métaphysique*, 18; see the English translation in Gabriel Marcel, *Metaphysical Journal*, trans. Bernard Wall (Chicago: Henry Regnery, 1952), 223.
46. Iwata, *Arisutoteresu no rinri shisō* (Ethical thought of Aristotle), 323–24, adopts this interpretation.
47. *NE* V, 9, 1136b21–22.
48. *NE* IX, 8, 1168b27.
49. *NE* VIII, 3, 1156b10–11.
50. Having followed Yasuo Iwata's brilliant interpretation of the structure of Aristotle's doctrine of love so far, on this point I differ with Iwata, who regards *philiā* as converging with *agapē*. Iwata, *Arisutoteresu no rinri shisō* (Ethical thought of Aristotle), 328.
51. P. Tillich, *Dynamics of Faith* (New York: Harper & Brothers, 1958).
52. See P. Ricœur, *De l'interprétation: Essai sur Freud* (Paris: Éditions du Seuil, 1965), 35.

Revisiting "Wonder"

Over the past fifteen chapters, we have studied various ethical ideas on the part of the Greeks and Hebrews, and this should yield plentiful insights when we ourselves consider ethical issues. In closing, I would like to narrow the focus down and ask just what is the most essential point that underlies these ideas and speaks to us today. As noted in the introduction and throughout this book, I believe this generally boils down to "wonder." I would like to conclude by reviewing and summarizing how "wonder" underpins these ideas, and also by presenting a perspective on its relevance to contemporary ethics.

1. The Common Thread in the Greeks and Hebrews

GREEK "WONDER"

Starting with the "water" of Thales the Ionian and moving on through Anaximander's discovery of "the Infinite" and Xenophanes' criticism of anthropomorphic views of the gods, up to Heraclitus's pursuit of the sole being behind all phenomena, what we first noted in the "practical philosophy of the Greeks" was a questioning of how people should live (i.e., ethics)—a questioning prompted by the thought of transcendency and a sense of awe at this (ch. 1, part I). Empedocles, an Italian Thracian, also philosophized about contemplating the gods, while Democritus regarded the idea of "reverence" based on a receptiveness to wonder at things transcending oneself as that which "embraces virtue" (ch. 2).

Socrates' famous statement (via Plato) that philosophy begins in wondering (*thaumazein*) also needs to be understood against this backdrop. Of course, there is a strong sense of "wonder" as intellectual curiosity in the immediate context of the *Theaetetus*,[1] but the *Symposium*[2]

259

and the *Phaedrus*³ discuss "wonder" in relation to Ideas, and there this concept is positioned as a yearning for transcendence (ch. 4). This also corresponds with wonder at Socrates' ethical decision, which overturns the common perception of wanting to avoid the death penalty (ch. 3). Aristotle, who declared in the *Metaphysics* that "It is through wonder that men . . . began to philosophize,"⁴ can be regarded as having distilled his views down to "contemplation" of "the divine" in the final chapter of the *Nicomachean Ethics*, and he speaks of the supreme ethical virtue as consisting of contemplation based on a wonder at and fervor for transcendence (ch. 7).

HEBREW "WONDER"

Equating this transcendent being with God is naturally a consistent foundation underlying "Hebrew religious ethics." Even more so than was the case with the Greeks, the Hebrews' awareness of this frequently took the form of "wonder."

First we noticed that observance of the ethical commands in the Ten Commandments becomes possible based on reverential "fear [*yir'ah*] of him" (ch. 9, part II).⁵ Both the Book of the Covenant and the Holiness Code spoke of "terror" of God in their respective contexts. Proverbs stated that "The fear [*yir'ah*] of the LORD is the beginning of knowledge,"⁶ and it was this very "wonder" that was regarded as making people "lowly in spirit" before God and that cultivated the ethical virtue of "humility" (ch. 11). After continuing to rebuke the God who failed to follow through on retribution ethics, Job, too, eventually arrived at a humble "repent[ance]" for having "uttered what I did not understand, things too wonderful for me [*pela'ot*], which I did not know" (ch. 12).⁷

Job's "wonder" was directed, so to speak, at the God of creation, who transcended retribution ethics. It seems to me, however, that the God of salvation, who was "revealed"⁸ first and foremost in this realm of retribution ethics and who truly "startle[d]" (*nazah*)⁹ people, was discovered in his ultimate form after various explorations by Qohelet and his redactor (ch. 13, part III) and by Deutero-Isaiah (ch. 14), for instance. This was the discovery of a sense of astonishment and awe at the God of redemption who, by having the Servant of Suffering vicariously redeem the ethical sins of the many, followed through on righteousness and also demonstrated his love. We need to reflect again on what is indicated by such symbolic expressions with their rich religious overtones, and these expressions need to be interpreted, while also retaining the urge behind this symbolic language (ch. 15).

I would suggest that this "wonder" at a transcendental being not only has universal relevance as a primal human idea before it was confined to a fixed faith, and that it also acts as the sole underpinning of the ethical ideas of the ancient Greeks and Hebrews, but that it continues to have a fundamental ethical significance that strikes a chord in our secular times today. I would like to conclude our discussion by briefly noting the meaning of "wonder" for us today.

2. Resonance with Our Times

1. A GIFT

What aroused wonder in the ancients was the workings in nature and history of something transcending human beings. The Greeks seem to have perceived these workings mainly in nature, while the Hebrews felt them more prominently in history.

Admittedly, the Greeks did have the histories by Herodotus and Thucydides, but these works parenthesized that which transcends human beings, and their interest consistently narrowed down to demonstrating the causal relationships behind events in this world.[10] Instead of in history, it seems to be in nature that the Greeks encountered something transcending humans, and they marveled at the "Infinite," who made nature what it is, and were driven to pursue this.

The Hebrews, too, marveled at nature, including human beings, as an amazing work of divine creation.[11] It was in history, however, that they perceived the work of God more deeply. They distilled this down to God's intention to forgive, which functioned through the one who, by means of his death, took on himself seemingly unreasonable suffering. The Hebrews were aware that, despite their sins deserving death, their lives were grounded in the transcendental love that forgave them these sins. This also seems to have imparted a depth to their view of life—one that went beyond an affirmation of the direct creation of life and passed through a disavowal that had encountered death—as well as a specificity in line with the breakdown of ethical reality.

In either case, the idea that life is bestowed on us by a being who transcends us in this way is not an illusion on the part of the ancients but a fact that is equally relevant to us today, so marveling anew at this reality should engender a sense of the limitless value of life, with its inviolable sanctity. This might bring about an awareness that harming life for humans' own sake is arrogant and something we have no right to do, being based on a failure to realize that life is a gift, and it might also lead to a clear intention to coexist with our fellow beings, so that "killing is inconceivable." As Heschel pointed out some time ago, "Perhaps this is the essence of human misery: to forget that life is a gift as well as a trust."[12]

2. HUMBLENESS

Some people who believe science to be almighty argue that it is a primitive myth of the ancients to say that life was given and entrusted to us by a transcendental being, and that we are now moving into a time when humans can even make cloned humans themselves. It should be noted, however, that this counterargument is itself merely a myth that overlooks the theoretical limitations of science. It is true that modern science has discovered ways of using enzymes to link DNA to specific viruses, for example, and ways to replicate these. Yet that is fundamentally the limit of scientific understanding. Science cannot understand why DNA is replicated when these operations are carried out, or why DNA exists in the first place. In other words, all science can do is accept nature and the laws at work therein as existing facts. Herein lie the limitations of science, as well as of humankind. The very fact that nature, the laws at work in nature, and above all, life itself are bestowed on us as "givens" is a wondrous mystery.

This should also awaken in us a sense of respect for life, and we should realize that the causes of environmental destruction lie precisely in our presumptuousness in overlooking the fact that the air, water, and sun are givens and in regarding human beings and science as the absolute rulers over these. Let me add that it is only through depriving other creatures, also "givens," of their lives that human beings—who are merely given life and cannot create it themselves—can sustain our own lives, and this fact of our existence means we are sinful.[13] That is exactly why we must consciously inquire into ethics as a means of transcending our fundamental sinfulness. In this way, a fundamental wonder at this givenness perhaps takes on even greater importance as something that makes us aware of our human finiteness and sinfulness and causes us to recover an appropriate humility.[14]

3. UNRAVELING MYSTERIES

Wonder is the emotion that arises when we become aware of a mystery to which we are usually oblivious. Examples include the question of why our very lives or the natural environment that keeps us alive are presented as a given here; the mystery of not knowing where we came from and where we go upon our death; or even the mystery of how the very idea of regarding this as a mystery occurs to me.[15] The fact that wonder at such mysteries sets us free is perhaps another point at issue.

In other words, wonder at the fact that countless such mysteries lie behind our humdrum daily life, set on its well-managed and fixed tracks, makes us realize that we also need to distance ourselves from utilitarian competition in the market mechanism, quit the hysteria of desire, and quietly ponder life. Eventually, wonder will entice us to an exciting adventure wherein these mysteries are solved. If we realize that our very lives are full of mystery and constitute the supreme enigma, and if we can take time to devote ourselves to solving this mystery, our lives will be that much more deeply affected by the encounter with this vital force.[16]

4. LOVE

Feeling wonder at something that transcends us makes us humble and gives us a sense of respect for our own lives and those of others, as well as for nature, and it adds color to our lives in the form of the pleasure of solving mysteries, but additionally—and perhaps most importantly in terms of ethical thought—this sense of wonder is also important in that it opens us up to relationships with others and allows us to love.

The source of our wonder is that a being who transcends us allows us to live with each other. The Other is itself an object of wonder in the sense that it cannot be placed under our control and collides with us beyond our expectations. The way in which love burgeons toward coexistence with others, transcending our innate egoism, is also a matter of wonder. Perhaps at the culmination of this the mystery of the death of the one who, after irrational suffering, died with love for others will fill us with wonder and shock. Will not our hearts experience love on coming into contact with such repeated wonders? In situations where people themselves become agents of active love after experiencing this passive love, are not wonder and ethics inextricably linked by an awareness of the transcendental love at work throughout history in retribution ethics or, rather, in its breakdown (i.e., the reality that sinners prosper and the just perish), as well as by an awareness of the love that provides us with nature as a given blessing?[17]

5. TRANSCENDENCY

In a time "after virtue,"[18] it is understandable that ethics restricts itself to applied ethics and contract jurisprudence. Dispassionately setting up various legal agreements relating to outward behavior is of course an important and significant task for our complex modern society. However, it is doubtful whether this alone is sufficient for moral science.[19] Unless we deliberately probe those inner parts of ourselves and cultivate ethical thoughts, ethics will merely act as an external means of legally binding people against their will, and it will lapse into formal agreements that lose sight of the substance. Ethics would then be observed unwillingly and would simply become a constraint in interpersonal relations so that, circumstances permitting, people would violate it without further thought. Yet for most of us in these secularized times, coercion by a fixed religious faith that might turn out to be a disguised desire for power or a matter of taste would be difficult to accept as such.

Yet—and this is something suggested in points (1) and (2), for instance, and something we verified in chapters 8 and 9 when questioning the grounds for ethics—if we suppose that even atheists believe in "God" as some kind of transcendental principle and that after all the foundation of our existence lies not in ourselves but in something transcending us, then surely it is acceptable to admit the fundamental fact that we have a relationship with transcendency in the broad sense of the word. "Wonder" at this fundamental fact holds its ground on the verge of being confined and entrenched in a set faith that transcends philosophical proof, and although it has universality as a primordial emotion, it does not exclude the freedom to restrict oneself to belief.[20] In that sense, I would suggest that "wonder" presents itself today—even more so today—as an effective concept that acts as a node linking ethics and transcendency.

These five points are, I believe, the main areas in which "wonder," the origin of ethical thought in ancient times, resonates with us today, but developing these points further lies beyond the goal of this book. As I stated in the preface, the main focus here has been to learn about the rich contents of the various ethical ideas entertained by the Greeks and the

Hebrews, and I leave it up to individual readers' discretion to draw their own conclusions. It is my humble but perhaps overly ambitious desire that these additional remarks about "wonder" here might stimulate such thinking on the part of readers.

Notes

1. Plato, *Theaetetus* 155D.
2. Plato, *Symposium* 210E.
3. Plato, *Phaedrus* 250A.
4. Aristotle, *Metaphysics* I, 2, 982b11–13.
5. Exod 20:20 = Deut 5:29.
6. Prov 1:7.
7. Job 42:3, 6.
8. Isa 53:1.
9. Isa 52:15.
10. See the comments in chapter 3 of my book *Transcendency and Symbols in the Old Testament: A Genealogy of the Hermeneutical Experiences*, trans. Judy Wakabayashi (BZAW 275; Berlin: Walter de Gruyter, 1999), originally published as *Kyūyaku ni okeru chōetsu to shōchō: kaishakugaku-teki keiken no keifu* (Tokyo: University of Tokyo Press, 1996).
11. See chapter 4 in my *Kyūyaku seisho no shisō: 24 no danshō* (The thought of the Old Testament: 24 fragments) (Tokyo: Iwanami Shoten, 1998). Thorleif Boman compares the creation myths of the Hebrews (Gen 1–3; Isa 40–55; etc.) and the Greeks, particularly Plato (*Timaeus*). After pointing out that they both belong not to the category of natural science but to the religious realm, Boman emphasizes the contrast between them: Hebrew myths discuss the creation of the world and human beings and regard people as achieving their acme when they return to primordial creation, whereas Greek myths discuss existence and maintain that people reach their acme when they are engaged in the eternal world. Thorleif Boman, *Hebrew Thought Compared with Greek*, trans. Jules L. Moreau (New York: Norton, 1960), 172–75, trans. of *Das hebräische Denken im Vergleich mit dem Griechischen*, 2nd ed. (Göttingen: Vandenhoeck & Ruprecht, 1954), 284–89.
12. A. J. Heschel, *God in Search of Man: A Philosophy of Judaism* (New York: Farrar, Straus & Cudahy, 1955), 352.
13. Although this is a crystallization of my own ethical thinking as well, I would like to quote the following startling comment from chapter 8 in Jirō Watanabe's *Gendaijin no tame no tetsugaku* (Philosophy for contemporary people) (Tokyo: Hōsō Daigaku Kyōiku Shinkōkai, 2000), where he comprehensively considers "the question of evil": "We must constantly nurture a sense of awareness and gratitude toward the 'sinful' and grave reality of our existence . . . whereby we take the lives of plants and other animals. I believe that as members of the universe who are placed within the great cycle of life and who did not

create ourselves, we must humbly accept, give thanks for, and constantly recall the 'sinful' inexorable fate whereby we are born, thrown down, and coexist with other beings in this universe—in fact, that it is only through depending on these lives that we can live our own lives" (140–41).

14. This brings to mind how, in his book *Rinrigaku* (Ethics) (Tokyo: Yūhi-kaku, 1971), Takeo Iwasaki, who rejects the introduction of a "transcendental being" into ethics, repeatedly emphasizes "wonder" at the "mystery" of existence, particularly of life (e.g., 315, 317, 319), when he tries to remain within the perspective of human beings and to find ethical principles in their "awareness of finiteness" (302ff.).

15. "Even our ability to wonder fills us with amazement." Heschel, *God in Search of Man*, 107.

16. Rachel Carson, the author of *Silent Spring* (Boston: Houghton Mifflin, 1962), the pioneering work in environmental ethics, wrote a small book called *The Sense of Wonder* (New York: Harper & Row, 1965) that was published posthumously. In it, Carson points out that "the value of preserving and strengthening this sense of awe and wonder, this recognition of something beyond the boundaries of human existence" lies in the fact that it means we "are never alone or weary of life" (88), and "a sense of wonder [is] an unfailing antidote against the boredom and disenchantments of later years, the sterile preoccupation with things that are artificial, the alienation from the sources of our strength" (43).

17. If we might be allowed to consider humans' negative aspects as well and to deliberately delve further in religious terms, Heschel's manner of speaking in *God in Search of Man* is suggestive. He makes virtually no mention of the Holocaust (except for pp. 170 and 221), but here is one of the rare occasions that he does allude to it, speaking of it from a broader perspective: "The idea of man's self-sufficiency, man's exaggerated consciousness of himself, was based upon a generalization; from the fact that technology could solve some problems it was deduced that technology could solve all problems. This proved to be a fallacy. Social reforms, it was thought, would cure all ills and eliminate all evils from our world. Yet we have finally discovered what prophets and saints have always known: bread and power alone will not save humanity. There is a passion and drive for cruel deeds which only the awe and fear of God can soothe; there is a suffocating selfishness in man which only holiness can ventilate" (169).

18. A. C. MacIntyre, *After Virtue: A Study in Moral Theory* (Notre Dame: University of Notre Dame Press, 1981).

19. In *Gendai rinrigaku nyūmon* (An introduction to modern ethics) (Tokyo: Kōdansha gakujutsu bunko, 1997, 187–88), Hisatake Katō—who has notched numerous achievements as a pioneer in applied ethics in Japan ever since he published *Ōyō rinrigaku no susume* (An encouragement to applied ethics) (Tokyo: Maruzen, 1994)—retains doubts about a MacIntyre-style ethics of communitarian virtue, but he also expresses concern over the lengths to which the right to folly has gone under liberal ethics. This merits close attention as being indicative of the future direction of Katō's ethics. See also chapter 11 in his *Rinrigaku no kiso* (The foundations of ethics) (Tokyo: Hōsō Daigaku Kyōiku Shinkōkai, 1993).

20. Heschel opens his book with this religious criticism: "It is customary to blame secular science and anti-religious philosophy for the eclipse of religion in modern society. It would be more honest to blame religion for its own defeats. Religion declined not because it was refuted, but because it became irrelevant, dull, oppressive, insipid." Heschel thus arouses interest in the fact that "*Religion is an answer to man's ultimate questions*," and he vividly reveals how the answer arises on the very basis of a fundamental "wonder" toward the philosophical mystery of human existence. Heschel, *God in Search of Man*, 3.

Index

196n120, 197, 198, 199, 200, 201,
202, 203, 204, 205, 206, 208n41, 211,
212, 213, 214, 215, 216, 218, 219,
220, 221, 222, 223n27, 225, 226, 227,
228, 229, 230, 231, 232, 233, 234,
236, 237, 239, 240, 241, 245, 252,
260, 261, 264, 266n17;
anthropomorphic views of, 12–13,
17, 114–15, 117n51, 149, 259;
personal, 115, 140, 148, 149, 155,
252; relations with, 137–39, 152n3,
160–61, 226, 230; of retribution,
189, 192, 205, 211, 213, 214, 218,
219, 220, 225, 232, 236, 240; view of
God, 12, 13, 113, 115, 149, 206, 221,
232, 241
gods, 12, 13, 14, 25, 33, 36, 53, 68, 110,
111, 114, 117n51, 122, 139, 140, 141,
142, 143, 144, 146, 160, 259
good, viii, x, 2, 14, 27, 29, 34, 35, 36,
37, 38, 39, 40, 41, 43, 44, 52, 53, 55,
59, 61, 63, 65, 66, 67, 68, 71, 74n65,
81, 82, 83, 84, 86, 90, 93, 97, 98, 99,
104, 105, 107, 108, 109, 112, 131,
140, 164, 174, 176, 179, 180, 182,
184, 186, 188, 190, 191, 192, 195n87,
199, 201, 202, 204, 206, 214, 217,
221, 246, 247, 248, 249, 250, 251,
252, 253; deeds, viii, 164, 179; and
noble deeds, 112; people, 98, 99,
204, 247, 248, 251, 252, 253; person,
109, 117n43, 250, 251; temper, 180,
184, 192, 195n87. *See also* goodness
good, the, 59, 60, 67, 81–84, 97, 109,
111, 179, 187, 189, 198, 246, 251
goodness, 34, 35, 36, 38, 52, 59, 60, 62,
65, 66, 67, 71, 82, 83, 93, 98, 189,
204, 211, 247, 250
Greece, vii, ix, 2, 26, 31n38, 79, 112,
175, 184, 185, 187, 195n106
guilt, 2, 228, 239
Gyges, 40, 41, 45, 46, 52, 56, 63

habit, viii, 55, 77n110, 85–87, 90, 104,
107, 112, 250
habituation, 85–86

happiness, x, 27, 36, 43, 45, 52–53, 56,
57, 60–61, 63, 71n2, 79, 80, 81,
83–84, 92, 93, 109–10, 114, 161,
162, 164, 189, 190, 192, 194n71, 205,
211, 213, 215, 249, 253
harm, 71, 124, 180
hate, 24, 25, 179
hatred, 87, 178, 188
health, 53, 82, 83, 89, 90, 104, 107, 108,
114, 198
heart-hardening prophecies, 225–27,
229
Hebraism, vii, ix, 12, 41, 77n110, 222,
245
Hebrews, viii, ix, xiii, xiv, 2, 3, 4, 119,
157, 158, 167n13, 184, 185, 191, 192,
194n55, 200, 211, 214, 215, 232, 233,
236, 255, 259, 260, 261, 265, 265n11
hedonics, 43, 44–45, 60, 75n73
hedonism, 61, 71n2, 74n65
Hegel, G. W. F., 129, 136n62, 237, 238,
244n58, 253
Heidegger, M., 18n16, 21, 22–23, 217,
218
Hellenism, vii, ix
Heraclitus, 9, 12, 13, 14–15, 16, 17, 26,
195n106, 259
hermeneutics, xi, 146, 155, 229, 254
Herodotus, 7, 261
Heschel, A. J., viii, 2, 77n110, 151,
152n3, 244n55, 262, 266n17, 267n20
Hesiod, 13, 14, 16, 114
hexis, 85, 86, 87, 90, 95, 104, 107, 250.
See also habit
highest good, the, 84, 108
high-mindedness, 80, 184, 185, 192
Hippias, 7
Hippolytus, 16
historical-critical, xiii, 229, 253
history, ix, xii, 3, 14, 21, 38, 48n56, 51,
94, 128, 133, 142, 144, 152, 163, 164,
211, 213, 214, 218, 220, 221, 226,
233, 237, 241, 243n38, 261, 263; of
philosophy, 38
Holiness Code, ix, 121, 155, 159, 161,
163–64, 165, 169n55, 260

Old Testament, viii, ix, xi, xviii, 3,
47n31, 120, 121, 122, 124, 125, 126,
128, 137, 139, 145, 146, 148, 149,
152, 154n28, 155, 159, 162, 165, 166,
179, 185, 201, 206, 218, 228, 230,
232, 234, 235, 236, 240; studies, xii,
128, 242n12
ontology, ix, 21, 247
oppressed, the, 181, 219, 220, 233
oppression, 43, 219, 254
oppressor, the, 181
ordinary men (people), xii, 81, 83, 112,
114, 115
origins, vii, x, xi, xii, 1, 4, 10, 41, 166,
175, 211, 228, 244n55, 255
other people, 60, 148, 221, 249
others, xi, 39, 42, 45, 60, 62, 67, 71n2,
75n73, 95, 96, 99, 113, 126, 132, 149,
161, 190, 212, 215, 219, 220, 221,
222, 229, 230, 231, 241, 249, 254,
257n34, 263

pacifism, 124, 125
pain, 44, 45, 74n65, 87, 90, 91, 94, 105,
106, 112, 201
panta rhei, 15
parainesis, 92
pariah nation, x, 234
Parmenides, 9, 21–23, 26, 27, 30n9, 67
passions, 96, 99, 246
Paul, 141, 179, 235, 241
peace, 46, 53, 56, 125, 177, 179, 186,
217, 240, 241, 244n55
people, the, x, 39, 43, 75n77, 145, 147,
151, 156, 161, 162, 164, 181, 184,
215, 225, 226, 227
Peripatetic School, 79
personal God, 115, 140, 144, 148, 149,
155, 252
personified God, viii, 115
persuasion, 29, 40
Phaedo, xvii, 31n38, 37, 47n34, 47n37,
51, 55, 66, 70, 72n2, 72n88
Phaedrus, 5n3, 51, 64, 68, 70, 72n2,
73n38, 74n59, 260
Philebus, 51, 61, 71, 108

philia, 97, 246, 250, 252–53, 257n50
philosopher(s), viii, ix, xvii, 1, 2, 38, 45,
46, 47n44, 51, 56, 57, 59, 62, 63, 68,
70, 75n77, 81, 84, 87n1, 114, 115,
253, 254
philosophical debate, 33, 39, 40, 108,
130
philosophical hermeneutics, 146, 229,
254
philosophy, 1, 2, 4n1, 9, 10, 11, 12, 17,
21, 25, 26, 35, 37, 38, 47n33, 51, 68,
69, 70, 75n73, 76n77, 79, 111, 113,
117n45, 120, 148, 218, 239, 241,
244n55, 245, 253, 255, 259, 267n20
physis, 40, 48n56, 247
Plato, viii, xvii, 1, 15, 17n2, 18n33, 25,
28, 31n38, 33–49, 51–77, 79, 81, 82,
83, 108, 111, 112, 113, 118n58, 212,
251, 252, 257n41, 259, 265n11
pleasure, xii, 28, 29, 44–45, 53, 55, 56,
57, 60–61, 63, 64, 71n2, 74n65,
75n73, 75n77, 80, 83, 87, 90, 91, 97,
98, 99, 105, 108–9, 110, 112,
117n43, 176, 183, 219, 220, 246, 248,
251, 263
politicians, xi, 34, 39
politics, 34, 39, 75n77, 79, 100n29,
111–12, 114
Politics, 18n4
poor, 83, 175, 178, 179, 181, 186, 190
Popper, K., 63, 75n77
poverty, 34, 53, 94, 157, 172, 175, 176,
185, 186
practical philosophy, ix, 1, 2, 9, 70,
120, 255, 259
practice, 25, 53, 82, 111, 112, 160, 214
prayer, 115, 165, 235
precaptivity prophets, 225
present, the, xi, 68, 70, 79, 95, 138, 142,
220
pre-Socratic philosophers, viii, ix, xvii,
9, 18n13, 21, 38, 51, 70
pride, 43, 93, 185, 186, 187, 188
priest, 162, 163, 167n1
Priestly materials, 164
principle, 11, 13, 36, 52, 66, 91, 92, 93,